FAITH AND REASON

Faith and Reason

Philosophers Explain Their
Turn to Catholicism

Edited by
Brian Besong
Jonathan Fuqua

IGNATIUS PRESS   SAN FRANCISCO

Cover photo:
The Philosopher
© iStockphoto

Cover design by Enrique J. Aguilar

© 2019 by Ignatius Press, San Francisco
All rights reserved
ISBN 978-1-62164-201-5
Library of Congress Control Number 2018948284
Printed in the United States of America ∞

CONTENTS

FOREWORD: TAKING FAITH SERIOUSLY

Francis J. Beckwith

It's not as easy as you think to choose to change your mind, literally to unbelieve something that you currently believe. Try it. Suppose today is Tuesday and I ask you if you believe that it really is Tuesday. If your cognitive powers are functioning properly (that's just fancy philosophy talk for "if your head is screwed on straight"), your answer will be, "Yes, I believe today is Tuesday." Now try your hardest to unbelieve it. Not so easy, eh?

But we all know that people do in fact change their beliefs. Yet, they don't do it in the way they change their clothes, doctor's appointments, or menu options. Belief change usually occurs slowly over time as a consequence of small and seemingly insignificant changes. You may, for example, at one point in your life consider yourself a political liberal, only to discover a decade later that you have in fact abandoned some of the central tenets of liberalism without even realizing it. Perhaps you were a strong proponent of the welfare state because you believed (correctly) that the community has an obligation to care for those who cannot care for themselves. You never actually reject that belief, but what happens is that you begin to doubt the effectiveness of the welfare state (or the current configuration and administration of it) to achieve your belief's moral end. Your doubts do not arise all at once, but begin to germinate in your mind as you acquaint yourself with writers and scholars who challenge you to consider the possibility that your account of social justice may not be the best way for the community to do its proper work in helping the needy and the downtrodden. Then one day when discussing politics with a friend, she says to you, "I can't believe how conservative you sound," and you realize at that moment that you had experienced a change of mind, even though you were never conspicuously aware of it throughout

7

the transformation process. From there, you may choose to make the conversion "official" by changing your political party affiliation. But make no mistake about it, your mind had changed long before you knew that it had changed. You did not change your beliefs by an act of will at some single moment—as you would change a flat tire, a light bulb, or your clothes—but rather, your careful study and reflection *over time* slowly informed your intellect so that it could offer to your will the only options your intellect had found to be the most reasonable from which the will could freely choose.

If politics isn't your thing, then pick any area in which you or anyone else probably holds a firm opinion, such as literature, sports, morality, entertainment, art, or family life. We can easily imagine one undergoing the same sort of belief transformation in these areas as one would in politics.

Can we extend the same analysis to religious beliefs? Yes and no. Yes, in the sense that conversion, like changing political views, is rarely a matter of exercising your will at a particular moment and literally "changing" your mind as a consequence. In my own story, I returned to the Catholic Church of my youth after years of slowly appropriating into my seemingly Protestant mind Catholic understandings of faith, reason, and the moral life until I was forced to ask myself the question, why aren't you Catholic?[1] (By the way, I actually don't think I had a Protestant mind, but I thought I did. What I had was a confused Catholic mind that would not rest until it found its way home.)

Before I had asked myself that question in December 2006, four other people had already posed it to me in previous years: my wife, Frankie Beckwith (1998); Amherst College political theorist Hadley Arkes (2003); my eight-year-old niece, Darby Beckwith (2005); and Boston College philosopher Laura Garcia (2006). My answer got worse each subsequent time I was asked the question, for as the years passed I had become more Catholic in my thinking, which meant that the set of plausible responses became smaller and each member that remained in the set became less convincing.

When I finally found the time to answer the question, why aren't you Catholic? I had concluded that there were four issues that kept

---

[1] See Francis J. Beckwith, *Return to Rome: Confessions of an Evangelical Catholic* (Grand Rapids, MI: Brazos, 2009).

me from returning to Catholicism: (1) apostolic succession, (2) Eucharistic realism, (3) the sacrament of penance, and (4) the doctrine of justification. On other matters that typically bother Protestants—purgatory, praying to the saints, Mariology, and so forth—I was not particularly troubled, since, in my mind, if the Catholic Church is right about apostolic succession, the Eucharist, penance, and justification, then it is surely right about these other matters. (A confession: while I was a Protestant, even though I didn't believe in purgatory, the doctrine did make a lot of sense to me. For when it comes to joining the saints in heaven, I tended to think like Woody Allen in *Annie Hall*: "I would never wanna belong to any club that would have someone like me for a member.")

Encouraged by my friend J. Budziszewski (one of the contributors to this volume) to examine carefully the Church Fathers on these four issues, I soon came to the conclusion (in March 2007) that the Catholic perspective on these questions was at least a permissible one for a Christian to hold. However, once I conceded that point, it did not take long for me to see that it was blindingly obvious that the issues that prevented me from returning to Rome—the very issues that have divided Protestants and Catholics for five centuries—had *united* the Church, both East and West, up until the Reformation. Thus, I knew immediately that it was me, and not the Catholic Church, that had the burden to justify my schism with it. So, on April 28, 2007, I went to confession for the first time in over thirty years.

But, for the Catholic, conversion involves more than a slow and extended process of intellectual adjustments in response to unexpected challenges. What I mean here is that if one truly believes in divine providence, that God acts through his creation including his free creatures to achieve his ends, then what may appear to many as an accident in the ordinary course of human affairs may in fact be a special act of divine grace. Consider this story from my own life.[2]

My wife and I had arrived in Rome on the evening of February 10, 2015. I had spoken to my parents moments before we had boarded our plane in Austin, Texas, on the prior afternoon. My

---

[2] The story that follows is adapted from Francis J. Beckwith, "St. Anthony, Pray for Us", *Catholic Thing*, May 21, 2015, https://www.thecatholicthing.org/2015/05/21/st-anthony -pray-for-us/.

eighty-four-year-old father, Harold "Pat" Beckwith, did not sound well. His voice, ordinarily poised and robust, crackled through the phone, as he seemed to struggle with every word he uttered.

My mother, ever the optimist, assured me that I should not worry. She said that she was confident that he would be okay. In my heart, I did not believe her, but I wanted to. She went on to insist that she had everything under control and that Frankie (my wife) and I should enjoy ourselves in Rome, where we were to live for three months while I was on research leave from Baylor University.

The flight from Texas to London and then to the Eternal City was the most difficult journey of my life. The thought that something was terribly wrong with my father, and that I was traveling in the opposite direction and away from that trouble, was nearly unbearable.

In December 2013, my father had been diagnosed with cancer. In the first six months of 2014, he underwent chemotherapy and radiation treatment. Subsequent monitoring had shown that the tumor had shrunk and did not seem to be growing. Because of his age, and the location of the tumor, surgery to remove it was too risky.

When my father first told us that he had cancer, I made it a point to pray for him each morning and each evening from that day forward. I wanted to do so by asking for the assistance of one of the great saints of the Church, but who that saint would be was not obvious. After a little research, I discovered that someone had composed a prayer to St. Anthony of Padua (1195–1231) for cancer patients. So, St. Anthony it was. I uttered the same prayer to him twice a day, and had not told anyone what I was doing, not even my wife.

My brother, James, contacted us two days after we had arrived in Rome. He told us that my parents had been to my father's oncologist, who informed him that he had no more than four to six weeks to live. Not only was the cancer back, but he had contracted leukemia as well. Upon hearing how many weeks he had remaining, my father, ever the comedian, replied, "Doc, can you give me two?"

After Frankie and I had talked with my parents via FaceTime, we knew we had to return to the United States as soon as possible. So, on February 16 we flew from Rome to Las Vegas, Nevada, where we had grown up and my parents still resided. From the airport, we drove immediately to their home.

My father was sitting at the dinner table, surrounded by family. Having already lost the ability to speak clearly, he nodded in my direction as I bent down to kiss him. He knew we had traveled all the way from Rome just for him.

After he had been moved to his hospice bed—which was set up in my parents' living room—I placed in his right hand the rosary beads I had received at the Vatican when I met Pope Francis on Father's Day, June 16, 2013. I leaned over and said into my dad's right ear, "The pope gave me these; I want you to have them."

For the next two nights, my mother, my sister-in-law Kimberly, and her son, Dylan, took turns staying watch next to my father. My mother rarely left the room, sleeping as much as she could on a couch to the right of the chair beside the bed.

At around two o'clock in the morning on February 18—Ash Wednesday—it was my turn to occupy the chair. I prayed the Divine Mercy Chaplet as well as the Sorrowful Mysteries of the Rosary. For the latter, I used the version suggested by the United States Conference of Catholic Bishops. Between the prayers were Scripture verses, perfectly suited for the task at hand. The last four were particularly powerful:

> Wait for the Lord, take courage;
> be stouthearted, wait for the Lord!
> > Psalm 27:14
>
> *Hail Mary* ...
> But the souls of the just are in the hand of God,
> and no torment shall touch them.
> > Wisdom 3:1
>
> *Hail Mary* ...
> They seemed, in the view of the foolish, to be dead;
> and their passing away was thought an affliction.
> > Wisdom 3:2
>
> *Hail Mary* ...
> But they are in peace.
> > Wisdom 3:3b
>
> *Glory Be* ...[3]

An hour after I had completed the Rosary, at 5:49 A.M.—on the first day of Lent—I witnessed my father take his last breath.

[3] United States Conference of Catholic Bishops, "Scriptural Rosary: The Sorrowful Mysteries", accessed August 3, 2018, http://www.usccb.org/prayer-and-worship/prayers-and-devotions/rosaries/scriptural-rosary-the-sorrowful-mysteries.cfm.

On the Saturday that followed, when my mother was going through his belongings, she handed me what looked like a tiny booklet, no more than two inches in height. She said that my father had carried it in his pocket for many years, though in the past fourteen months he seemed more insistent that he always have it on his person. I never knew this about my dad, and my mother confessed that she had never looked closely at the item and thus was not sure what it was. As she handed it to me, I noticed that on the front it read, "St. Anthony of Padua, Pray for Us". On the inside was a medal and relic of St. Anthony, along with this prayer: "St. Anthony, help me experience peace of mind and heart in my present needs. Free me from needless worry and burdensome fears. Grant me unfailing trust and an awareness of God's loving mercy. Amen."

If this had not happened to me, I would not have believed it. But it did happen, and I will never fail to see it as a gift of God by way of my father.

And yet, the unbeliever or the Protestant will likely cling to the "accident of history" account to explain away what seems to me (and other Catholics) to be a kind of miracle. He will not "see" the "miracle" because his intellect has not been formed by the small though seemingly insignificant changes in faith that we Catholics attribute to the cooperating grace that God imparts to us. As St. Thomas Aquinas writes: "As regards ... man's assent to the things which are of faith, we may observe a twofold cause, one of external inducement, such as seeing a miracle, or being persuaded by someone to embrace the faith: neither of which is a sufficient cause, since of those who see the same miracle, or who hear the same sermon, some believe, and some do not. Hence we must assert another internal cause, which moves man inwardly to assent to matters of faith."[4]

This is a book consisting of autobiographical accounts of people who have changed their minds about matters of faith and have become Catholic. What these authors also have in common is that they are professional philosophers. They are trained in an academic discipline that prizes reason and logic. And yet, they believe in the sorts of

---

[4] St. Thomas Aquinas, *The Summa Theologica of St. Thomas Aquinas*, trans. Fathers of the English Dominican Province, 2nd and rev. ed. (London: Burns, Oates, and Washbourne, 1920), II–II, q. 6, a. 1, http://www.newadvent.org/summa/3006.htm.

things—like the efficaciousness of praying to St. Anthony of Padua—that most self-styled sophisticates (including many of their philosophical peers) do not consider reasonable or logical.

In the professorate, the conventional wisdom is that beliefs arising from faith are by their very nature contrary to the deliverances of reason. But for those Catholic academics, like the contributors to this volume, who have both a deep faith and a sophisticated mastery of philosophy, that's not at all how they understand the relationship between faith and reason. They see them as complementary, that we can know some things by both faith and reason (e.g., that God exists, that there is a natural moral law), some things only by reason (e.g., that water is H_2O, George Washington was the first U.S. president), and some things only by faith (e.g., that God is a Trinity, that Jesus died for our sins). Because everything that is not God must ultimately come from God—including what we know by reason and believe by faith—the two cannot be inconsistent with each other. This is why the Catholic philosopher maintains that although reason is the limit of the human intellect's power, it is not the limit of what the human intellect may reasonably believe. If this is true, then to shut oneself off from faith is to deny oneself access to important truths about reality.

Consider an example offered by one of my former students who is now a history professor at a small Catholic college in the northeast United States. While she was studying for her Ph.D. at a prestigious secular university in Maryland, she taught an undergraduate course in medieval history. One of the figures she covered was St. Francis of Assisi (1181–1226). In class she asked her students about what they thought of the claim that St. Francis, in the last two years of his life, bore the "stigmata", five wounds in his feet, hands, and side, seemingly identical to descriptions in the New Testament of the wounds borne by the crucified Jesus. Rather than entertaining the possibility that St. Francis' stigmata may actually be a divine sign,[5] which is what

---

[5] I am using the phrase "divine sign" rather than "miracle" or "nonnatural cause", since one could give a scientifically exhaustive account of St. Francis' stigmata and still reasonably believe that it was a divine sign. The combination of timing, persons involved, and meanings communicated by the event or circumstance can be very powerful. This is exactly what I believe about my experience with the St. Anthony medal. I do not think any scientific laws were violated, nor would they have to be. The idea that divine action requires gaps in nature is a mistake made by many atheists and theists.

his contemporaries believed,[6] the students tried to explain it away by offering alternative accounts that did not take the faith of the medieval saint seriously. In reply, my former student noted to her students that it turns out that the well-educated Catholic, when confronted with the story of St. Francis, *must* take seriously the possibility that the stigmata is a divine sign, which no one can say a priori is impossible. But in that case, the well-educated Catholic, though willing to abandon the divine sign account if the evidence tells her otherwise,[7] is more rational than the so-called rational sophisticate who reflexively rejects that option from the start.

So, if your aim is to be rational, you must take faith seriously.

---

[6] See Lawrence S. Cunningham, "The Strange Stigmata", *Christian History* 42 (1994), http://www.christianitytoday.com/history/issues/issue-42/strange-stigmata.html.

[7] For example, miracles attributed to prospective saints are rigorously investigated by the Church, which has no problem rejecting claims that do not pass muster. See Michael O'Neill, "A Church of Miracles", *Our Sunday Visitor*, July 6, 2016, https://www.osv.com/osvnews weekly/article/tabid/535/artmid/13567/articleid/20182/a-church-of-miracles.aspx.

INTRODUCTION

Brian Besong

In his *Prescription against Heretics*, Tertullian infamously quipped, "What indeed has Athens to do with Jerusalem? What concord is there between the Academy and the Church?"[1] Behind the bombast was a serious complaint: that established philosophy was, for Tertullian, a source of trouble for the Church, being a fount of corrupt wisdom spoiling the pure stream coming from Christ. Tertullian's philosophical contemporaries make his attitude somewhat understandable, even if shortsighted. Luminaries such as St. Augustine, St. Anselm, St. Bonaventure, and St. Thomas Aquinas (among a great many others) prove that being a first-rate philosopher does not involve being a second-rate Christian. And yet, Christians today—and perhaps for the last century or two—find themselves once more in a situation not unlike Tertullian's when it comes to professional philosophy. In brief, one is far more likely to encounter hostility to religion generally and to Catholic orthodoxy specifically among philosophers than one is to find fair and intellectually serious engagement. The contemporary caricature of the aggressive atheist philosophy professor is not so wide of the mark.

In the most prominent research of its kind, philosophers David Bourget and David J. Chalmers surveyed established contemporary philosophers on a variety of subjects related to the discipline.[2] Some results were surprising, and some merely confirmed armchair suspicions: 72.8 percent of those surveyed were self-declared atheists—that is, they believe God does not exist; 56.5 percent were self-described

---

[1] Tertullian, *Prescription against Heretics* 7.
[2] David Bourget and David J. Chalmers, "What Do Philosophers Believe?", *Philosophical Studies* 170, no. 3 (2014): 465–500.

physicalists about the mind—that is, they believe that the human person is a purely physical thing, without an immaterial soul or intellect; and 49.8 percent reported an underlying commitment to naturalism—that is, they believe that the natural (i.e., nonsupernatural) world is all that there is.[3] In the relevant areas, these three positions represented either the majority or the plurality view among professional philosophers. At the same time, the numbers reveal a nuance that resists easy caricature, or makes a contemporary Tertullian-like attitude toward professional philosophy as excessive today as it was when Tertullian first expressed it. As a simple example, when one looks narrowly at contemporary philosophers whose main research area is the philosophy of religion, the survey results paint a very different picture. Only 20.87 percent of this group—philosophers whose specialization involves their deeply considering arguments for and against God's existence—are self-described atheists.[4] Openly religious philosophers such as Alvin Plantinga, William Alston, Alasdair MacIntyre, and Eleonore Stump (to name a few) have ranked as some of the most prominent members of the profession.[5] And anecdotally, there are signs that a younger (i.e., Gen-X and forward) generation of philosophers are much more open to God's existence and to the truth of traditional religious claims than are their older philosophical counterparts. Only time will tell if the trend lasts, and if the more openly religious young philosophers will be able to find and keep jobs when—so common lore goes—a large number of university hiring committees have at least one closeted or openly antireligious professor willing to stifle an applicant's job prospects if he detects some hint of religiosity. The broader shift toward a "progressive" or "liberal" political ideology in Western universities has not made it any easier to profess belief and adherence to any traditional religion openly—with Catholicism in particular often being targeted with special animosity, given its male hierarchy and manifestly nonprogressive sexual ethic.[6]

---

[3] Ibid., 476.

[4] Ibid., 483.

[5] For a sample, see Thomas V. Morris, ed., *God and the Philosophers: The Reconciliation of Faith and Reason* (New York: Oxford University Press, 1996), and Kelly James Clark, ed., *Philosophers Who Believe: The Spiritual Journeys of 11 Leading Thinkers* (Downers Grove, IL: IVP Academic, 1997).

[6] See, for instance, Philip Jenkins, *The New Anti-Catholicism: The Last Acceptable Prejudice* (Oxford; New York: Oxford University Press, 2003).

Understanding the background intellectual climate of the contemporary university and a typical philosophy department helps put the present collection of essays in its proper context. For the typical philosophy department is not an open forum in which all ideas are aired and discussed in a calm and reasoned way, without fear of public scrutiny or reprisal. Quite the contrary, religious philosophers of nearly every creed find themselves in a mostly hostile environment. For this reason, religious philosophers often keep their heads down, so to speak, when it comes to religion. Given the prevailing pressures, religious philosophers as a group tend also to be intellectually serious about their religious commitments (particularly when the commitments have survived the scrutinies of graduate school). Although they may not want to subject their religious views to a public debate with colleagues, even the most nonconfrontational of religious philosophers have typically thought through the various arguments (or irrational prejudices) that could be raised by their colleagues were a debate to take place. Hence, unlike the broader professional world, relatively few professional philosophers remain religious simply because it was part of their upbringing or background culture. Religious inertia is typically not a sufficiently powerful force to stand against the pressures of the contemporary philosophical academy. On the whole, religious philosophers have reasoned through their theological beliefs and believe them to be rational, despite what the majority of their peers say.

In the context of the contemporary university, professional philosophers being moved to embrace the Catholic faith—without perverting that faith to make peace with the ideologies that rule the day—is far from what one would expect. And yet, this is exactly what one finds. The movement is difficult to document, especially given the pressures explained above. All the same, anecdotes of such conversions[7] are commonplace among professional philosophers, and

---

[7] Terms such as "convert" or "conversion" can carry with them negative associations about the non-Catholic religious backgrounds of those who later embrace the Catholic faith. For this reason, the National Statutes for the Catechumenate (in the United States) explains that "the term 'convert' should be reserved strictly for those converted from unbelief to Christian belief and never used of those baptized Christians who are received into the full communion of the Catholic Church." Michael S. Driscoll et al., *The Liturgy Documents: Essential Documents for Parish Worship*, 5th ed. (Chicago, IL: Liturgy Training Publications, 2012), 119. Proportionately fewer philosophers who have become Catholic are converts in this highly narrow

they range across a broad spectrum of backgrounds: graduate students through full professors, moral and political philosophers through philosophers of science, atheists through Protestants. Some conversions happened recently, and some many years ago. Given no common clearinghouse of such conversions—besides the proverbial water cooler—it is very difficult to get a full sense of the whos and the whys. Some are common knowledge, and some conversions might be known only to a handful of colleagues. As a simple illustration, after coming up with the list of contributors for the present collection, we have come to discover such a large number of additional philosopher converts that we could easily compile several more volumes of similar accounts. Hence, the essays contained here comprise only a small (but hopefully representative) sample of a phenomenon that is not widely known outside of academia, but should be.

Among Catholics, it should come as little surprise that intellectuals whose professional training has honed their reasoning skills and whose vocation calls them to pursue the truth—come what may— should embrace Catholicism. God has revealed it and God is Truth. Through what precise means God drew the wise men to follow the star to Bethlehem, we can only speculate. We need not speculate here, for the essays contained herein detail the various perceptible means of grace that God has used to draw these lovers of wisdom to himself. In every case, reason has played a primary role. And this is fitting, for reason is our most noble faculty; fitting too, because God uses the bait most appropriate to those he seeks to lure. Of course, reason never forces faith upon a person. Still, it was the reasonableness of the Catholic faith, especially in contrast to other claimants (or wholesale denials) of supernatural revelation, that captured the attention of these professional philosophers and that cleared a space into which the seed of supernatural faith could be planted.

Considered on its own, it is not so very impressive that some individuals find a faith rationally compelling. Our natural ability to reason is, after all, fallible, and broad experience teaches us that individuals

---

sense of the term. Yet, terms of conversion are commonly used in a much broader sense and without negative implications (e.g., we speak of political conversions, scientific conversions, etc.). For lack of a suitable alternative, we shall adopt terms of conversion—to be understood in the latter, broader sense.

travel in a multitude of directions with each claiming reason as their guide. What makes the present situation different is that all the present contributors (and, for reasons explained above, likely all philosopher converts to Catholicism) took their preconversion outlook on the supernatural world seriously—that is, their pre-Catholic religious outlooks were weighed conclusions that would not be given up without a more rationally compelling alternative. And the individuals evaluating the alternatives are sophisticated and methodical thinkers, highly capable of developing and mentally pursuing arguments on both sides of a debate.

That Catholicism is the collective conclusion of these individuals, who were each pursuing their inquires in relative isolation from the rest, is worthy of serious consideration. Also worthy of consideration is the relative absence of a *considered* Catholic exodus. For although one can find a large number of individuals—professional philosophers among them—who have left the Catholic faith, it is rare to find in this set individuals who have done so after coming to a proportionately deep understanding of the Catholic faith and finding in its claims something at least initially compelling. Much more commonly, one will find fallen-away Catholics who were raised in nominally religious homes (i.e., homes in which Catholic faith was centrally a matter of routine) and who had either a superficial or an irrationally dogmatic religious education. That many of these lose their Catholic faith is not surprising, even though it is deeply lamentable. For individuals like these, Catholicism seems to have never had a genuine rational appeal. The seed of faith appears to have only ever grown shallow roots. In stark contrast, one finds a great many converts to Catholicism whose allegiance was a hard-won battle of mind against a rationally settled former conclusion.[8]

What grips the minds of these philosophers to embrace Catholicism? A list of the ordinary reasons will sound commonplace to anyone familiar with conversions to Catholicism: that the Catholic faith is evident in the earliest Church, that it makes better sense of the

---

[8] For example, Francis J. Beckwith, the author of this volume's foreword, converted to Catholicism while serving as the president-elect of the Evangelical Theological Society and is a professor of philosophy and church-state studies at Baylor University. Beckwith's story of conversion can be found in his *Return to Rome: Confessions of an Evangelical Catholic* (Grand Rapids, MI: Brazos Press, 2008).

Scriptures (internally considered and as a collection), that it better diagnoses and responds to the human condition, that it has a beauty as difficult to describe as it is to overstate, that it solves or avoids vexing problems inherent in alternative religions, that it remains despite intense and repeated waves of persecution on the outside and extreme corruption and wickedness among some of the Church's members on the inside. The four marks of Christ's Church are that it is one, holy, catholic, and apostolic. And one can see in the many reasons drawing individuals to Catholicism one or another of these marks at work: the oneness of the Church throughout history; the unspotted purity, beauty, and moral goodness of the faith even when proclaimed by the most wicked and filthy of men; the universal appeal of the faith as a response to a shared human condition; and the unbroken line of authority capable of settling disputes and thus transmitting the complete deposit of faith to all generations.

The first essay of the collection is by Edward Feser, an associate professor of philosophy at Pasadena City College. Although Feser was raised Catholic, as a young man his faith gave way against Protestant objections. The Protestant beliefs he adopted in turn gave way under the influence of existentialist and (later) atheist philosophers. Yet in his professional philosophical research, Feser began to see serious problems in the purely physicalist view of the person that fit most naturally with the atheism he had embraced, as well as broader problems with the project of explaining everything in purely material terms. And as a professor, Feser began to seek more robust reasons to believe in God's existence so to make his teaching involve a more interesting debate. Rather than discovering the cartoonish errors that he was accustomed to seeing in the arguments for God, Feser instead found powerful reasoning that won him over by degree. But it was his teaching of a class on world religions that channeled his emerging belief in God toward a worship of God revealed through the Catholic Church. For Feser saw in Catholicism a rational and historically authentic structure, and in every alternative religion, irresolvable problems: a false view of the self common in Eastern religions, for instance, an ambiguity on central points of the human condition found in non-Christian Abrahamic religions, and an implausible view of authority and revelation present in non-Catholic Christianity.

In the second essay, J. Budziszewski explains how his childhood Christianity also gave way in early adulthood to atheism, influenced especially by a materialism that accompanied his understanding of the natural sciences, along with a political ideology that recast Christianity in this-worldly terms. Like Feser, Budziszewski saw deep connections between his views on God and his views on the self. Unlike Feser, Budziszewski was willing to bite the physicalist bullet regarding himself—or at least to attempt to do so, even if it killed him internally. Yet Budziszewski's conscience pulled him back from using his position as a professor of government and philosophy at the University of Texas at Austin as a pulpit for nihilistic materialism. In his hesitations, he reflected and found his condition deeply wanting. So, too, he saw in the classical Christian literature that his courses covered an intimation of what—or whom—his soul had been wanting, and he was drawn in by this goodness and beauty. Thereafter, Budziszewski and his wife became Episcopalian, where they remained for some years. But the crises that shook the Episcopalian communion also shook Budziszewski, and led him and his wife both to reflect much more deeply upon the necessity of legitimate doctrinal authority, capable of maintaining truth and settling disagreement. These reflections led to their collective embrace of the Catholic faith, secured upon the rock that is Peter and the apostolic authority that descended from him.

The third essay is written by Brian Cutter, an assistant professor of philosophy at the University of Notre Dame. Like many, Cutter was raised in a home where religion was neither wholly present nor wholly absent. In high school, he was positively exposed to a more serious presentation of Protestant Christianity in the works of C. S. Lewis and through friends, but this exposure did not lead to the development of serious commitments, and by the time he entered graduate school, Cutter was a thoroughgoing atheist and materialist. Much like Feser and Budziszewski, Cutter's first steps toward Catholicism consisted in an increasing disillusionment with the philosophical "companion" views that went together with atheism. In particular, Cutter saw methodological (or metaphilosophical) problems with his approach to philosophy as something akin to naturalistic puzzle-solving. He also became increasingly convinced that physicalism about the person is an error. The Christian alternative appeared far more plausible on a number of fronts, but especially regarding the condition of the human person. But whereas the movement from atheism to a general sort of Christianity proceeded relatively slowly, it did not take long for Cutter to embrace Catholicism as the most plausible form of Christianity, motivated by the internal plausibility of its doctrinal claims, the historical continuity of Catholicism with the early Church, and Christ's manifest intention to leave a visibly united Church on earth, among others.

Neal Judisch, an associate professor of philosophy at the University of Oklahoma, was raised in a pious Baptist household and, despite some youthful waywardness, retained the religiosity of his youth into adulthood. What changed were the particularities of his convictions, for as he explains in the fourth essay of the volume, the cohesive systematicity of so-called Reformed (or Calvinist) theology supplemented the more piecemeal teaching he found in his Baptist instruction. Thereafter, Judisch joined the Presbyterian Church in America (PCA), where Calvinism is more officially embraced, and here he (and later his wife) remained for some years. Yet, lingering doubts about central parts of the "Reformed" story weighed on Judisch during his early years as a professor. These concerns became inquiries, and the inquiries saw their resolution in the embrace of Roman Catholicism. Most centrally, Judisch saw the unavoidable and undeniable necessity of genuine ecclesiastical authority to preserve both truth and unity in Christianity.

The popular Catholic intellectual Peter Kreeft, professor of philosophy at Boston College, converted to Catholicism while a graduate student at Yale, and in his contribution he explains how he was raised and educated in the Dutch wing of the Reformed tradition (specifically, in the Reformed Church in America). But even while a student at a college firmly committed to this tradition—Calvin College (so named after the early Protestant John Calvin)—his philosophical mind turned to thinking about the justification of this tradition, especially in light of Church history and in contrast to core Catholic teachings, like that of the Real Presence of Christ in the Eucharist. He was surprised on point after point at the greater reasonableness of the Catholic faith and converted as soon as he left the Dutch Calvinist stronghold in which he had been raised.

The sixth essay of the volume is written by Logan Paul Gage, assistant professor of philosophy at Franciscan University of Steubenville.

Gage grew up in a deeply religious home as a "preacher's kid" of an Assemblies of God (and later Baptist) minister. Although preachers' kids commonly have reputations among Protestants as spiritually complacent or even rebellious, Gage took his religious upbringing seriously, committing himself to Christ in an authentic way, especially as a teenager and attending a Protestant college. In his first job out of college, Gage was exposed for the first time to serious Catholicism by way of a colleague, and the challenging conversations that followed made Gage reflect more deeply than he had previously on the foundational elements of Protestant belief. Most central, in Gage's mind, was the Bible—both as a collection and in its proper interpretation. After considerable study on the formation of the canon (or set of books that are recognized as inspired by God), and reflection on the need for a living authority necessary for establishing what is included in the canon, Gage found the only plausible resolution in acceptance of the authority of the papacy, and by extension, the Catholic Church.

Robert C. Koons, professor of philosophy at the University of Texas at Austin, came to Catholicism as a member of the Lutheran Church–Missouri Synod. In the seventh essay of the volume, Koons explains how he—following Luther—thought that the rupture of Christianity that occurred in the sixteenth century stood or fell upon the proper understanding of the doctrine of justification (i.e., the doctrine pertaining to our having a right relationship with God, sufficient to enter his company after death). For it was the dispute over justification centrally that provided the first and central impetus for large numbers of European Catholics to "protest" and leave the Church. If this protest stood upon a mistake, then the resulting break in Christian unity (i.e., the Protestant movement) was indefensible. In an essay primarily written as a Lutheran working through the rival views on justification, Koons explains how he sees the traditional Protestant understanding of this doctrine to be an error and the rival Catholic view to be much more reasonable.

W. Scott and Lindsay K. Cleveland were raised in religious homes and took their Christian belief seriously throughout their college studies—seriously enough to have met while participating in a post-college Protestant formation program aimed at aspiring Christian leaders (Trinity Forum Academy) and then both going on to pursue

master's degrees at Yale Divinity School. Subsequently, they both
entered Ph.D. programs at Baylor, with Scott pursuing a degree in
philosophy and Lindsay a degree in theology. Yet Lindsay increasingly noticed deep problems in the theology that formed the core of
her study—the shallowness of Protestant ethics, the misunderstanding of St. Paul's writings that underpinned the characteristic Protestant notion(s) of justification, the inescapability of tradition, among
others—problems that were all resolved in an embrace of the Catholic faith. While Lindsay was ready to embrace the faith to which
her reasoning pointed, Scott had serious reservations about Catholicism. To ease any possible tension, Scott began to work through
his reservations independently of Lindsay, and on point after point
he saw mistakes inherent in his background Protestant views, and a
greater reasonableness in Catholicism. While still at Baylor, they both
entered the Catholic Church. Presently, Scott is an assistant professor
of philosophy at University of Mary, and in the spring of 2018, Lindsay received her Ph.D. in philosophy from Baylor University.

The ninth essay of the collection is written by Bryan Cross, assistant professor of philosophy at Mount Mercy University. Cross was
raised in a pious Pentecostal home, and his formation inclined him to
a strong love of God from an early age, which grew in time as a college student and thereafter as a leader in a student fellowship program.
While discerning a call to be either a Protestant minister or missionary, Cross began studies at Covenant Theological Seminary, where
his theological training deepened his understanding of and commitment to the Reformed theology he had begun immersing himself
in since high school. Both family tragedy as well as apologetical and
doctrinal concerns began to pull Cross to pay increasing attention to
philosophy and how philosophy comes in to thinking about suffering
and other foundational aspects of Christian teaching. It was an apparently happenstance series of conversations with Mormon missionaries that prompted Cross and his wife to begin thinking about what
resources, if any, they as Protestants had to vindicate appeals to the
early Church as the appropriate lens through which to interpret the
Bible—more so, at least, than the rival Book of Mormon interpretation being offered. Providentially, these reflections deepened over
time for Cross as illustrations of the role paradigms play in theology
and—following arguments from the prolific philosopher (and fellow

Catholic convert) Alasdair MacIntyre—Cross eventually saw that it was the Catholic paradigm that better explained its rivals (with their related objections) and made intelligible myriad theological truths. Soon after, both Cross and his wife came into full communion with the Catholic Church.

In the final essay of the collection, Candace Vogler, David B. and Clara E. Stern Professor of Philosophy at the University of Chicago, recounts the providential way in which she was drawn closer to Christ in her sufferings and was persuaded of the truth of Catholicism by its commitment to the biblical doctrine of the Eucharist. The victim of profound abuse at the hands of her father, Candace saw in Christ a model of true masculinity, fundamentally at odds with the specter of a man that tormented her. Abandoned by her mother, she was not alone. For by the magnificent inner working of grace, she embraced the love and forgiveness even of one's enemies that she found in the life of Christ and was able to bring that light to the darkness of her troubled family, among many others.

In each of these essays, the attentive reader will find a fully human story. For as humans we are rational beings, but we are not disembodied intellects. We are driven by reason, but not by reason alone. Rational considerations captured the attention of our contributors, but their intellects were actuated by more than what's appropriately subject to cross-examination and scrutiny. In other words, the contributions contained herein are not merely a collection of arguments for Catholicism; they are stories of grace.

The God of a Philosopher

Edward Feser

It is sometimes said that teaching something to others is the best way to learn it yourself. In large part, that is how I returned to the Catholic faith, in which I had been raised but which I had abandoned as a teenager. I only came genuinely to understand and accept it in the course of trying to explain to students why anyone else would ever accept it. Making the explanation as convincing as I could for pedagogical purposes, I inadvertently converted myself.

My Apostasy

Some backstory: In elementary school in the 1970s, I was taught by nuns of the traditional stripe. They wore the habit, used the Baltimore Catechism, tried to instill piety, and were just stern enough to lend a little bit of credence to the stereotypes (though I was never struck with a ruler). Naturally, the religious instruction we received was clear, substantive, and orthodox. The real stuff. Catholic high school was a different story. There, "spirit of Vatican II" liberalism was the rule. Standout memories include the priest who spent part of a Scripture class cheerfully explaining various pornographic slang terms, the Mass where ordinary honey wheat bread was used for the hosts, and the theology lecture based on the lyrics to the Rolling Stones' "Sympathy for the Devil". Unsurprisingly, several of the clergy would, years later, be exposed as sexual abusers, though I never saw or heard of any of that myself at the time.

I came to reject orthodox and liberal Catholicism alike, however, after a relative introduced me to some of the Protestant objections against Catholicism. There were two that seemed especially powerful. The first was the claim that many central Catholic doctrines had no foundation in Scripture. The second was the claim that the true source of these doctrines was paganism. I discovered books like Alexander Hislop's *The Two Babylons* (1853), which seemed to show that Catholicism is essentially a continuation of precisely the sort of religion condemned throughout the Bible, and thus something any true Christian had to oppose.

Hence, my teenage rejection of Catholicism was based on (what I would later discover was) an unfounded prejudice—*sola scriptura*—and on crackpot historical scholarship. In any event, the thing to emphasize for the moment is that my objections were essentially theoretical rather than practical. Though certain distinctive Catholic moral doctrines were among the teachings I rejected, my motivation was not to find a way to justify looser morals, but rather I judged that the teachings in question were unscriptural. I was then, and always have been, conservative on moral and political issues. Nor was I looking for an emotional "born again" experience of the sort associated with Evangelical Protestantism. I have always found highly sentimental religiosity distasteful. In short, my falling away from Catholicism, like my later reversion, was a fairly cerebral affair.

I don't say this by way of either self-congratulation or self-criticism, but just matter-of-factly. It is also important not to misunderstand what I am saying. There was nothing bloodless in either my falling away or my later reversion. On the contrary, where religion, morality, and other serious matters are concerned, I am prone to rather visceral responses. But one of the things I seem always to have had a visceral attachment to is the idea of the objective pursuit of the true and the good. If you want to appeal to my emotions, the best way to do so is to give me a knock-down rational argument. By the same token, fideism, sophistry, subjectivism, and the like have always aroused in me a profound revulsion.

Unsurprisingly, then, though in college I fell hard for the woman who would become my wife, she had competition. For that is when I also fell deeply in love with philosophy. The occasion was a course on Greek literature, which devoted a unit to the Pre-Socratics.

Thales, Anaximander, Heraclitus, and company—and most especially the arch rationalists Parmenides and Zeno—immediately and utterly fascinated me. From that point on, I have never been able to take seriously the notion of being anything but a philosopher.

Philosophy can be overwhelming when you first delve into it. The novice is inevitably pulled in several directions at once as he reads different writers and finds much of what they say interesting and plausible, but also finds that some of the ideas to which he is attracted are not compatible with others. Sorting things out takes time. Though no longer a Catholic, I was for the time still a Christian. Naturally, then, I wanted to see what Christian philosophers had to say, and the one who first drew my attention was St. Anselm. I was, for a time, obsessed with his ontological argument for the existence of God. It was the high-octane rationalist method of Parmenides applied to the defense of a conclusion that (unlike Parmenides' own notorious position, which denied the reality of change) I still found plausible. Anselm's *Cur Deus Homo*, wherein he takes the same approach to explaining why the Second Person of the Trinity had to become incarnate and die on the Cross, exerted a similar fascination.

However, I was also a young man, and there are no thinkers more attractive to a young person just getting into philosophy than the existentialists. Søren Kierkegaard's writings became another enthusiasm— *Fear and Trembling* (1843) was an especially strong influence—as did those of the Protestant theologians Karl Barth and Paul Tillich, who, in their very different ways, developed some of Kierkegaard's ideas. The standout theme was that neither God nor the Christian's relationship to him could be captured in a philosophical system. God transcends the categories of any such system, his revelation comes to us from a place beyond them, and thus our response to it must involve a "leap of faith" rather than rational deliberation. I gradually became convinced that such a leap is indeed what Christianity requires.

I also gradually became convinced that, precisely for that reason, Christianity had to be rejected. Christian existentialism was thus the gateway drug that would lead me to atheism, and German philosopher Friedrich Nietzsche replaced Kierkegaard as my existentialist hero. To be sure, there were other influences on my atheism. There was Bertrand Russell's essay *Why I Am Not a Christian* (1927) and its potted (and, as I would come to realize only much later, laughably superficial) criticisms of arguments for God's existence. There were also more serious philosophical works, like J. L. Mackie's *The Miracle of Theism.*[1] There was Hyam Maccoby's *The Mythmaker,*[2] which purported to show that St. Paul had invented Christianity by grafting themes from the Hellenistic mystery religions onto Judaism. This was Hislop 2.0: Christianity as a whole, and not just Catholicism, was really just an adaptation of pagan superstition. Like Hislop, it was crackpot stuff, but more mainstream historical-critical study of the New Testament also led me to reject the key historical claims of Christianity, as did Scottish philosopher David Hume's (1711–1776) famous argument regarding miracles.[3]

But the overarching theme for me was the idea that Christianity requires an irrational faith commitment. An epigram from Nietzsche's notebooks became a favorite motto:

> A very popular error: having the courage of one's convictions; rather, it is a matter of having the courage for an attack on one's convictions!!![4]

As my philosophical education progressed and I became more immersed in analytic philosophy, my enthusiasm for and interest in the bombastic and unsystematic Nietzsche would wane considerably. But the spirit of the epigram stayed with me, and religion, I believed, was incompatible with it. To be a true philosopher required testing one's convictions by reference to evidence and rational argument, whereas to be religious required the opposite. Hence, as a philosopher, I could not be religious.

The irony is that the very sentiment that led me to this conclusion would eventually lead me away from it. For I would come to do something that few people who thrill to Nietzsche's epigram ever

---

[1] J. L. Mackie, *The Miracle of Theism: Arguments for and against the Existence of God* (New York: Oxford University Press, 1982).

[2] Hyam Maccoby, *The Mythmaker: Paul and the Invention of Christianity* (New York: Harper & Row, 1986).

[3] David Hume, "Of Miracles", in *An Enquiry concerning Human Understanding* (1748), section 10.

[4] Quoted in Walter Kaufmann, *Nietzsche: Philosopher, Psychologist, Antichrist,* 4th ed. (Princeton, NJ: Princeton University Press, 1974), 354. As Kaufmann notes, the three exclamation points are in the original.

seem to: I applied it to atheism itself, and to my skeptical assumptions about Catholicism. And what I found is that they could not withstand rational attack.

Rethinking Atheism

I was an atheist for about ten years—roughly, the 1990s. Several developments in my philosophical thinking during that period prepared the ground for my eventual rethink. First, arguments developed by John Searle and other philosophers of mind convinced me that none of the existing attempts to explain the human mind in materialist terms could work. Second, arguments from the logician Gottlob Frege and others convinced me that attempts to explain language and meaning in materialist terms also failed. Third, the work of the later Bertrand Russell convinced me that mathematical physics tells us little about the nature of matter beyond its abstract structure. Now, materialism is a key component of modern atheism and was a component of my own atheism. Materialists tend to think that they have a very clear idea of what matter is and of how to explain all phenomena in materialist terms. I came to see that neither of these suppositions is true, so that the standard metaphysical alternative to theism was not nearly as well worked out as I had thought. It was as riddled with difficulties, unanswered questions, and dogmatic assumptions as atheists take theism to be.

That softened me up for the next big revelation, which was that theism, by contrast, was in fact much *more* philosophically sophisticated and worked out than I had supposed. Now, I have told this story of my gradual philosophical disillusionment with materialism and reversion to theism at length elsewhere, and I won't repeat much of it here.[5] What I want to focus on are the aspects most relevant to my reversion to Catholicism, specifically.

While still a graduate student at the University of California at Santa Barbara in the late 1990s, I had several opportunities to teach

---

[5] See "The Road from Atheism" in my anthology *Neo-Scholastic Essays* (South Bend, IN: St. Augustine's Press, 2015), 200–214. The essay first appeared at my blog in a post from July 17, 2012, at http://edwardfeser.blogspot.com/2012/07/road-from-atheism.html.

the Introduction to Philosophy course. Because the course was geared toward nonmajors, I made sure that the topics covered would be of the sort anyone might find interesting. The classic arguments for God's existence filled the bill, since everyone cares *whether* God exists, even those who are convinced that he does not. So I devoted a part of the course to them. Around the same time, I had the opportunity to teach a Philosophy of Religion course as an adjunct instructor at Pasadena City College, and naturally we covered the theistic arguments in that class too.

Unsurprisingly, given that I was an atheist, my approach to the subject in the classroom was essentially negative. I would line up the arguments and then shoot them down, running through the list of stock objections that so many people, including perhaps most philosophy professors, suppose are fatal (e.g., "If everything has a cause, what caused God?" "Even if there were a first cause, why should we think it is God?"). I did not do so in a polemical way. My atheism was matter-of-fact at that point, the zeal that typically accompanies the adoption of any big new idea having long since worn off. I simply dutifully conveyed the conventional wisdom about the arguments and then moved on. Students dutifully swallowed it, having been conditioned by the surrounding intellectual culture to believe that religion was not in any case the sort of thing that could be supported through reason.

It was boring as hell. There was a quiz show on TV in those days called *Win Ben Stein's Money*, and I remember Stein once jokingly referring to the competition between contestants on the show as an "intellectual street fight". My view was that the most interesting way to teach a philosophy class, especially for novices in the subject, was to present a philosophical dispute as something like an intellectual street fight. In particular, I thought that the students would be most engaged if they saw the issue being debated as one where the stakes were high, and where the intellectual firepower on both sides was impressive. But the debate over God's existence, as I was presenting it and as probably most philosophy professors present it, seemed the opposite of that. It came across as one side presenting some manifestly lame arguments for a silly superstition, and the other side responding with some obvious objections that an eight-year-old could have come up with.

Nor was this *merely* boring. It put the subject of philosophy in a bad light and didn't sit well with the fact that Aquinas, G. W. Leibniz, and other defenders of arguments for God's existence rightly had reputations as men of genius. Why study the subject if this trivial sort of exchange is all it amounted to? Why are these thinkers so highly regarded if they are so easily refuted? *This is no way to teach a philosophy class*, I concluded.

So, I decided to jazz things up. As my dissertation supervisor Tony Anderson once emphasized to me, when evaluating the ideas and arguments of a philosopher, it is important always to consider not merely what he *did* in fact say in support of them, but what *could be* said in support of them. This method is characteristic of analytic philosophy at its best, and it is essential to the objective pursuit of truth, to which any genuine philosopher must be committed. You cannot be confident that you have given an idea a fair hearing until you make a serious effort to understand how a rational person could find it plausible. This is especially important when considering ideas you find alien or unattractive. Perhaps deeper investigation will simply confirm your original judgment that they are implausible. But it could turn out that they contain some insight you have overlooked. It could turn out that it is only unexamined prejudices of your own that have kept you from taking the idea seriously. Certainly you will understand the ideas better as a result of having made the effort.

I decided, as a pedagogical exercise, to apply this method to the classic arguments for God's existence, which I had long before decided were no good. How might an Aquinas or a Leibniz respond to the various standard objections, which seemed so obvious and devastating? Was there some way to turn the debate between atheism and theism into a horse race, at least for a few lectures, so that class might be more interesting and challenging for the students?

In order to answer these questions and to prepare better lectures, I began to revisit the literature on the theistic arguments—and, more to the point, to look at materials I had not considered before. Another graduate student who was a friend and fellow atheist introduced me to William Lane Craig's book *The Cosmological Argument from Plato to Leibniz*,[6] which contained a wealth of material showing how much more philosophically rich and complex than I had realized were the various medieval versions of the argument, such as Aquinas'.

[6] William Lane Craig, *The Cosmological Argument from Plato to Leibniz* (London: Macmillan Press, 1980).

Frederick Copleston's work on the history of medieval philosophy[7] helped me to get up to speed on heretofore alien notions such as the theory of act and potency. I also discovered contemporary "analytical Thomist" writers like John Haldane[8] and David Braine,[9] who were still defending arguments like Aquinas'.

Material like this gradually revealed to me that Aquinas' Five Ways were saying *nothing like* what I and most other contemporary philosophy professors supposed they were. Modern readers, including most academics, typically make assumptions like the following:

1. Aquinas thinks that everything has a cause, but arbitrarily makes an exception in the case of God.
2. He traces the universe back to a temporal beginning point and then argues that God must be the cause of that beginning.
3. He simply assumes without argument that a series of causes cannot regress infinitely.
4. He gives no reason for thinking that there can be only one first cause, or that the first cause possesses omnipotence, omniscience, and the other divine attributes.
5. His Fifth Way is an early version of a William Paley–style watchmaker argument.
6. The Five Ways were meant by Aquinas to be complete, stand-alone arguments for God's existence.

The stock objections to Aquinas' arguments reflect these assumptions. But I came to find out that they were not only wrong, but laughably incompetent. In fact, Aquinas does not rest his arguments on the premise that everything has a cause and indeed would deny that everything has a cause. He is not arguing for a temporal beginning of the universe and in fact explicitly denies that such a beginning can be established through philosophical argument. He has a careful analysis of different types of causal series and admits that some series can indeed be infinite while arguing that the nature of the kind of

---

[7] Cf. F. C. Copleston, *Aquinas* (London: Penguin Books, 1991), and Frederick Copleston, *A History of Philosophy, Volume II: Medieval Philosophy* (New York: Doubleday, 1993).

[8] Cf. J. J. C. Smart and J. J. Haldane, *Atheism and Theism* (Oxford: Blackwell, 1996).

[9] Cf. David Braine, *The Reality of Time and the Existence of God: The Project of Proving God's Existence* (Oxford: Clarendon Press, 1988).

causation involved in the other type makes an infinite series impossible in principle. He devotes literally hundreds of pages to arguing that a first cause would have to have the various divine attributes. He does not think of natural objects on the model of watches or other human artifacts and is not arguing that they are unlikely to have arisen via natural processes. The Five Ways are merely summaries, and presuppose various background metaphysical theses, and answers to various objections, that Aquinas develops in detail elsewhere. And so on.[10]

In short, no one who has actually studied Aquinas' natural theology could think that he believes the things commonly attributed to him or that the standard objections have any force at all. It became clear that most philosophers who criticize Aquinas are simply parroting what they had read in textbooks or heard in lectures while undergraduates, from people who were themselves ignorant of what Aquinas had really said. They had never read Aquinas or other Thomists for themselves, or at best had read in an anthology only the very short selection from the *Summa Theologiae* summarizing the Five Ways. Ignorant of the larger context, they read their false assumptions into Aquinas' text and then based their objections on this misreading. This had been happening for generations, until misconceptions like the ones noted settled into widely believed and unquestioned dogmas. To dispel these misconceptions, all one needs to do is make the effort to read Aquinas and other Thomists more carefully. But most philosophers do not do that, because they think, precisely on the basis of the common misconceptions, that the arguments are not interesting enough to warrant further investigation.

This reexamination of Aquinas had two immediate effects on me. First, it enabled me to improve my teaching. Though initially I was still not quite convinced by Aquinas' arguments, covering the Five Ways no longer seemed like shooting fish in a barrel, and I was able to present the debate between theism and atheism in a more philosophically substantive and interesting way. Second, it hammered home the lesson that academic philosophers, even when speaking on philosophical topics, often don't know what they are talking about. They are as prone to prejudice, ignorance, and circular reasoning as

---

[10] I have since written a lot about how properly to understand Aquinas' arguments. See, for example, my book *Aquinas* (Oxford: Oneworld Publications, 2009).

anyone else. To be sure, I already knew this from my experience of
the political climate in universities. Again, I was conservative even
in my atheist days, which put me out of step with most academics. I
found that left-wing philosophers, like left-wing academics in general, are often ill-informed and prejudiced when it comes to conservative ideas and arguments. But I had been accustomed to thinking
that on religious matters, at least, the academic conventional wisdom
was well-founded and the self-confidence of secular philosophers justified. Now I found out that, at least with respect to Aquinas, that
was not the case. "What else have they gotten wrong?" I began to
ask myself.

But Aquinas' arguments were not the only ones in which I came to
have a renewed interest. In the course of preparing my lectures, I also
began to revisit the rationalist style of cosmological argument developed by Leibniz and Samuel Clarke. I found what Richard Taylor
and William Rowe had to say about the subject especially helpful.[11]
The basic thrust of the argument is that there can be no ultimate
explanation of why any world exists at all unless we affirm the existence of something that exists in an absolutely necessary rather than
contingent way. Leibniz and Clarke also argue that this necessary
being must have the key divine attributes. Now, there are various
technical issues that arise in discussions of this argument, such as the
question of how exactly to formulate the principle of sufficient reason
(roughly, the thesis that everything has an explanation, which is the
foundation of the argument). Defenders of the argument, it seemed,
had various ways to deal with the technical objections that might be
raised. But the key atheist objection to the argument, it seemed to
me, was the one pressed by Russell and Mackie. That was the idea
that it may be that the world simply has no explanation at all, but is
just an unintelligible brute fact. The theist, Russell and Mackie claim,
has not shown otherwise, and in that case the rationalist cosmological
argument fails.

When I had originally thought about the argument in the course
of becoming an atheist, this objection seemed to me to be strong.

[11] Richard Taylor, *Metaphysics*, 2nd ed. (Englewood Cliffs, NJ: Prentice-Hall, 1974),
chap. 10; William L. Rowe, "The Cosmological Argument", in Joel Feinberg, ed., *Reason
and Responsibility*, 9th ed. (Belmont, CA: Wadsworth, 1996).

But again, I was now trying to make the debate between theism and atheism more interesting for classroom purposes, so I started to think seriously about how a defender of the argument might respond. As I did so, the objection raised by Russell and Mackie came to seem increasingly problematic, in two respects.

First, why should anyone take seriously the suggestion that the existence of the world is just an unintelligible brute fact? The atheist seemed vulnerable to the charge that he had no reason for doing so other than as a means of avoiding theism. After all, in no other context would anyone take such a suggestion seriously. If the waiter serves you a steak that has been burned to a crisp, you would never be satisfied with the response: "Don't blame the cook; maybe it's just an unintelligible brute fact that it came out that way." If the mixing of certain chemicals was followed by an explosion, no chemist would say: "Maybe it's just an unintelligible brute fact that the explosion occurred." So why should we make an exception when evaluating the rationalist cosmological argument? The atheist could be accused of simply trying to find a loophole by which he might avoid having to accept the argument, rather than believing the "brute fact" view because it really was plausible. This might be good lawyering, but it seemed to be bad philosophy.

Second, it seemed hard to contain unintelligibility once you let it get its foot in the door. If the very existence of the material universe and the fundamental laws of nature were merely "brute facts" without rhyme or reason, why should we believe that more particular phenomena within the universe are any more intelligible? Why not regard all explanations as no less illusory than the atheist takes the cosmological argument to be? Theism and the very possibility of explanation—in philosophy, science, and everyday common sense—stand or fall together. Or so the theist could argue.

Once again, the immediate effect these considerations had on me was twofold. First, they enabled me to make of the debate between atheism and theism a much more interesting subject for classroom lecture and discussion. Second, it increasingly dawned on me that atheism no less than theism could be motivated by wishful thinking, special pleading, and otherwise irrational habits of mind—and that theism could be motivated by entirely *rational* considerations no less than atheism could be.

As all this was going on, my thinking about the mind-body problem—which, in graduate school, had been my main interest and the subject of my doctoral dissertation—was also evolving. Searle, as I have already noted, was a big influence. One of the themes of his work that stood out was the idea that materialist attempts to explain the mind always really implicitly end up ignoring or even denying the existence of the mind. In other words, purportedly reductionist forms of materialism are, ultimately, disguised forms of eliminative materialism—the thesis that the mind does not really exist at all, but is an illusion. And eliminativism, I have always thought, is a ludicrous and indeed self-refuting position.

Now, philosophers distinguish various aspects of the mind. Our capacity for conscious awareness is one aspect, and an aspect we share with nonhuman animals. Our capacity for abstract thought is another, and in the animal kingdom it is unique to us. I believed that there was a way that consciousness might after all be understood in purely material terms, but abstract thought was another thing entirely. Here I resorted to a variation on a view known as *mysterianism*, according to which there is an explanation of how the human intellect can arise from purely material processes, but the intellect is too limited to understand that explanation. The problem with this approach as a way to salvage materialism, however, is that the most important antimaterialist arguments show, if they are correct, that the intellect simply *cannot be* material, not merely that we cannot know *how* it can be. Frege's arguments, for example, purport to show that the meanings of our thoughts simply cannot be identified with brain processes, sensations, or anything else bodily. Again, I had come to regard such arguments as very powerful.

The bottom line is that it gradually came to seem to me impossible to fit the existence of our rational thought processes into a purely material world—at the very same time as it was gradually coming to seem to me impossible to deny the principle of sufficient reason, and the divine necessary being the principle entailed, without denying the intelligibility of the world altogether. My investigations in the philosophy of mind and philosophy of religion, which had always been at the center of my philosophical interests and which had originally led me to materialism and atheism, were now leading me in the opposite direction. And as with my youthful atheism, a kind of rationalism was the driving force. How could it be *rational* to deny the existence of rational thought processes themselves? How could it be *rational* to deny the very intelligibility of the world?

I vividly remember lying on my bed one quiet afternoon and staring intently into the corner of the room as I pondered these matters. There was nothing there but cobwebs and tiny bits of dust and other debris lying on the carpet. I turned the scene over in my mind, and the more I did so, the more this little corner of the room came to seem entirely devoid of any sort of intelligibility or meaning. The exercise was not unlike that of repeating a word over and over to yourself until it starts to sound like gibberish. I started to conceptualize the scene the way it seemed one ought to if eliminative materialism were true and if the principle of sufficient reason were false. I thought of it as just *brute mindless stuff* devoid of any explanation, devoid of consciousness, devoid of moral or aesthetic value, devoid of any of the cognitive significance we know from our thoughts. Given the utterly banal character of the scene—again, just cobwebs, dust, a bit of carpet—this was fairly easy to do. I then continued this little thought experiment by extending the conceptualization to the entire universe. That is to say, I concentrated on the thought that absolutely every square millimeter of the universe was as utterly pointless and inexplicable—as completely devoid of meaning, purpose, intelligibility, or significance—as this stupid little patch of dust and cobwebs was. That included everything going on in every human brain and every human action, including my own, including what I was doing at that very moment—all just further brute mindless stuff, in no significant way different from the dust and cobwebs.

The effect was surreal, indeed chilling. It just seemed an utterly insane way to think about the world. Yet it also seemed to be what one was ultimately committed to if one was to be a consistent atheist.[12]

Eventually I drew the conclusion that it was indeed insane. The more I mulled over the arguments for theism and against materialism through the course of the late nineties and the beginning of the new century, I gradually went from thinking, "These arguments are a little better than they are given credit for," to thinking, "These

---

[12] Some atheists would agree. See, e.g., Alex Rosenberg, *The Atheist's Guide to Reality* (New York: W.W. Norton, 2011).

arguments are actually kind of interesting," and then, "These arguments are pretty plausible." Finally it hit me that *the arguments were,
after all, simply correct*, and that I had gone badly wrong about the most
fundamental philosophical questions for a decade or so.[13]

As with my apostasy, I was simply following the arguments where
they were leading me. Ten years before I had judged: *I am a philosopher, therefore I cannot believe in God.* Now, as committed as ever
to the rational and objective pursuit of truth but better informed, I
drew a very different conclusion: *I am a philosopher, therefore I cannot
be an atheist.*

As before, the effect was as visceral as it was cerebral. Rational
explanation, pursued consistently, led to the conclusion that there is
a single, infinite, eternal, necessary, immutable, immaterial, omnipotent, omniscient, perfectly good ultimate cause of things—one that,
as I learned from Aquinas' arguments in particular, is sustaining
everything in existence, including me, *right now and at every moment.*
The entire world, again including me and all my current thoughts
and actions, would blink out in an instant if God were not keeping
it all in being, just as you would fall to the floor if the chair you
were sitting on gave way, or a movie would disappear from the
screen if the projector stopped. Contemplating this can produce a
strange, almost dizzying experience. More than that, contemplating
the utter existential dependence of everything at every moment on
this divine cause, and that cause's unfathomable infinite nature, can
move one to worship. Everything else seems second-rate, indeed
trivial, in comparison.

It is sometimes alleged that the God of the philosophers is a mere
abstraction that can only ever appeal to us as an intellectual curiosity and never move the heart or the will. One need only read an

[13] See my book *Five Proofs of the Existence of God* (San Francisco: Ignatius Press, 2017) for
my most recent and detailed exposition and defense of what I take to be the most compelling
arguments for God's existence. What I there call "the Aristotelian proof" (see chap. 1) and
"the rationalist proof" (see chap. 5) are formulations of the two kinds of theistic argument
that I found most persuasive at the time of my reversion to theism. See the essays collected
in the philosophy of mind section of my *Neo-Scholastic Essays* for exposition and defense
of what I take to be the most important arguments for the immateriality of the intellect
(pp. 217–86). The failure of naturalistic accounts of intentionality, which I discuss in a couple
of those essays, was the main consideration that convinced me at the time of my rethinking of
materialism that the mind is immaterial.

Aristotle or Plotinus to see how silly and ill-informed this cliché is. In any event, I know from experience that it is false.

God of Abraham, Aristotle, and Aquinas

During the years in which I was rethinking atheism and materialism, I was also rethinking the world religions. Part of this had to do with the fact that, as I said above, I started to wonder what else my fellow atheists were wrong about, given that they had gotten Aquinas and other theistic philosophers so badly wrong. But once again, part of it had to do with teaching. As an adjunct instructor at Pasadena City College, I was assigned a world religions class, and I taught it several times over the years.

Being an atheist, I decided at first to use a textbook I had heard about that was published by Prometheus Books, well known as a publisher of atheist literature. It was Charles Monroe's *World Religions: An Introduction,* and I soon found out to my horror that it was absolutely dreadful, badly written, and inaccurate. Finding more accurate and fair-minded texts to assign was easy enough, but the real challenge and interest came in going beyond what even a good religious studies textbook would give the students. As with my teaching of the theistic arguments, I wanted to give students a sense of how a rational person could be attracted to any of the seven world religions we covered in the class—Confucianism, Taoism, Hinduism, Buddhism, Judaism, Christianity, and Islam. Accordingly, I focused on the doctrinal side of each religion and approached the material the way a philosopher would—laying out the logical connections between the key ideas, identifying arguments that have been given or could be given for the foundational beliefs of a given religion, and so forth.

This was easier to do with some religions than with others, because they are not all equally interested in abstract theoretical issues. Still, there are serious thinkers associated with each one of these religions, and they informed my thinking about, and teaching of, the religions. In part this reflected my personal interest, as a philosopher, in ideas and arguments. But as with the approach I was taking in my Introduction to Philosophy and Philosophy of Religion courses, I also wanted to do justice to the material and make it as interesting as possible to students. Badly taught, a religion can seem to an outsider to be merely a random collection of superstitions and strange practices, perhaps of historical and sociological interest but unattractive to anyone who hadn't been born into it. My view was that it was much more fair-minded and interesting to see how the doctrinal system of a world religion might seem to follow from premises that a reasonable person might find plausible. It was a matter of applying the philosophical method of asking *what could be said* in favor of an idea, so as to understand it better and find out whether it is on to something.

I found that while for some students this approach was a little dry and abstract for their tastes, for others it was a revelation. They hadn't been accustomed to thinking of a body of religious ideas as having logical structure and grounds. That there was a *rationale* to this or that doctrine or practice of Buddhism, Christianity, or Confucianism helped them to understand these religions and their attraction to some people.

Still an atheist, I did not accept any of these religions myself. It was initially for me an intellectual exercise, comparable to the way one might try one's best, in a history of philosophy class, to help students see why someone might find plausible an odd view like eighteenth-century Anglo-Irish philosopher George Berkeley's idealism or Leibniz's theory of monads. But it increased my respect for all of the religions in question. (A student once remarked to me after class that she believed in God but not in religion. I playfully replied: "That's interesting, because I believe in religion, but not in God.")

This was all going on, however, as I was rethinking atheism and materialism. Hence, as the semesters and years passed, I increasingly started to wonder whether one of the world religions might after all be *true*. Now, since I eventually became convinced by the theistic arguments of philosophers like Aquinas and Leibniz, that ruled out certain religions right away. God, the arguments showed, is utterly distinct from the world, and there is in him something analogous to what we call intellect and will in us. I concluded that pantheistic religions, like Hinduism in most of its forms, are therefore mistaken at a fundamental level. So too are religions that conceive of the ultimate principle of reality in impersonal terms, as Confucianism and Taoism do. Buddhism is even more deeply mistaken insofar as it denies that there is *any* permanent divine reality underlying the world of appearances. So, while I respected the great thinkers of the Eastern religions, I decided that these religions were too deeply in error with respect to the nature of God to be acceptable.

A second problem with the Eastern religions was what they had to say about the nature of *man*. For another thing that I had become convinced of, you'll recall, is the immateriality of the human intellect. The core of the individual human being, I had concluded, is an incorporeal self that stands apart from the entire material world in which we are embedded. And since this self is *rational*, it is like God in a way that nothing else in the material world is. I also eventually became convinced by the traditional philosophical arguments to the effect that this self's incorporeal nature made it incorruptible. All of this makes human beings unique in nature; yet this uniqueness did not seem to me to be recognized in the Eastern religions. Even those having a doctrine of reincarnation, such as Hinduism and Buddhism, held that the individual person *ultimately* disappears, like a water droplet absorbed back into the ocean. There is no abiding self at all in Buddhism; and though there is an abiding self in Hinduism, what strictly abides is the deep *core* of the self that is taken to be identical to God, and not anything that is distinctive of this or that particular man or woman. For pantheistic Hinduism, *everything* is ultimately God-like, because everything is ultimately God. There's nothing special about human beings.

So, if any of the world religions is true, I judged, it had to be one that recognized that God was a creator utterly distinct from the world he creates, and that human beings do have a special destiny within that creation. Hence, I concluded that it is the view of God and the soul that one finds in the Abrahamic religions that was most in accord with what we could know through philosophical arguments. But were any of these religions true?

There were several considerations that, though they did not by themselves demonstrate the truth of Christianity, gradually came to make Christianity seem far more plausible to me than either Judaism or Islam, let alone any of the Eastern religions. The first was that Christianity had a far more plausible conception of the point of human existence. As an undergrad I had read St. Athanasius' *On the Incarnation*, and John Hick's book *Evil and the God of Love*,[14] which introduced me to the thought of St. Irenaeus. These early

[14] John Hick, *Evil and the God of Love*, rev. ed. (San Francisco: Harper & Row, 1977).

Church Fathers were associated with the thesis of salvation as *theosis* or divinization. The idea, as Athanasius put it, was that "the Son of God became man so that we might become God."[15]

What this means is, in part, that human beings are not only analogous to God in having intellect and will, but are also intended by God to *perfect* our intellects and wills to a point that they will be as *like* the divine intellect and will as possible (even if, as created things, we can never *literally* be God). The way our intellects are to be perfected is by achieving as direct an apprehension as possible of the very essence of God, the source from which all reality derives—what is traditionally called the *beatific vision*. The way our wills are to be perfected is to be fixed forever only on the good, and on the highest good—namely, God. The knowledge the human mind craves and the goodness the human will yearns for will thereby be realized to the maximum possible extent. We can attain, as far as is possible for creatures of our kind, *God-like* knowledge and goodness.

The other part of what Athanasius had in mind is that in order to help us realize this end, God put himself in our position by becoming incarnate. Human beings have both a special dignity and a special weakness. Our dignity lies in our having intellects and wills that are capable of the divinization just described. Our weakness lies in the fact that those intellects and wills are finite and tied to the flesh, with all the limitations, temptations, and sufferings that that entails. Our bodies and the material world in general are good, but they easily distract us from our higher end and naturally make us prone to errors and harms of various kinds. We are *rational* animals, but still animals, and that means that our perfection has to be worked out in the life span and circumstances characteristic of an animal. This is very hard, and in solidarity with us in our sorry state, God took on flesh himself. He wants to raise us up to his level and is willing to get down in the dirt with us to do it. He is like a father who gets down on his hands and knees with a child who has fallen down and badly skinned himself, the better gently and compassionately to help him to his feet.

This makes it intelligible why God would go to the bother of creating us, and how the sufferings of this life have a point. The other

---

[15] Athanasius, *On the Incarnation* 54.3.

religions, I judged, had nothing to compare to it. Judaism and Islam seemed either vague on the point of human existence, or at best to characterize our ultimate destiny in terms of rewards that were too crude and this-worldly. Hinduism and Buddhism, again, held that what is unique and individual to any particular human being was destined to disappear. Christianity, by contrast, taught that the point of human existence was for the *unique, individual* human being to become like God. It couldn't get any better than that—*if* Christianity was true, anyway. But was it?

There was a second feature that gradually made Christianity seem to me much more attractive than its rivals. In my early atheist days, I had come to reject Christianity because I thought it made too many doctrinal claims that could not be supported by rational arguments but required a leap of faith—several leaps of faith, in fact. I recall telling a Christian friend of mine that if I ever were to take any religion seriously again, it would probably be either Judaism or Buddhism. The reason is that these religions tended to emphasize practice over doctrine, so that there was far less in the way of dubious truth claims that one had to swallow. I had also come to think of Christianity as a hodgepodge of claims thrown together without rhyme or reason, no doubt in part because I had thought of many of them as borrowed in an ad hoc way from paganism.

Actually having to teach students about Christianity in my world religions class changed my mind. As I have said, my method was to try as far as possible to make it clear how a rational person might find a religion plausible, and that required setting out the logical relationships between the teachings and the sorts of arguments that have been or could be given for them. This turned out to be easiest to do in the case of Christianity, precisely because it puts such an emphasis on doctrine. As an undergrad, I had read about, and taken courses on, the history of Christian doctrine. As I revisited that material in preparing lectures, I came to see how logical and systematic the structure of Christian doctrine was. There were *reasons* why the core claims were hammered out over the centuries in just the way they were, and it had to do with the implications one doctrine had for other doctrines. If you are going to insist on monotheism but also on the Incarnation, you are going to be led in a Trinitarian direction, and once you are led in that direction, you are going to have to affirm just the sorts of things the tradition ended up affirming, and denying just the things it ended up denying. If you are going to insist that Jesus was God in the flesh, that is going to have implications for what you say about his mother—such as whether she, functioning as essentially the tabernacle of God, could have been stained by sin. And so on. One could of course dispute this or that particular chain of reasoning, but the point was that there *was* reasoning involved, and very carefully considered reasoning, in the case of each doctrine that came to define orthodoxy.

This was one of several considerations that also led me gradually to see how silly were the claims that Christianity in general or Catholicism in particular derived its key doctrines from paganism. To be sure, I found out early on in my undergrad days that Hislop's scholarship was not reputable. I also gradually found out that even more modest claims about purported borrowings from paganism were problematic in various ways. In some cases, the parallels between Christian and pagan ideas were, on careful inspection, not as strong as was claimed; in some cases there was in any event no evidence of any historical influence of the one on the other; and in yet other cases the borrowing could have gone in the *other* direction, from Christianity to paganism. But the systematic, logical structure of Christian doctrine was also a very powerful counterargument. A bundle of arbitrary piecemeal borrowings just wouldn't have the natural, logical connections to one another that, as I came to discover, the doctrines of Christianity had.

The fact that Christianity was *so* systematically doctrinal a religion also made it especially attractive to a philosopher. If there is a true religion, I thought, it ought to appeal strongly to our intellects as well as to the other aspects of our nature, and I came increasingly to see how Christianity did that. But again, was it all *true*? *If* one accepted certain fundamental claims—such as the Resurrection of Jesus and his divinity—then the rest of the structure of Christian teaching fell into place like pieces of a puzzle. But *why* accept those claims?

From St. Paul onward, Christianity has appealed to Christ's Resurrection as the linchpin of the whole religion. A true resurrection from the dead could only be brought about by God himself. Hence, if Christ really was resurrected, this served as a divine seal of approval of him and of what he taught. And if he taught that he is God in the flesh, then that claim, too, and everything that follows from it, had the same divine backing. Hence, if the Resurrection did not occur, then Christianity was a fraud. But if it did occur, then one had to become a Christian.

There had been two remaining obstacles in the way of my doing so. The first was Hume's argument against the rationality of accepting any claim to the effect that a miracle has occurred. The second was the now common view that historical-critical study of the Bible has shown that Christ had not really made the sorts of claims about himself traditionally ascribed to him. But both of these obstacles, as I gradually came to see, essentially presuppose naturalism—the thesis that nothing supernatural exists and that everything that does exist or occur can therefore be explained in terms of the laws of nature—and I now knew that naturalism is false.

Hume's argument is that since a miracle would be a suspension of a law of nature, the evidence that a miracle has occurred, no matter how strong, is always trumped by the evidence that it has not occurred. For example, suppose it is claimed that a resurrection from the dead has occurred. This would involve a suspension of the law that dead people stay dead. But the reason we call this generalization a law is that the empirical evidence for it is as strong as can be. Hence we have empirical evidence of the strongest possible kind that, if in some particular case it seems as if some dead person did not stay dead, that must not really be what happened. We can rule out the miracle claim tout court, precisely *because* it would involve the suspension of a law of nature.

This has a certain plausibility *if* one presupposes that the laws of nature are the fundamental reality in terms of which everything else can be explained, which is of course what naturalists suppose. But if we already know independently that there is a divine First Cause who is more fundamental than the laws of nature, and indeed who created those laws and can suspend them, then Hume's argument collapses. Given that independent knowledge, the evidence for a particular miracle claim cannot be dismissed a priori, but has to be considered on its own merits. Now, Hume's argument had been my main reason for rejecting the claim that Jesus rose from the dead. Once that argument was abandoned, the arguments for the Resurrection took

on a new complexion. William Lane Craig's presentation of those
arguments was especially powerful and convinced me that the Resurrection really had occurred.

Craig's arguments also convinced me that Christ really had
claimed divinity for himself. He showed that, even if the evidence
is limited to sayings of Jesus and stories about him that the majority
of contemporary New Testament scholars are willing to accept as
authentic, it is hard to sustain the thesis that he thought of himself as a mere man.[16] But I had, in any event, come to doubt that
there is any good reason to limit the evidence in this way. Even
as an atheist, I had found many of the arguments put forward by
contemporary New Testament scholars to be ridiculous. The whole
field seemed given to wild speculation. The most famous and widely
accepted of these speculations is the thesis that the Gospels attributed
to Matthew and Luke are based on Mark's Gospel together with a
hypothetical document labeled Q. Some scholars went well beyond
this—for example, claiming to identity further distinct collections
of sayings of Jesus within this imagined document Q (labeled Q1,
Q2, and Q3), coming up with fanciful reconstructions of the communities that purportedly gave rise to these collections, and then
conjuring up fantastic revisionary accounts of the history of early
Christianity on the basis of all this speculation. I had always rolled
my eyes at this kind of stuff.

What I *did* find plausible when I was an atheist was simply the
methodological principle that, given that naturalism is true (and thus
that miracles do not occur, etc.), it is reasonable to reject or reinter-
pret New Testament historical claims where this is necessary in order
to come up with a naturalistic reconstruction of the history of early
Christianity. It was this philosophical commitment to naturalism that,
in my view, justified modern skeptical and revisionist claims about
the self-understanding of Jesus, the dating of the New Testament
documents, and so forth. But when one rejects naturalism, as I had
come to do, the ground for these skeptical and revisionist claims is
undermined, and there is no good reason to reject the traditional

---

[16] Craig has addressed the Resurrection and self-understanding of Jesus in several works.
His book *Reasonable Faith*, rev. ed. (Wheaton, IL: Crossway Books, 1994), contains useful
summaries of the main arguments.

reading of the New Testament—including the traditional understanding of what Jesus claimed about himself.[17]

Full Circle

Thus did I come to accept Christianity. But why Catholicism, specifically? Eastern Orthodoxy had its attractions, especially given my aforementioned interest in some of the Greek Fathers. But Catholicism had greater appeal. The Latin approach to the Trinity, which begins with God's unity and works to the Persons, seemed to me more in the spirit of monotheism, and the *filioque* (and the Son) a more satisfactory way of making sense of the distinctness of the Persons. The intellectual rigor and systematic thinking of the Scholastic tradition were also highly attractive to me as a philosopher.

By far the most important consideration, however, was the Catholic understanding of revelation and authority. A divine revelation is of no effect unless one can know both what counts as part of the revelation, and whether one has properly understood it. I came to see that the Protestant doctrine of *sola scriptura* makes such knowledge impossible. A book cannot interpret itself, and it cannot even tell you what counts as part of the book. For even if there were some passage in it that said, "Here is a list of the materials that should be counted as part of this book," that would only raise the further question of how we can know that *that* passage should really be counted as part of the book. Obviously, to answer that question, we could not appeal to the book itself without begging the question.

A book is merely the expression of the thoughts of the person who wrote the book. In order to know for sure what he intended as part of the book and what he meant by it, you have to ask him. Or you might ask someone who knows him, or someone he has given authority to represent him. The point is that you have to be able to *ask*, and you can't literally ask a book anything. You can only ask, and get answers from, something *personal* rather than impersonal. It could

---

[17] For an excellent recent Catholic defense of the traditional view that Jesus claimed divinity for himself, see Brant Pitre, *The Case for Jesus: The Biblical and Historical Evidence for Christ* (New York: Image, 2016).

be what Scholastic philosophers call a "moral person"—an institution like a state or a corporation. But even these institutions are run by persons in the ordinary sense—human beings who can be asked questions and answer them as representatives of the institution, can make authoritative decisions, and so forth.

Now, when Christ was on earth, he could obviously be asked by his disciples about his revelation. After he departed, these disciples themselves could do the job for others who had questions. Unless these disciples themselves left successors, in each succeeding generation, with the authority to do the same, those later generations would be unable to get an answer to the question of what is truly part of Christ's revelation and how to understand it. Hence, that revelation would be ineffective unless there is some "moral person" or ongoing institution that can interpret it authoritatively. But such an institution is run by persons in the ordinary sense, and where these persons disagree, the institution cannot function unless there is some chief executive with authority to break any deadlock. In short, divine revelation, to be effective, requires something like apostolic succession and a papacy—that is, of course, exactly what Catholicism maintains.[18]

This, too, appealed to me as a philosopher. The reason is that without such an institutional authority, whether to accept something as part of divine revelation, and how to interpret revelation, ultimately seem arbitrary, subjective, and fideistic—tendencies that, as I have said, I have always found strongly off-putting. Primarily for this reason, when I began during my atheist years to reconsider Christianity, I was never really attracted to Protestantism. Once I judged *sola scriptura* a nonstarter, that was pretty much that. There were secondary considerations too. The emotionalism associated with much Evangelical Protestantism remained as off-putting to me as it had when I was an atheist. The more cerebral kind of Protestantism represented by Calvinist presuppositionalism seemed to me hopelessly locked in fallaciously circular reasoning. And even other, less fideistic and sentimental brands of Protestantism simply seemed to me to

---

[18] A useful popular exposition and defense of the Catholic position, which I had read during the course of my reversion to Catholicism, is Mark Shea's *By What Authority?* (Huntington, IN: Our Sunday Visitor, 1996).

lack the sheer intellectual, spiritual, and liturgical gravitas of Catholicism and Eastern Orthodoxy. Again, though, the failure of *sola scriptura* and the power of the Catholic conception of revelation and authority were the decisive issues.

But *had* Catholicism really preserved the teaching of the early Church whole and undefiled? My study of the development of doctrine convinced me that it had. As I was on the cusp of returning to the Catholic Church but still wavering, there was one particular issue that stood out: contraception. Paradoxically, that was the issue that both delayed my reversion but ultimately also sealed the deal.

Even when I was an atheist, I had found the Aristotelian teleological approach to ethics compelling, Alasdair MacIntyre and British philosopher Philippa Foot being the big influences on my thinking in those days. When I started taking Catholicism seriously, I naturally took great interest also in British philosopher Elizabeth Anscombe's writings on sexual morality and in Catholic natural law theory, which was grounded in Aristotelian philosophy. I saw the logic of natural law arguments against contraception and was convinced by the historical arguments that Christianity had indeed condemned contraception from the beginning.

But the flesh is weak, and I dithered. I knew the sacrifices that accepting and living by this doctrine would entail, and thus I was open to hearing out arguments for wiggle room in this area. What convinced me that this was hopeless was my study of how thinking about contraception had evolved within Christianity during the course of the twentieth century. By the end of the century, Protestants had essentially caved in completely on the issue, and the Eastern Orthodox were increasingly wobbly. Use of contraception was also widespread among Catholics, of course. But *doctrinally*, the Church had not changed her teaching. Indeed, the Catholic Church was the last, stubborn institutional holdout.

This bothered me, but also impressed me. Especially impressive was what had happened with Pope Paul VI's 1968 encyclical *Humanae Vitae*, which reaffirmed traditional teaching, to the great consternation of liberal Catholics and the secular world. Paul VI was hardly a conservative pope. He made dramatic changes to the liturgy and oversaw the great disruptions in Catholic teaching and practice that followed upon the Second Vatican Council. He was under enormous pressure to change Catholic doctrine on contraception and had theological advisors telling him that this was possible. That he would in fact change it was widely regarded as inevitable. Even when he finally reaffirmed the traditional teaching, he didn't enforce it and tolerated vociferous dissent.

And yet for all that, *he did reaffirm it.* In his person, the Catholic Church did exactly what you would expect her to do if she was what she claimed to be—under great pressure, she held fast to the deposit of faith even when everyone else was doing the opposite. This utter, intransigent insistence on doctrinal consistency, even in the face of massive countervailing cultural pressures, spoke to the truth and rationality of the Catholic faith. I realized that if I wasn't emotionally comfortable with this perennial doctrine, the problem was with my emotions and not with the doctrine. In resisting it, I was not being reasonable, not being intellectually honest. It was as if a voice was telling me: *You* know *what you need to do. Get with the program, already.*

And so I did, in late 2001, in a confessional in the Catholic church nearest our house. The priest asked me what led me to return to the Church, and I gave him the two-minute version of the story I've been telling here. Mostly, though, we didn't talk about philosophy.

2

A Rake's Progress

J. Budziszewski

Introduction

Since this book is about philosophers who have become Catholics, it would be splendid to present a steady intellectual advance from birth to Catholic faith. This I cannot do, since both philosophically and spiritually, much of my life was a rake's progress. For this reason, I am not sure how edifying the tale will be. Then again, perhaps most lives have something of this messy character, so I am emboldened to proceed.[1]

Writing about oneself has never seemed to me helpful to spiritual discipline. The compilers of the book seem to think it may be a good idea for other reasons. So I will trust them. Besides, it is too late to back out now.

Perhaps I should begin by saying something about what sort of person I am. Though does anyone know what sort of person he is? We speak of finding or even "inventing" ourselves, but we are already invented, and only God can find us. I find it immensely comforting that in this life I don't have to know who I am. God knows and will tell me in the next.

---

[1] When one is telling the same story, one inevitably repeats himself. Some portions of this narrative are adapted from "Escape from Nihilism" (campus lecture, 1997); an essay entitled "Why I Am Not an Atheist", in *Why I Am a Christian: Leading Thinkers Explain Why They Believe*, ed. Norman Geisler and Paul Hoffman (Grand Rapids, MI: Baker Books, 2001), 49–61; and "Objections, Obstacles, Acceptance", *Catholic World Report* (January 2005). I am grateful to the editors.

Some people claim to know God's will for them in minute detail. Though I have a strong sense of his providential care, I have never possessed such knowledge. I can count on the fingers of one hand the occasions on which I have "heard his voice", although they have been powerful. Perhaps some few spiritual luminaries have always known down which pathway to walk and at which door to turn in. I use a method better adapted to fools: "Lord, show me the door, but if I can't see it, please push me on through."

This works surprisingly well.

I suppose I am what is called an intellectual. I can hardly now imagine another life for myself, although when I was a little Baptist boy, working my way through the Old Testament stories, I was enamored of the idea of being a Jewish priest, and when I was a young socialist, after I had dropped out of college to pretend at being proletarian, I spent some time as a welder. I would like to say I crave understanding like food and drink, but those who know my weakness for chocolate would laugh. People have always thought I was smart, probably less because of my real intellectual gifts than because I have a precise manner of speaking. Curiously, those who think I am intelligent—there are numerous dissenters—have sometimes assumed I must be cold. Actually, I feel strongly about things, I am sentimental about my family, I cherish my wife, and I am of the personality type sometimes called romantic. Men, of course, were the inventors of romance. Women, who are more practical, said, "This is a good thing. Let's push it along."

Though in early adulthood I suffered strongly from acedia, today I am almost always cheerful. This cheerfulness, a product of faith and hope, is not native to my temperament, since I am predisposed to a certain melancholy in which the sense of the fall of man and the feeling of things passing away are very strong. Unless he is careful, such a disposition can make a person a crashing bore, and some people would say that I am one. However, dispositions are also gifts to be used, and if I lost mine, I would miss it. I tend to be more acutely aware than most people of how things go awry in our culture. Now and then, the memory of the many ways in which I have personally gone awry provides some small insight into the travails of others. I don't object to the description of the world as a "vale of tears"; it seems to me refreshing, because honest. The acknowledgment of sin does not burden me. I would be burdened if there were no cure.

I am not telling everything; some things are only for God and one's confessor. Besides, one cannot do everything at once. There already exist books about philosophers who come to accept the reasonableness of Christian revelation, so for the most part, this essay presupposes that belief is reasonable rather than arguing the point. Since I am describing how I became Catholic, inevitably it includes thoughts about what I found missing from Protestantism, but I would not wish these reflections to be misunderstood. It was in Protestantism that I first learned the Gospel, and I will be forever grateful. Christ prayed that his followers would be one.[2]

Childhood

Aristotle says philosophy begins in wonder. This includes all people, certainly children. I remember how puzzled I was as a child that one continuous substance could interpenetrate another, as when cream is poured into coffee. The theory that matter is made of particles came as a revelation, because it spared me the need to suppose that the little bits of cream and coffee interpenetrated; instead, they slid past each other.

Yet if matter is made of particles, what are particles made of? Is everything matter? Is the act of will matter? I used to think to myself, "Arm, move," then note that my arm did not move, and puzzle over how thinking "move" was different from willing movement. Knowledge puzzled me too. At age eight or nine, it struck me that for all I knew, what other people "saw" when looking at an object that I called green might be the color that I called red. How could I know? Not until many years later did I learn that this quandary is old hat. In the meantime, it was maddening not to be able to make the puzzle clear to others, even to the adults of my admittedly limited acquaintance. When you look at something green, they said, you see green. Did you expect to see puce?

Yet the power of wonder was strongly mixed with what can only be called the wonder of power. I was very much taken with the

[2]Jn 17:11, 21–23.

descriptions of the so-called primordial soup in the science books
I borrowed from the public library. A pint-sized mad alchemist, I
endlessly mixed various disgusting things together in the attempt, as
I supposed, to "create life". The closest I came was to create a mess.
With encouragement of authors who wrote for boys like me, I also
confused wonder, which is the laudable desire to know the truth of
things, with empty curiosity, which, as the great Augustine teaches,
is a vice. Years later, when I read C. S. Lewis' opening remark in
The Abolition of Man, "I doubt whether we are sufficiently attentive
to the importance of elementary text books," I knew exactly what
he meant. My school library contained a book, written to stir boyish
scientific interest, that commended to our awe certain neurobiolo-
gists who had cut off the heads and tails of centipedes and stitched
the stumps together to make loops, just to see if the hapless creatures
would run in circles. (Dreadfully, they did.)

But my greatest questions were about God. Why did he create?
How *could* he create? Who created him? It goes without saying that
although I could pose such questions, I had none of the intellectual
equipment necessary to frame them well or think about them clearly.
I had heard of cyclotrons and synchrotrons, novae and supernovae,
random mutation and natural selection, but no one had mentioned
essences and accidents, first and second causes, or the difference
between necessary and contingent beings.

Concerning the God questions, my encouragement was neither
philosophy, of which I had never heard, nor science, or what I
thought was science, but Christianity. I was the sort of boy sometimes called "pious, but not holy"—that is, I was just as crass, selfish,
and inconsiderate as other boys; one Sunday I got into the organ loft,
removed some pipes to play with them, and put them back in the
wrong order so that the organ was off-key. Yet I was serious about
faith. I devoured all 608 pages of *Egermeier's Bible Story Book,* began
on the Holy Scriptures, and made myself obnoxious to my Sunday
school teachers by asking why we didn't read the Bible instead of dull
lesson books that rehashed it.

I also read the myths of the Greeks and other ancient peoples,
which raised interesting questions. But the myths did not have the
savor of the Scriptures, and I was never in danger of thinking that
God was a Hebrew version of Zeus. Reading the Old Testament,

I was particularly awed by the dealings of God with Moses. In one epochal encounter, Moses protests that if he comes to the sons of Israel and says to them that the God of their fathers has sent him, they will want to know His name. What shall he say to them? God replies, "I AM THAT I AM.'"[3] How I struggled with that demonstrative pronoun! Though I did not know the words for it, this was my first glimpse of God's ontological self-existence and nondependence.

The family faith was exclusively Protestant. When I read in the Old Testament about the institution of the Mosaic priesthood, I told my parents and grandparents, "I want to be a priest." This vastly amused everyone. As Baptists, we had pastors, not priests. But I did not want to be a minister like Pastor White, much less a Catholic priest, whatever that was. I wanted to be a priest like Aaron, and did not get the joke.

Though I played with Catholic kids, I was taught that Catholics worshipped idols, like pagans. My remote Polish and Ukrainian ancestors had been Catholic, but my relatives on both sides became Protestant a short time after arriving in America. One relative is supposed to have turned to the Baptist church in disgust after finding the priest drunk in the sanctuary. Since he is supposed to have been a drinker himself, when I reached adulthood I came to wonder just who had found whom.

My maternal grandfather was a very different case. Upon his arrival in the country as a teenager, he was converted by the Baptist aunt who took him in. After marrying and working various jobs—for example, as a tailor and a railroad laborer—he was admitted to Crozer Theological Seminary, as part of an outreach of the American Baptist Association to the immigrant communities. Later he was pastor to what I am told may have been the first Polish-language Baptist congregation in America. I still venerate my grandfather, a good man who had fully as much influence on my spiritual formation as my parents. It was he who baptized me in my tenth year.

Considering the stress that Protestants have historically placed on the insufficiency of "works" for salvation, it is curious that this doctrine made no impression on me when I was small. I clearly remember conversations about the afterlife with my little friends, most of them,

[3] Ex 3:13–14.

I think, Baptist and Lutheran. Every last one of us took for granted that we would have to earn our way into heaven. At death, God weighed each person's deeds, like Anubis of the Egyptians weighing the heart on a scale, and if the person had done more good than evil, he was in. At that age, I had no idea that this scenario would have been anathema to the Protestant Reformers. Indeed, I didn't know that there had been Reformers; I thought the Baptist church went all the way back to Jesus. (After all, wasn't Jesus baptized?) Still less did I know that it wasn't Catholic doctrine either.

Eventually I absorbed the Protestant idea that we become acceptable to God by faith "alone". However, what I understood by faith was not the Catholic understanding of faith as the assent of the whole person to Christ, heart and mind and will, but sheer belief. But if sheer belief makes us acceptable to Christ, what did St. James mean when he wrote that faith without works is "dead"?[4] My elders responded that *if* we have faith, *then we will* behave differently, but what matters is faith. But if faith, as such, is mere belief, then it was not clear why this should be so. Besides, why then did St. Paul urge his readers to "work out" their salvation with fear and trembling?[5]

Music made a great impression—everything from the polyphonic doxology and the majestic "Holy, Holy, Holy", to sentimental old Baptist favorites like "The Old Rugged Cross" and black spirituals like "Go Down, Moses". On road trips, my family would sing hymns in harmony. I was also moved by holy communion. We called it the "ordinance" of communion, to show that we didn't consider it a sacrament, although, since I had never heard of a sacrament, I didn't know that.

My grandfather and I spent hours in conversation about God. He never doubted the words, deeds, and divinity of Jesus, but surprised me in other ways. For example, he thought that when Jesus multiplied the loaves and fishes,[6] what really happened was that the people who had secretly hoarded food began to share it with others. To put the difficulty in terms I would use today, I was uncomfortable with

---

[4] Js 2:14–26.

[5] Phil 2:12–13.

[6] First miracle, feeding of the five thousand: Mt 14:13–21; Mk 6:32–44; Lk 9:10–17; Jn 6:1–13; second miracle, feeding of the four thousand: Mt 15:32–39; Mk 8:1–10.

the attempt to naturalize the supernatural. If that's the game, why stop with loaves and fishes? But this did make me realize that any given passage could be interpreted in more than one way. Many years later I realized that this fact is one of the reasons why the Protestant maxim *sola scriptura*, "Scripture alone", must be mistaken, because Scripture does not interpret itself. That does not make it wrong or untrue, but it makes it incomplete.

During my early teens, my parents moved South and my grandparents followed, leaving the purview of the American Baptists and entering the ambit of the Southern Baptists. By this time my grandfather had retired, and though he grumbled about "fundamentalists", a term I did not understand, he was content to worship with the rest of us.

Tumult

In adolescence, my interior life began to fissure. By this time my passions were divided between religion and what I thought was science. John Paul II famously wrote that faith and reason are like the two wings of a bird: it needs both to fly.[7] My Baptist forebears were far from rejecting reason, but except for biblical exegesis, they lacked a strong and critical intellectual culture. Consequently, I was not prepared for what was about to happen.

Even so, I was taught, and believe, that there is no conflict in principle between science and faith. But it depends on what one means by science and by faith. The method of science should be following the evidence wherever it leads. But the scientific investigation of material things is often confused with dogmatic materialism, which is not at all the same. Materialists do not follow the evidence wherever it leads; they accept only material explanations, even if the evidence is against them. This attitude has been expressed in a morbidly defiant way in an essay by the Harvard paleontologist Richard Lewontin:

> We take the side of science *in spite* of the patent absurdity of some of its constructs, *in spite* of its failure to fulfill many of its extravagant

[7] John Paul II, encyclical letter *Fides et Ratio* (September 14, 1998), blessing remarks.

promises of health and life, *in spite* of the tolerance of the scientific
community for unsubstantiated just-so stories, because we have a
prior commitment, a commitment to materialism. It is not that the
methods and institutions of science somehow compel us to accept a
material explanation of the phenomenal world, but, on the contrary,
that we are forced by our *a priori* adherence to material causes to create
an apparatus of investigation and a set of concepts that produce material explanations, no matter how counter-intuitive, no matter how
mystifying to the uninitiated. Moreover, that materialism is absolute,
for we cannot allow a Divine Foot in the door.[8]

I do not fault scientists like Lewontin for being materialists, but
for being unconsidered materialists. Suppose we follow the evidence
wherever it leads a little further. I think we discover that so-called
material explanations are not always the best explanations.

Though what I say would be widely accepted among philosophers, even so materialism grips many minds with surprising force.
To use a helpful distinction of Hilaire Belloc, it functions more as
a mood than as a premise.[9] If their materialist suppositions were
pointed out to them, many people would deny holding them; yet
they do. For example, we hear every day that modern science has
no need for explanations that refer to the purposes of things. Surprisingly, this statement expresses more a wish than a fact. Not only
biology and psychology, but also, from optics to quantum mechan-
ics, even physics makes use of teleology. This is especially clear in its
extensive use of variational principles, such as the principle of least
action. A variational principle is one that proposes that physical systems always tend to behave in such a way as to minimize, maximize,
or hold constant some quantity—for example, the "optical length"
of the path taken by a beam of light, which is the physical length
multiplied by the index of refraction of the material through which
the beam passes. Always remembering that we are not supposing
such systems to have minds, these extrema (*not* the terminal points
of the paths followed) may be considered the ends or goals to which
they are directed.

[8] Richard C. Lewontin, "Billions and Billions of Demons", *The New York Review of Books*
44:1 (January 9, 1997): 28–32 (emphasis in original).
[9] Hilaire Belloc, *Survivals and New Arrivals* (London: Sheed and Ward, 1929), chap. 4.

But I was taught science through a materialistic filter, and materialism is not congruent with faith. At first I was not aware of the materialistic assumptions underlying what was taught to me, probably because materialism was often dished up with a dash of vitalism to make it more palatable. Life is merely a complex chemical reaction— *but if you like, you can believe that a divine spark got it going.* That sort of thing. The vitalist sauce could not long disguise the flavor of the materialist meat. So though, as a teen, I was even more a religious enthusiast than as a child, I was increasingly torn apart.

Materialism was not the only difficulty. For example, most of what passed for my schooling in "critical thinking" was really the inculcation of prejudices. It was not all wrong. For instance, I was rightly warned of the *ad populum* fallacy: the fact that the majority believes something does not prove that the belief is true. But the textbooks insinuated that popular beliefs are *irrelevant*, an elite prejudice that is certainly mistaken. For example, what most people believe about free will is plainly evidential, because they have personal experience of making choices. But I developed the habit of ignoring such considerations.

Another difficulty was how I was taught to use language. My high school English teachers were determined to teach me the difference between what they called facts and what they called "opinions", and moral and theological propositions were always included among the opinions. Protons are a fact; God is only an opinion. Later, my college social-science teachers were equally determined to teach me the difference between what they called facts and what they called "values", and to much the same effect. The prevalence of marriage is a fact; its importance is only a value. I thought that to think in this fashion was to be logical. Actually it was obfuscation. I should have been told that an opinion is a hypothesis about a fact, a fact is what really is true, and a value, when true, is a moral fact. I do not think my high school teachers realized that they were denying the reality of moral and theological facts. My college teachers did.

Moreover, everything I read taught me that even the most basic ideas about good and evil are different everywhere. This is empirically false. As C. S. Lewis remarked, cultures may disagree about whether a man may have one wife or four, but all of them know about marriage; they may disagree about which actions are most courageous, but none of them ranks cowardice as a virtue.[10] But by the time I was taught cultural relativism, I wanted very much to believe it.

All these things tore me in two, but by the end of high school, I found a distraction. Having been caught up in the radical politics of the late sixties, I had acquired a new passion. I now had my own ideas about redeeming the world. By means of the mantra "Jesus was a cultural revolutionary", I tried to hide the contradiction between my ideas and his. Actually, Christian faith made him important, political radicalism made me important, and that settled it for me. For something else had been happening within; I did not want God to be God. I wanted myself to be God. I preferred my way to his.

Every day Christ became less a personal reality, more an abstraction. As I drifted from him, I also drifted from common sense about moral law and personal responsibility. This fact set the stage for the next phase of my rake's progress.

Apostasy

The apostasy that I am about to describe spanned my years as an undergrad, a dropout, and a grad student, along with my first year and a half of teaching. One day during my second year of college— the same year that I married—I realized that I no longer believed Jesus to be the Son of God and Savior. There was no moment at which I was aware of arriving at disbelief; rather, there was a moment at which I became aware that for some time I had not believed. Although in my intellectual pride, I took for granted that my disbelief must be reasonable, it was more a state of mind than a rational conclusion of argument. The atmosphere of my life provided no air for faith to breathe.

Not much longer after discovering that I no longer believed in the Son of God, I discovered that I no longer believed in God. This change in belief was equally without rational warrant. I never became what is called a theoretical atheist; I was a practical atheist. In other words, I didn't claim that I could show there was no God; I understood the near impossibility of proving a universal negative. In this

---

[10] C. S. Lewis, *Mere Christianity* (New York: HarperCollins, 2001), 6.

sense I conceded that there could be a God, and when the mood struck me, I called myself only an agnostic. But I didn't think there were any good reasons to believe God existed, and I lived as though he didn't. My pretense was that we cannot know anything about God, including whether he exists.

There is a great difficulty in asserting God's unknowability. To say that we cannot know anything about God is to say something about God: "If there is a God, he is unknowable." But why should this one thing be an exception? The agnostic would have to know quite a few things about God in order to know that he couldn't know anything else about God. In fact, doesn't he have an elaborate picture of God in his mind, full of all sorts of colorful details that render God either impossible or unknowable, apart from the colorful details themselves?

The agnostic must suppose that any possible God is infinitely remote—otherwise, he couldn't know that he couldn't know him. He must suppose that any possible God is either powerless to make himself known, unwilling to do so, or unconcerned about whether he is known—otherwise he would have provided means to know him. He must suppose that any possible God would be completely unlike the Pauline portrayal of him—because in that account, God is anything but remote, he desires to be known, he has already provided the means for the agnostic to know of him, and in fact the agnostic does know of him.[11]

But if I did know of him, then when I told myself I "no longer believed" this and that, these were self-deceptions. In retrospect I see that at some level I knew very well that God existed and that good and evil were real. I only told myself I didn't.

Self-deception is a variety of lie, and the universe is so tightly constructed that in order to cover up one lie, we usually have to tell another. Deception begets deception; self-deception begets more self-deception. And that happened to me. Not much longer after discovering that I "no longer believed" in God, I discovered that I "no

[11] "For what can be known about God is plain to them, because God has shown it to them. Ever since the creation of the world his invisible nature, namely, his eternal power and deity, has been clearly perceived in the things that have been made. So they are without excuse." Rom 1:19–20.

longer believed" in objective moral law. Law supposes a lawgiver; how could I affirm the one while denying the other?[12] Of course sophisticated replies may be given to this question, for many thinkers do regard morality as something other than real law. Yet repeatedly and revealingly they slip back into the language of law. Conscience speaks the language of law because she is the lawgiver's representative.

Crisis

So the agnostic has a pretty thick theology after all. He views the Heavenly Father as rather like one of the absentee fathers of our generation: he isn't there, he doesn't care, or he's powerless. I too reached this conclusion, but I began by arguing that *I myself* was transfixed on two tines of that fork: *I myself* was either nonexistent or powerless. If to deny God's reality I had to deny my own, so be it. My thinking went something like this.

First, I insisted that if the principle of causality is true, then the chain of causes and effects is an unbreakable fetter. It would make no difference even if the fetter were probabilistic, as in quantum theory, because I do not choose how the dice will fall. My mind is nothing more than an activity of my brain, my brain nothing more than a computational device. We don't experience ourselves as machines, but I told myself we are under a double curse—the illusion of being more, and the desire for the illusion to be true.

How a machine could suffer such things as desires and illusions deeply troubled me. In fact *all* of the phenomena of consciousness troubled me. I was troubled by the redness of red; the preciousness of the beloved; the sense I sometimes had of exerting my will *against* an inclination, as though free—even by the experience of being troubled. I knew I couldn't fit these things into the machine theory, and that the intuition that I was more than a machine fit reality better. Like Professor Lewontin, I had reached my conclusions not because of the data, but in spite of them.

---

[12] G. E. M. Anscombe, "Modern Moral Philosophy", *Philosophy* 33, no. 124 (1958): 1–19, has interesting things to say about law presupposing a lawgiver, but I had not read the article at that time.

But if I *was* in the grip of a blind causality, then it followed that I had no freedom, no responsibility, no *Self*. These too were illusions. "I" didn't produce my activity; I was its product. In a sense, I thought, "I" didn't exist. What then of God? If he existed, then how could he escape what I called "causality" any more than I could? He was no freer than I.

That fact, I thought, showed that something else about him was like me too. For if I have no free will, then I believe what I believe, not because I recognize its concordance with reality, but because it is cranked out by a mental mechanism over which "I" have no control. That mechanism may have evolved to accomplish certain functions, but there was no reason to think that arriving at the truth of things was one of them. Unlike, say, an ability to find food or outwit predators, the capacity to arrive at the truth of things would make no contribution to its own survival.[13] But if I am really in the dark about everything, then, I thought, God too must be in the dark about everything. How could he make himself known if he didn't even know himself?

You see where this leads. Although I couldn't prove the non-existence of God, I thought I could prove the nonexistence of a God that mattered. I pictured God like the blinded monarch in *King Lear*, helpless, raving, a pawn to fatalities he didn't understand. It wasn't Satan who was frozen in the ice at the center of hell, as Dante thought; it was God.

If my imprisonment in a blind causality made my reasoning so unreliable that I couldn't trust my beliefs, then of course I shouldn't have trusted my beliefs about imprisonment in a blind causality. In that case I had no business denying free will in the first place. But if I did have free will, then perhaps I could trust my beliefs—in which case I didn't have free will. Because of the incoherence of my reasoning, I should have rejected it. I didn't.

---

[13] C. S. Lewis developed an argument to this effect in *The Case for Christianity* (New York: Touchstone Books, 1996). A more rigorous version was later developed by the philosopher Alvin Plantinga; see his *Warrant and Proper Function* (New York: Oxford University Press, 1993), 216–38; cf. James Beilby, ed., *Naturalism Defeated? Essays on Plantinga's Evolutionary Argument against Naturalism* (Ithaca, NY: Cornell University Press, 2002). Though the point seemed intuitively obvious to me, such was my ignorance that I was not at this point in my life aware of either version of the argument.

My picture of the universe did not make me an idolater. I was an idolater already. It only offered me an idol. I used the idol of matter until it broke, and then made an idol of the breakage. Did nothing make sense? Then I would make an idol of Nothing.

Though a million idols are adored by the sons of men, in the end there is only one, for they are but a million masks for the one idol of Self. Finding that we are made in God's image, we worship the image in place of God. Our own time is unusual in its tendency to adore the Self openly, according to its proper name. The classical pattern, however, is to disguise the adoration of Self under the adoration of one of its representatives. The idol of Reason is the Self represented by its rational powers; of Sex, the Self represented by its animal powers; of Duty, the Self represented by its moral powers; of Race and Nation, the Self represented in the millionfold mirror of the group.

My own idolatries followed the classical rather than the contemporary pattern. I didn't consciously think, "I shall adore Myself"; nevertheless, the real significance of my idolatries was that they seemed to annihilate God *so that I myself could be God.* This explanation of their significance may seem unbelievable, for as we have seen, in order to annihilate God, I had to annihilate myself; my road to deicide was through suicide. How could that be a worship of Self?

Because we misunderstand what suicide is. Killing oneself is not supreme self-resignation, as we suppose, but extreme self-assertion. As Chesterton pointed out, God may have called everything into being, but the suicide imagines that he can make it all go away.[14] My suicide was just like that, but more violent still. The conventional suicide can destroy the universe only once, but for me each day was suicide. There was no need to bother with the slashing of wrists, because it was all going on in my mind. In one long prolongation of nightfall, the light went out, and went out, and went out, all without the inconvenience of physical death.

Besides, to commit suicide *was* to commit deicide, symbolically. I said above that self-adoration is the worship of God's image in God's

---

[14] G. K. Chesterton, *Orthodoxy*, in *The Collected Works of G. K. Chesterton*, vol. 1 (San Francisco, Ignatius Press, 1986), chap. 6.

place. By now my wish to replace him was so strong that I resented even his image in me.

Conceive what a person has to do to himself to go on like that. St. Paul said that the knowledge of God's law is written on our hearts, our consciences also bearing witness.[15] The way this is put by natural law philosophers—such as I am now—is that the law is the deepest predisposition of the practical intellect: so long as we have minds, we *can't not know* it. Since I was unusually determined not to know it, I had to destroy my mind. I resisted the temptation to believe in good with as much energy as some saints resist the temptation to neglect good. I loved my wife and children (I had married at nineteen), but I was determined to regard this love as merely a subjective preference with no real and objective value. Think what this did to my capacity to love them. Love is a commitment of the will to the true good of another person. How can one's will be committed to the true good of another person if he denies the reality of good, denies the reality of persons, and denies that his commitments are in his control?

I knew that the name of my malady was acedia, and I even had an image: I too was frozen in the ice. But the name and the image did not cure it. I knew that I was in agony, but the agony did not return me to God. Because I believed things that filled me with dread, I thought I was smarter and braver than the people who didn't believe them. I thought I saw an emptiness at the heart of the universe that was hidden from their foolish eyes. Of course I was the fool.

Return

By this point I had received my political theory doctorate from Yale and been hired at the University of Texas. I won the position by giving a talk in which I maintained two theses: we merely make up the difference between good and evil, and second, we aren't responsible for what we do anyway. Good talk, son. Here's a job.

Yet I found that I couldn't teach these things to my students. Paradoxically, I felt too responsible for them to teach them there is no

---

[15] Rom 2:15.

personal responsibility, and too conscious of my duty to do no harm to teach that there is no good or harm.

Strangely, it was only after I had apostatized that I read much classical Christian literature. This literature had strongly shaped the Western tradition and was plainly worth teaching. So in the introductory course I designed on political philosophy, I included a unit on Thomas Aquinas. To dramatize his vision of the unity of eternal, divine, and natural law, I read to them from Dante's *Paradiso*:

> I saw within Its depth how It conceives
> all things in a single volume bound by love,
> of which the universe is the scattered leaves.[16]

Some days while lecturing on St. Thomas, it took all the control that I could muster to conceal the fact that I felt like weeping for the sheer beauty of the appearance of truth, an appearance I bitterly told myself was an illusion. Something of the strain must have been evident. One day after class a student approached. Could he ask a question? "I've been listening to you every day," he said, "and I figure that you're either a Catholic or an atheist. Which is it?"

One evening, in tears but ashamed of my weakness, I prayed. I told God, "I don't believe you're there. I think I'm talking to the wall. But if you do exist, *you can have me.*" In desperation, I added, "But you will have to show me, because I can't tell anymore."

I don't know what I expected. The room was silent. The ceiling did not part to reveal a choir of angels. The wall looked more and more like a wall. I felt like an idiot. I went to bed.

Yet when I said he could have me, I meant it. Could he have heard my prayer after all? I think so. Months passed before I noticed, but something happened. I began to experience an intuition that my condition was objectively evil. It grew stronger every day until it was overpowering. It did not present itself as an emotion, but as a perception: *This is what a fact looks like.* It was as though a man were to notice for the first time that the sky is not red, but blue. Finally I accepted it. Yes. It was factual indeed. My condition was objectively evil.

[16] Dante, *Paradiso*, trans. John Ciardo (New York: Penguin, 2003), canto 33, lines 85–87.

In letting that one through, my mental censors blundered. Augustine of Hippo had argued that although evil is real, it is derivative; the only way to get something horrible is to ruin something wonderful.[17] "Pure" evil makes no sense, because evil is a privation in what would otherwise be good. We say disease is something missing from health; we would never say health is something missing from disease. I had always considered this argument a neat piece of reasoning, but with a defective premise. Granted evil, there had to exist good, of which evil was a disorder. But I didn't grant evil, so I didn't grant good. Now I saw that there was such a thing as evil after all. It was right behind my eyes. But in that case there must be a good, of which the evil was a perversion.

I still could not have told you *what* was good. But the insight that there was such a thing dizzied me. It meant I had been so wrong, for so long, about so many things, that for all I knew, almost anything might be true.

As time passed, I began to think forgotten thoughts and *unforget* suppressed memories. In particular, I came to remember that I had never had good reasons to apostatize. My self-knowledge—in which I had arrogantly continued to believe, even when I thought I had no Self—had come to nothing. That was a shock. One by one, various pieces of buried knowledge reasserted themselves: the good of this, the evil of that, the reality of God. Even the memories of experiences began to change. Imagine looking at an old and familiar photograph, but suddenly seeing in it a figure whom you had refused to notice before. The recollection of God's goodness to me was like that.

Just as I had come to realize one day that some time before, I had stopped believing, now I came to realize one day that some time before, I had begun again.

Of course I had to repudiate my dissertation. At the time, I thought my scholarly career was over. I couldn't possibly retool, rethink, and get anything published before my tenure review came up. By God's grace and providence, that turned out to be untrue, but I did not yet know that. If in penance I had to wash dishes the rest of my life, I thought, then so be it, but I was daily assaulted by the thought that

---

[17] St. Augustine of Hippo, *City of God Against the Pagans*, bk. 12, chap. 9.

I had wasted my gifts. No one is useless to God—but I thought I had become useless to him. My state of mind was black.

I could not remain long in that state of mind. This was my convalescence, because I was relearning all sorts of experiences the capacities for which I had tried to tear out of myself. It was as though I had lived in a dark garret for a very long time, and someone was flinging back the shutters. Shafts of light lanced in. The experience was almost physical. I was learning again how to feel, and for the first time, really, how to think.

Although I had understood that first Augustinian step, several years passed before I was able rationally to reconstruct the rest of what was happening. The movement was not irrational, but it exceeded the movements I had hitherto called reason. Just because I could not yet explain all my reasons, I was humiliated. It was a humiliation to come back to God and *then* begin gaining understanding. I wanted to have gained understanding, and then, for my own reasons, come back to God. But all love is like that. True, I had to know something about my wife to believe in her; but I had to believe in her to know more about her. So too with God.

Besides, I now understand that my humiliation was necessary. Since I had deserted God not through the proper use of my intellect, but through its pride, in his mercy he chose means of restoring me that starved that pride. Any other way would have left me too vulnerable to relapse. I had to be left no opportunity of taking credit for my return.

I had worked so hard over the years to forget all the good reasons for faith and all the sane mental principles that I had thrown away. Now by the grace of God, I remembered them—and recognized that their force was unimpaired.

Attraction

A few paragraphs ago I mentioned my wife, a ruby among women, who had been an anchor during the prodigal years. She too had wandered from Christ before returning to him, but she had never been so foolish as to tell herself that there was no God, or that there was no good, or to deny the reality of persons. In fact, when I expressed such thoughts, she laughed at me. "You don't believe those things," she said. "No one can." This irritated me, but she was right. At some level I had known I was lying to myself.

By God's mercy, despite the difference in our paths, we two were drawn back to faith at the same time. We came all the way. Was Christ real? Then we would have to be Christians. One morning we told our children that from now on we would be worshipping on Sundays. I expected them to resent the interruption of their play, but they were delighted. My oldest child told me years later, "I had always wanted our family to go to church, but I had never told you." So strange are God's mercies.

The last church we attended before apostasy had been an empty social-Gospel congregation, in which what had once been holy communion had degenerated into a celebration of the grape boycott. Though we had nothing against unionizing migrant farm workers, there was no returning to that sort of thing.

So where would we go? Thank God, my Baptist family had taught me enough that even after abandoning Christ, I knew what it meant to return. Yet I did not want to reenter the Baptist fold, because its understanding of the faith seemed somehow incomplete. I mentioned that I had discovered classical Christian literature only after apostatizing. But writers like Augustine, Thomas Aquinas, and Dante were all Catholic. I could no longer believe with my old Baptist teachers that Catholicism was not Christian. In fact, I wanted to have one foot in the richness of Catholic tradition.

Yet I couldn't see my way to Catholicism proper, for I also wanted one foot in the Reformation. I still had the misconception that the Church teaches "works righteousness"—that if only we earn enough virtue points, we're in. Had you asked me, "If you still think that about Catholics, then how can you now believe that they are Christians?" I would have replied that even though they misunderstood the faith that reconciles us with God, somehow, they possessed it.

So we became Episcopalian. The Anglican world presented itself as a *via media*, a middle way, between Catholicism and the Reformation, which seemed just the thing. We had not yet discovered how John Henry Newman came to realize that there can be no *via media*, nor had we yet discovered its impossibility through our own experience.[18] During this time, I wrote a few articles for *First Things*, the journal of religion and public life. One day during a telephone conversation, one of the editors asked me to settle a bet. Some of the staff were sure I must be Protestant. Others were sure I must be Catholic. Which was I? If he would pardon the oxymoron, I told him, I would call myself an Evangelical Anglo-Catholic. He paused, then drily quipped, "That's not an oxymoron. It's a material heresy." I found this very funny. But I was not yet convinced.

The Anglican choice made sense to my wife too. She had been raised in a religiously indifferent family, but had found her way to the Episcopal church as a teenager and been baptized and confirmed in it. I had visited the church with her in those days and had found the liturgy both moving and instructive. Just by a certain mode of worship, one is formed in a certain way. Or one should have been.

Yet as we went on, we discovered that Anglicanism was dying and all but dead. We naturally assumed that the reason the congregation recited the Nicene Creed together was that they believed it. After years of exile, this was indescribably wonderful. The "cloud of witnesses" of which St. Paul speaks was almost visible;[19] I felt as though I could reach out and touch those millions of Christians from bygone generations. Then came the day when the priest who was giving the homily that day announced to the congregation that he was "no longer able" to believe in the Resurrection. I wanted to ask, "What happened to your vows?" and, "How can you call yourself a priest?" But appealing to him by name after the service, I confined myself to asking, "I see you every week, reciting the Nicene Creed like the rest of us. If you don't believe it, how can you?" He responded, "I do it as an act of solidarity with the community."

I think I was the only person in the sanctuary who heard him deny the Resurrection. Apparently no one listened during homilies. I came to realize that this was a divine mercy.

Doctrinal education in our parish followed the principle "anything goes". One year a proposal was made in the education committee

---

[18] In a series of tracts entitled *Via Media*, written while he was an Anglican, Newman had argued that there can be a middle way. However, by the time he wrote his *Apologia Pro Vita Sua*, he had abandoned this view.

[19] Heb 12:1.

to teach a series for adults on the various theories that held that the Resurrection never happened. I am afraid I made myself obnoxious in opposition (I have that talent). On another occasion a better idea was hatched, to teach an Advent series for children on the various biblical prophecies of the birth of the Messiah. An Old Testament expert from the local Episcopal seminary was invited to speak to the Sunday school teachers. His message: there were no such prophecies. They were all about other things. The roomful of dazed faces was a spectacle to behold. Finally a woman asked, "How are we supposed to teach this to children?" He shrugged.

Another year, a student from the seminary signed on to lead the youth group. Someone made a casual remark about orthodoxy to her. "There is no such thing as orthodoxy," she sneered.

The question my wife and I faced was whether it would be more pleasing to God to get out of the Anglican Communion, or to stay as a "faithful remnant". For the time, we remained Anglicans. However, we transferred our membership to another Episcopal parish where it seemed that historic Christian doctrine was still taught. We remained in that parish for years and still bear a deep love for the people we knew there.

When people asked, we said we belonged to the Christian wing of the Episcopal church. But the ongoing collapse of the Anglican enterprise forced us to ask deeper questions about the nature of the true Church. At a convocation of the Diocese of Texas I attended as a lay delegate, a resolution was moved that priests should abstain from sexual intercourse out of marriage. The majority of lay delegates voted in favor; the majority of priests, against. Really.

Christ had promised that the gates of hell would not prevail against his Church,[20] but they were prevailing here. Where then was the Church? What would it have to look like? There seemed only one plausible candidate: Catholicism. No other ecclesial body even believed in the Church's unity and authority. The Eastern Orthodox communions were divided. The Reformation had led to tens of thousands of "denominations", each of them believing different things, most of them drifting like the wrack of gale-struck ships. According to the Protestant idea, all of them together are the

[20] Mt 16:18.

Church. But St. Paul had called the Church the Body of Christ.[21] A bloody arm here, a severed leg there, a torso floating in the river—no matter how many such things were added into the total, they could not make up his Body.

So our ecclesiology was very nearly Catholic, long before we joined the Catholic Church. This fact made our theory of being a "faithful remnant" inside Anglicanism harder and harder to take seriously. After all, if what the Catholic Church teaches about her nature and authority is true, how could we justify *not* becoming part of her? Although we continued to disagree with a number of Catholic dogmas, this was a poor answer, for we suffered a growing suspicion that it was we who were wrong, not the Church.

Sometimes my wife was closer to accepting Catholicism than I was, and I balked. Sometimes I was closer, and she balked. Sometimes we were both close. But neither of us was truly ready.

Not all converts come into the Catholic fold in the same way. For most, the ecclesiastical objection is the last one to topple. First they become convinced about doctrine A, then doctrine B, then doctrine C. At last, they accept that the Church has authority to teach doctrine.

For me it was the other way around. First I became convinced that the Church has authority to teach doctrine. That didn't mean that my difficulties about doctrine A, doctrine B, and doctrine C disappeared, but it converted my "objections" into "obstacles". In the meantime, Protestant theology was becoming implausible. After several years of wrestling, becoming convinced on one point after another, I finally found myself able to say about the remaining issues, "I am ready to obey." That turned out to be crucial. As St. Augustine said, we believe in order to know.[22] There are some things you have to understand before you can accept them—but there are others you have to accept, and live, before you can understand them.

It took about eight years to reach this point, ending in 2003. We made God wait. Two of our Catholic friends said to us, "Your whole understanding of things is Catholic. You think like Catholics. You sound like Catholics. You have a Catholic sensibility. Why aren't you Catholics?" During a long conversation with another Catholic

---

[21] I Cor 12:27; Eph 1:23; 4:12; 5:30; Col 1:18, 24.
[22] St. Augustine, *Sermo* 43.9.

friend who knew of my attraction to the Church, I bellyached. "I can't call this an objection to Catholic doctrine," I said, "but you can't deny the flatness and tonelessness of the language coming from some of the liturgical reforms. Besides, the Church puts up with forms of popular piety that are utterly inconsistent with her own teachings." I gave an example: devotion to Mary should be all about Christ, but sometimes it is all about Mary. I was coming to love Mary too, but I could not imagine that she approved. I asked, "Why is this tolerated?"

My friend leaned back and answered, "All of this is true. These are real problems. The Church knows about them. But in two hundred years they'll all be taken care of."

It was a preposterous reply, and on another evening, in another mood, I might have considered it glib. That evening, though, it struck me that my friend was viewing things from the perspective of the Church. I realized that as a Protestant, I had a much shorter timeline, and much of what I considered wisdom might actually be impatience. The mystery of the endurance of the Church through centuries of heresies and assaults sank in a little deeper.

The last three of those eight years were quite difficult, because my wife and I had not reached that point of obedience, but needed to. We decided that if the Episcopal church ever came to incorporate the prevalent abominations into its canons, that would be our signal to get out.

The signal came unmistakably during the summer of 2003. It was bad enough that the Episcopal general convention ordained as bishop a man who had abandoned his wife and children in order to live in sin with another man. Yet that might have been viewed as an aberration. After all, even in the Catholic Church there have been bad popes and bishops, and there will be in the future. Much worse was the fact that the general convention authorized drawing up rites for the blessing of same-sex unions, because that converted the aberration into a rule.

But the signal turned out to have been unnecessary, because we had already crossed our Rubicon. That summer, we had visited an Episcopal church while out of town. The "tract table" offered visitors free pro-abortion bumper stickers bearing the Episcopal shield. We turned and walked out. Never again.

Friends sometimes ask, "Why didn't you consider one of the Anglican denominations that split from the Episcopalians?" The answer is that we could not see how a schism could be fixed by a schism. A dear friend who had joined one of these denominations told my wife how wonderful it was to have found a congregation "where everyone is just like me". We did not want to belong to a congregation where everyone was just like us; we wanted to belong to the Church.[23]

My analytical habit makes this story seem more orderly than the actual tumble of experience, but the movement of our lives did possess an underlying unity. The beauty of Catholic truth was ever more evident, and its gravitational attraction ever stronger. All else is detail.

Conversion

We met with a priest. The first reason, frankly, was to take his measure—to make sure he believed Catholic doctrine himself. Thank God, this was not my old arrogance reawakening. But you must remember how much rank disbelief we had encountered among Episcopalian priests. An ordained friend related the tale of how the Episcopal seminary he had attended gave students who were about to graduate tips on how to keep congregations from learning what they really believed. The only good thing about the story was that he too had been disturbed.

Although we expected conditions to be different in the Catholic Church, we were under no illusions that there would be no troubles. The New Testament warns that there will always be wolves in the flock. Our Catholic friends, who had lived through various ecclesiastical disorders, told us, "Welcome aboard! It's a mess!" Actually, we found conditions to be much less a "mess" than we had expected.

To this day, the priest with whom we spoke loves to tell how we "interviewed" him. He was enormously amused. After it became obvious that he was a good priest, we told him that we wanted to begin preparation to enter the Catholic Church, but that we were still troubled by certain obstacles that we hoped he could assist us in overcoming.

---

[23] Our friend later came to the same conclusion.

For me, the last such obstacle concerned the title of "co-mediatrix" often given to Mary. By using such a title, was the Church contradicting her own teaching that Christ is *the* mediator between God and men? He was most helpful. A convert himself—Methodist, then Anglican, then Catholic—he understood the difficulty immediately, discussed it with me, and encouraged me to read chapter 8 of Vatican II's 1964 Dogmatic Constitution on the Church, *Lumen Gentium*. As he expected, it resolved my difficulties. I considered that people can be mediators in many ways. If you pray for someone in prayer, you are a sort of mediator. If you explain the Gospel to someone, you are a sort of mediator. If a priest offers the sacrament of reconciliation, he is a sort of mediator. As the vessel through which Christ entered the world, Mary has a still more exalted role in this economy of grace. But to confess this neither lessens nor compromises the uniqueness of what he did on the Cross.

Although at one time, the doctrine of justification had presented an even greater obstacle for me, by this time that iceberg had already broken up. The Church's approval in 1999 of the Joint Declaration on the Doctrine of Justification—an accord between the Catholic Church and the Lutheran World Federation—had been especially helpful. At the time, when I was still firmly Protestant, it had struck me like a thunderclap. Recalling Luther's words that justification was the article on which the Church stands or falls, I thought as I read it, "The Reformation is over."

Reaction among well-informed Protestant friends had been quite different. Most were simply indifferent; intuitively if not theoretically congregationalist, they viewed all faith as local. Others held that the agreement was merely verbal, a trick of ambiguous wording, signifying nothing. Others, my Calvinist acquaintances, held that it was real but unimportant, because the article on which the Church stands or falls is not justification, but the sovereignty of God (what has Wittenburg to do with Geneva?). Still others held that it was real, but that the Lutheran World Federation did not represent their views. A sizable group conceded that the declaration would be important if the Catholic Church meant what she said, but meaning it would have required renunciation of the Council of Trent; therefore, the Church had been lying. All this seemed preposterous. I came to realize that the Church's actual teaching about justification is quite different from what I had always taken it to be—and that it made sense.

An uneasy fear persisted that in the Church I would find less Scripture, less prayer, and less Jesus. The reality has turned out differently. I have found more Scripture, more prayer, and more Jesus. The greatest surprise, though, has not been in the doctrine, morals, or devotion of the Church, but in her culture. To give but a single example, the warmth of the parish community expresses itself differently. We were accustomed to Protestant ways, according to which a new person is surrounded by well-wishers the instant he walks into the church building. By contrast, the Catholic Church seemed chilly. But then one Sunday after Mass, before our reception into the Church, we found our perspective turning upside-down when a new acquaintance warmly said to us, "I've noticed you coming for several months, and I've wanted to talk with you so much, *but I was afraid of speaking for fear of scaring you away.*" I am absolutely convinced that she was sincere. This devout woman plainly wanted us to become part of the community, but we wouldn't have known it before then. What might have seemed like chilliness was really an expression of her warmth. She didn't want to be so aggressive that we took alarm and fled. This consideration was touching, amusing, and a little bit bizarre, like finding yourself in a tribe where you express your gratitude for the meal by belching loudly.

Our cradle Catholic friends sometimes tell us, "It's good to talk to people like you, because people think we're crazy to be Catholic. We're so encouraged to find people who weren't Catholic discovering that Catholic faith makes sense." To me it makes more than sense. All the pieces that were missing from my faith have come together. The sacraments are channels of God's blessing. Possibilities of grace have opened up of which I had never been aware. I understand a little more what my marriage, my family, my teaching, and my life are about.

To what can I compare being received into the Church? Think of a man who has been living for a long time in a little cottage on the grounds of a palace. One day he stumbles across the palace threshold and falls flat on his face; yet he finds, to his astonishment, that he is welcome.

The best is to meet His Majesty in every Mass. Yet this sacramental meal is only a foretaste of what Scripture calls the wedding feast of the Lamb. I will be satisfied, when I am satisfied in him.

3

Down the Labyrinthine Ways

Brian Cutter

> I fled Him, down the nights and down the days;
>   I fled Him, down the arches of the years;
> I fled Him, down the labyrinthine ways
>   Of my own mind; and in the midst of tears
> I hid from Him, and under running laughter.
>   Up vistaed hopes I sped;
>   And shot, precipitated,
> Adown Titanic glooms of chasmed fears,
>   From those strong Feet that followed, followed after.
>   But with unhurrying chase,
>   And unperturbèd pace,
>   Deliberate speed, majestic instancy,
>   They beat—and a Voice beat
>   More instant than the Feet—
> 'All things betray thee, who betrayest Me
>
>   —Francis Thompson, "The Hound of Heaven"

I entered graduate school in philosophy as an atheist and a naturalist. In my third year of graduate school I converted to Christianity, and at the end of my fourth year I was received into the Catholic Church. Here I recount the story of these conversions. There is a lot I could say about my relationship to Christianity prior to graduate school, but due to space limitations I shall touch only very briefly on my pre-graduate-school life. Growing up, I was not much exposed to

Christian ideas. My father was not religious. My mother attended a
Methodist church, where I went to Sunday school until age ten, but
I did not receive any meaningful religious instruction there, probably
because (as I would later find out) the leaders of the church were not
particularly keen on Christianity. Their view of Jesus, I gather, was
that he was a morally impressive man, and although he was *merely* a
man (he was not divine, was not born of a virgin, did not perform
miracles, and was not raised from the dead), his life of love and com-
passion can serve as a model for us today. Or, more accurately, a small
subset of the stories about him in the Gospels can serve as a model
for us; we cannot know whether Jesus himself was especially morally
impressive, since the Gospels were never intended as accurate repre-
sentations of the words and deeds of the historical Jesus, if there even
was a historical Jesus.

My first real exposure to serious Christian thought came through
reading C.S. Lewis in high school. I was introduced to Lewis
through my best friend, Jesse Hinde, who had converted to Christianity during our sophomore year of high school. Reading Lewis and
arguing about his ideas with Jesse was my first foray into philosophy.
Early in college I developed close friendships with several very intelligent and morally admirable Christians, including my future wife,
and I started attending the worship meetings put on by the campus
ministry. For a few years in college I identified as a Christian before
gradually moving away from the faith. I recall a recurrent train of
thought that nagged at me during the months when I was growing
cold on the faith in college: that there was no firm ground to stand on
in thinking about theological matters, and in particular, no obvious
grounds for giving the Bible the sort of authority it would need in
order to speak to any number of important and disputed theological
questions. While this was by no means the only cause for my drift
away from the faith, on this particular point I may not have been so
despairing if Catholicism had been a live possibility for me. Unfortunately, it wasn't. At the time I hardly knew any serious Catholics,
and although I knew a bit about Catholicism, and even felt an affection for the Roman Church (largely from studying Church history,
visiting Western Europe, and reading a lot of G.K. Chesterton), I
don't recall ever seriously considering becoming Catholic during my
undergraduate years.

A large part of the story of my later (re)conversion to Christianity, at least insofar as it was an intellectual process, is a story of losing some of the core philosophical commitments with which I began graduate school, specifically commitments to metaphysical naturalism (the view, roughly, that there is nothing to reality beyond the natural world, which consists entirely of physical stuff acting in accordance with the laws of nature) and a physicalist view of the mind (roughly, the view that all aspects of the mind are reducible to physical processes in the brain). My approach to philosophy when I entered graduate school was an approach that might be called "fixed-point naturalism", a (unfortunately very popular) philosophical methodology that takes naturalism as a fixed point and judges all other philosophical issues by how things look from this immoveable foundation, aspiring in all things to make one's commitments on specific issues as naturalistic-sounding as possible. When one takes this stance, the business of philosophy largely becomes a matter of finding a "naturalistically respectable account" of this or that troubling phenomenon—consciousness, intentionality, meaning, teleology, morality, rationality, free will, mathematical knowledge, etc.—within the naturalistic scheme, or else discarding the alleged phenomenon as "naturalistically unacceptable".

An important intellectual shift that would eventually lead me to abandon naturalism entirely occurred early on in graduate school. I became convinced that, even if naturalism is true as a metaphysical thesis—and I still held to this metaphysical thesis—the philosophical methodology just described is simply not a rational way to approach philosophical questions. I was persuaded (largely by philosopher David Lewis, if memory serves) that, ultimately, the only rational approach there could be to philosophical questions was the "Moorean" or "conservative" approach, which might be expressed as follows: one comes to philosophy with a prior stock of opinions, including those that make up the hard core of common sense. When doing philosophy, it's okay—indeed, it's mandatory—to start with what one initially finds plausible, or with what one takes to be obvious prior to philosophical inquiry. (Where else can one start? With what is antecedently *implausible*?) To say we can start with these beliefs is not to say we must end with them. But one should only abandon one's prephilosophical convictions if they can be shown to conflict with claims that are even more plausible. Perhaps every opinion is rationally revisable *in principle*, but I was convinced by David Lewis that, in practice, there is a large class of prephilosophical convictions that have the status of "Moorean truths". A Moorean truth is "one of those things that we know better than we know the premises of any philosophical argument to the contrary"[1] and therefore cannot be rationally rejected on the basis of any philosophical argument.

It took some time for this Moorean philosophical reorientation to ramify across my web of beliefs. At first its effects were local and piecemeal, leading me to revise my views on this or that particular question. But eventually this philosophical reorientation would lead me to rethink issues closer to the heart of my overall naturalistic worldview, especially the questions of philosophical anthropology to be discussed below.

Another important intellectual shift occurred when I became convinced that physicalism about the mind was false. The shift happened quite suddenly near the end of my second year of graduate school. I was sitting in my house, thinking about the metaphysics of consciousness and introspecting my visual experience (philosophers of mind do this a lot), and I was struck with a strong and sudden conviction that consciousness *obviously* isn't reducible to physical processes, that subjective experience is clearly something quite different in kind from the movements of matter, and that by officially committing to reductive physicalism about consciousness (as I had in some previously published work) I was just lying to myself. The seeds for this shift were laid, I think, by reading David Chalmers' *The Conscious Mind* several months earlier.[2] In the introductory chapter, "Taking Consciousness Seriously", he criticizes much of the theorizing about consciousness in the latter half of the twentieth century for either denying the self-evident data of introspection or simply ignoring the really difficult questions about consciousness. I remember reading this chapter with a vague feeling of being "called out", a feeling that there was something fundamentally dishonest about my attachment to physicalism. My immediate response to

---

[1] David Lewis, "Elusive Knowledge", *Australasian Journal of Philosophy* 74, no. 4 (1996): 549.

[2] David J. Chalmers, *The Conscious Mind: In Search of a Fundamental Theory* (New York: Oxford University Press, 1996).

the book, however, was not to abandon physicalism, but to engage his arguments at a technical level and try to come up with the best physicalist response. This whole project of trying to "make physicalism work" would later strike me as a kind of intellectual perversion. I came to feel as though I had been playing lawyer to a client without regard to whether the client was in the right, and without any clear reason, other than the winds of intellectual fashion, for defending this particular client rather than another. I don't want to disparage this approach to philosophy in general. Philosophy can be done in an exploratory spirit, and there can be significant value in giving the best possible defense of a view even if one is unsure of its truth. But on a question like physicalism, which is so closely tied to existentially fundamental questions of what we are and what life is about, my whole prior approach seemed to me to involve an unwholesome lack of seriousness about serious things.

This all happened shortly before some family troubles led me to take a semester off from my Ph.D. program at the beginning of my third year of graduate school to live near my family in Seattle for four months. In many respects, this was a difficult and emotionally tumultuous time. But when I recall this period now, it is hard for me to think of it as anything other than a time of coming out of darkness and into the light. This was a time when the Holy Spirit was moving palpably and powerfully in my life. There is no hope of adequately summarizing the various emotional and interpersonal and intellectual currents over the course of these four months that led to my conversion, but I'll say what I can within the constraints imposed by my expressive abilities, word limits, and a due respect for others' privacy.

There was, first, an experience of seeing God transform certain people close to me in ways that defied any reasonable hope on my part, like there was a living principle from outside nature, a vitality against the stream of this world in bondage to decay. There were also powerful experiences of Christian friends ministering to me and praying for me through a personally difficult time. There is a lovely passage in Peter van Inwagen's autobiographical essay, "Quam Dilecta", in which he perfectly captures my attitude toward a number of Christian friends and acquaintances of mine, including many who played a significant role in this period of my life:

There are five or six Christian I know who, for all the rich indi-
viduality of their lives and personalities, are like lamps, each shining
with the same dearly familiar, uncreated light that shines in the pages
of the New Testament. I can no more doubt this judgment than I
can doubt many of my much more everyday sorts of judgment to
the effect that this or that person is kind or generous or honest or
loving. When one is in the presence of this light—when one so much
as listens to one of these people speak—it is very difficult indeed to
believe that one is not in the presence of a living reality that transcends their individual lives.[3]

I also recall being haunted during this time by the thought that, by
renouncing religion, I had made myself into a truncated and stunted
human being. I came to feel that a life without worship was a
half-human life. Against the backdrop of this nagging thought, I
came to see the intellectual posture I had effected toward religion
as bordering on moral perversity. I have in mind specifically the
habit I had developed of systematically discounting my own (not
uncommon) religious experiences. (I do not mean strange visions
or booming voices or anything like that. I mean experiences like
the feeling of being in touch with things transcendent.) I came
to see my habit of discounting these experiences on analogy with
one who, having decided that the philosophical arguments for the
existence of other minds are unconvincing, proceeds to cut himself off from the interpersonal domain by consciously discounting,
and gradually dulling, his natural sense that there are other minds
behind the faces he sees.[4]

There were, in addition to these interpersonal and emotional
influences, several considerations of a more purely intellectual character that moved me away from naturalism and toward Christianity.
Many of these had to do with philosophical anthropology—that is,
with questions about the nature of the human person. It seemed to
me there were a number of considerations that told strongly against

---

[3] Peter van Inwagen, "Quam Dilectica", in *God and the Philosophers: The Reconciliation of Faith and Reason*, ed. Thomas V. Morris (New York: Oxford University Press, 1994), 57–58.

[4] The philosopher Alvin Plantinga explores a similar analogy in a number of places, e.g., in *God and Other Minds* (Ithaca, NY: Cornell University Press, 1967), though I don't remember whether this thought was inspired by reading his work.

a naturalistic anthropology and in favor of a theistic and specifically Christian anthropology. One such consideration had to do with free will. It's a commonplace that the existence of free will and naturalism are at least in *prima facie* conflict. If naturalism is true, then my actions are fully constituted by the motions and interactions of atoms in my brain and body, atoms whose behavior is governed entirely by laws of nature over which I have no control. In my view, the conflict here is genuine, not merely apparent, but this is not the place to argue the point.[5] Of course, a conflict between free will and naturalism is only a problem for naturalism if free will exists. But I don't think the existence of free will can be reasonably denied. (Here I understand "free will" in the minimal sense of having the ability to choose among multiple mutually incompatible courses of action.) To deny free will, we would need to deny one of the following claims (from which the reality of free will follows): (1) We sometimes do things that we are morally obligated not to do. (2) We are morally obligated to do something only if we are able to do it. (In other words, "ought" implies "can".) But (1) and (2) are both extremely plausible. They should certainly command more confidence than the premises of any argument that has yet been given for naturalism.

A second set of considerations that seemed to me to tell against naturalistic anthropology and in favor of Christian anthropology had to do with the cognitive capacities of human beings. Here most of my thinking centered on two cognitive capacities in particular: our capacity to know objective moral truths and our capacity to do science. I had been thinking a fair amount about the first in connection with so-called evolutionary debunking arguments against moral realism due to philosopher Sharon Street, among others.[6] Moral realism is the view that there are objective moral truths—that is, truths about what's right and wrong that hold independently of anyone's preferences or opinions. Evolutionary debunking arguments against moral realism come in various forms, but the basic idea is this: Anyone who thinks

---

[5] If I were to argue the point, my argument would not differ much in substance from that given in Jason Turner's excellent paper "The Incompatibility of Free Will and Naturalism", *Australasian Journal of Philosophy* 87, no. 4 (December 1, 2009): 565–87, https://doi.org/10.1080/00048400802598652.

[6] Sharon Street, "A Darwinian Dilemma for Realist Theories of Value", *Philosophical Studies* 127, no. 1 (2006): 109–66.

there are objective moral truths will presumably think that when we
make moral judgments—when we judge, for instance, that stealing is
wrong, or that we ought to keep our promises, or that parents ought
to provide for their children—we get the moral facts right, at least
approximately and for the most part. But on a naturalistic view of
the nature and origins of humans, we must admit that our faculties
of moral judgment are purely the result of natural selection, a process
that selects traits for their conduciveness to survival and reproduction
and is entirely insensitive to whatever objective moral facts there may
be. It would therefore seem to be a wildly fortuitous coincidence if
our faculties of moral judgement typically got the moral facts even
approximately right. Since we should avoid believing in cosmic coin-
cidences of this kind, we should therefore reject moral realism.

Now, it is commonly noted that this argument is no threat to moral
realists who also accept theism. If our faculty of moral judgment was
designed by God to be a reliable guide to the moral dimension of
reality, as most theists suppose, then the correspondence between
our moral judgments and the moral facts would not be an incredible
coincidence. But after making this concession to the theist, proponents of the evolutionary debunking argument typically follow up
with some or other dismissive remark: "Most of us, however, are
good naturalists and atheists, so we can ignore this escape hatch." But
I don't think the naturalist can rationally ignore the theistic response
to the evolutionary debunking argument, for it may be that the most
reasonable response to the argument is to give up naturalism. The
evolutionary debunking argument is, in effect, an argument from
naturalistic assumptions to the conclusion (roughly) that moral realism is false. There are, then, three possible responses. (1) We can
reject the naturalistic assumptions. (2) We can find a flaw in the argument, thereby showing that naturalism need not lead to the rejection
of moral realism. (3) We can accept the conclusion that moral realism
is false. I became convinced that (1) and (2) are the only reasonable
options. For to accept option (3) is to deny claims such as the following: (T) Torturing infants for fun is wrong (and it would still be
wrong if we came under the spell of an ideology that approved of
torturing infants).

Now, to call (T) plausible would be an understatement. It would
be hard to think of a claim more plausible than (T), and there are
certainly no arguments for naturalism with premises that a reasonable

person could find more plausible than (T). If the evolutionary debunking argument succeeds, it succeeds as a "reductio" argument against naturalistic anthropology, not as an argument against moral realism. Taken in this way, I think the evolutionary debunking argument is reasonably strong, so I think it provides good grounds for rejecting its naturalistic assumptions.[7]

A second epistemic capacity of humans that seemed to me to tell against naturalism is our capacity to do science. One often hears naturalists marvel at the astounding success of the scientific enterprise. To take one of many examples, consider the following remarks from Sam Harris:

> Within the Darwinian conception of how we got here there's no reason to believe that our cognitive faculties have evolved to put us in error-free contact with reality; that's not how they evolved.... We are designed by a happenstance of evolution to function within a very narrow band of light intensities and physical parameters. The things we are designed to do very well are, you know, recognize the facial expressions of apes just like ourselves and to throw objects in parabolic arcs within 100 meters and all of that, and so the fact that we are able to succeed to the degree that we have been in creating a vision of scientific truth and the structure of the cosmos at large that radically exceeds those narrow parameters, that is a kind of miracle. It is an amazing fact about us that seems not to be true, remotely true, of many other species we know about and that's something to be celebrated.[8]

Here the reason why Harris finds the success of science surprising ("a kind of miracle") is that he assumes that the naturalistic story of the nature and origins of humans is correct. I think Harris is right that

---

[7] Philosophers will notice a resemblance between this argument (as well as the argument in the following paragraphs) and Plantinga's evolutionary argument against naturalism, e.g., in *Warrant and Proper Function* (New York: Oxford University Press, 1993), chap. 12. But there are also important differences. For example, Plantinga argues that the assumption of naturalism and evolution leads to the conclusion that *all* our beliefs (not just our moral beliefs) are unlikely to be true. I am not convinced that such a strong conclusion can be justified, and while I endorse some of the core ideas underlying Plantinga's evolutionary argument, I do not wish to endorse the details of his formulation of it.

[8] "What Is True? A Conversation with Jordan B. Peterson", episode number 62 of the podcast *Waking Up*, hosted by Sam Harris, January 21, 2017, https://samharris.org/podcasts /what-is-true/.

the human capacity to do science is quite unexpected, quite improbable, on the assumption of naturalism. By contrast, this is not nearly so unlikely conditional on Christian theism. Here I think it's helpful to see that there are really two sides to the human capacity for science, only one of which is emphasized in the passage above. The first is the fact that the universe is intrinsically intelligible—that nature is structured in a way that admits of rational comprehension. This, I take it, is the fact at which Einstein marveled when he said that "the most incomprehensible thing about the universe is that it is comprehensible",[9] and is closely related to physicist Eugene Wigner's famous remark about "the unreasonable effectiveness of mathematics" in science.[10] The second, which is the focus on Harris' remarks above, is that our actual cognitive equipment, such as it is, allows us to discern the broad lineaments of nature, to plumb the deep structure of reality at levels well outside those relevant to life on the savannah. Both of these facts seem much more like what we should expect if Christian theism were true than if naturalism were true. The first fact fits comfortably with the theistic idea that the universe has its source in a Rational Mind, and is really quite surprising on the opposite assumption. And the second fact accords nicely with the Christian doctrine that human beings are made in the image of God, where bearing the image of God has traditionally been supposed to involve, among other things, the possession of an intellectual nature by which we partake in the divine reason.

There is a lot more to be said about the relationship between science and Christian belief, including the alleged conflicts between science and religion. I won't say much more about those issues here, except to record my conviction that the scientific discovery that bears most powerfully on religious questions is the metadiscovery that science is humanly possible, and this discovery strongly supports theistic belief for the reasons just given. The first-order discoveries of science for the most part have very little bearing on religious questions, and

[9] Albert Einstein, "Physics and Reality" (1936), in *Ideas and Opinions*, trans. Sonja Bargmann (New York: Bonanza, 1954), 292.

[10] Eugene Wigner, "The Unreasonable Effectiveness of Mathematics in the Natural Sciences: Richard Courant Lecture in Mathematical Sciences Delivered at New York University, May 11, 1959", *Communications on Pure and Applied Mathematics* 13, no. 1 (February 1960).

the few exceptions to this generalization (e.g., the discovery that the universe had a beginning, or the discovery that various fundamental physical parameters are fine-tuned for life) tend to be more friendly to theism than to naturalism.

A third consideration that seemed to me to tell against naturalistic anthropology and in favor of Christian anthropology had to do with a commonly held moral view that we might call "human moral exceptionalism", the view that (all) human beings have significantly greater moral worth than nonhuman animals. Nearly everyone (at least implicitly) believes this, at least if we set aside controversies about the moral status of the unborn and focus exclusively on human beings outside the womb. There is an obvious congruity between human moral exceptionalism and the Christian teaching that humans are made in the image of God and are, in that respect, set apart from all other creatures of the earth. On the other hand, human moral exceptionalism cannot be easily combined with a naturalistic anthropology. The naturalist may be able to salvage the *generic* claim that humans *typically* or *generally* have a higher moral status than nonhuman animals—for example, by holding that moral status is an increasing function of cognitive sophistication and noting that, as a matter of empirical fact, humans are typically more cognitively sophisticated than nonhuman animals. But this view has difficulty accommodating the nearly universally held belief that newborn infants have greater moral worth than animals. We would all agree, for example, that performing painful experiments on human infants is far more morally objectionable than performing similar experiments on animals, or that killing human infants for human consumption is morally worse than killing animals for human consumption. But the view under consideration implies that this attitude is unjustified, for it is certainly not clear that a newborn human infant is, in the relevant sense, more intelligent or cognitively sophisticated than a mature pig. A naturalist might instead say that moral status depends on a creature's *potential* for intelligence, or perhaps that moral status depends on having a nature that is teleologically ordered toward a certain level of intelligence. But it's doubtful that naturalism is consistent with the sort of robust teleology needed to make the second suggestion work, and the first suggestion seems unable to accommodate the distinctive moral worth of severely and permanently mentally disabled humans.

At this point, it seems the naturalist has two options (short of abandoning naturalism). First, he could follow philosopher Peter Singer and reject human moral exceptionalism, holding in particular that human infants and the severely mentally disabled have no more moral importance than animals, and that there is no significant moral difference between (say) killing babies and killing cows for human consumption, or between subjecting mentally disabled adults to painful involuntary scientific testing and doing the same to animals. I don't think this option merits serious consideration. Whatever moral objections there may be to our current treatment of animals (and for my part, I think much of what we routinely do to animals *is* morally objectionable), it is simply beyond question that it would be vastly worse, morally speaking, to subject humans to the same treatment. Second, the naturalist could say that moral status is determined by what we collectively value, and for biological and cultural reasons it so happens that we value human lives more than nonhuman lives. But the problem with this suggestion is obvious: it implies that, were we to stop collectively valuing certain groups of people, these people would no longer warrant moral consideration and it would no longer be wrong to treat them like animals (or worse, if we happened to value them less than animals). This is a deeply implausible position. It is far more plausible that the naturalistic assumptions that led us here are false. One should sooner abandon naturalism than follow it into such dark holes.

For the reasons given above, and various other supporting reasons too numerous to spell out in any detail (e.g., the existential resonance of Jesus' life and teaching, the fruits of the Church, the historical evidence for the Resurrection and for the general credibility of the Gospel narratives, and the fact that Christianity is almost unique, at least among philosophies taken seriously in the modern world, in correctly perceiving the depth and durability of human evil[11]), I came to find Christianity plausible. This is not to say that I found these considerations to *compel* belief. The Church teaches that faith involves the

---

[11] For a brief and accessible discussion of the historical reliability of the Gospels and the evidence for the Resurrection, see Peter Kreeft and Ronald K. Tacelli, *Handbook of Christian Apologetics*, repr. ed. (Downers Grove, IL: IVP Academic, 1994), chaps. 8–9. On the religious significance of the depth and durability of human evil, see van Inwagen, "Quam Dilectica".

will, and certainly in my case there was an element of choice in taking on Christian belief. I felt, if not compelled, then urged or called to submit my life to Christ, and whatever uncertainties remained, I felt that there was, apart from Christ, nothing else worthy of devoting a life to anyway. For weeks, St. Peter's words played through my mind: "Lord, to whom shall we go? You have the words of eternal life."[12] My feelings during this period of indecision could perhaps be summarized by the following broadly Pascalian line of thought: "Christianity is, by my lights, very likely to be true. If it is true, and I go on withholding belief, I will be missing out on the most important truth to my life. I will not be able to give myself fully in worship or obedience. I will probably revert to living as a practical atheist and live on in wretched ignorance of the glorious truths of the Gospel. I will be on the outside of life. If, on the other hand, Christianity is not true, I do not lose much by being a Christian, for in that case (so it seemed to me) there is no great significance in anything, and nothing of great value is to be had in this world. True, I would in that case live my life in error, and error, I suppose, is always an evil. But how great an evil it is depends on what the truth is. And if the truth is as drab and dispiriting as the atheist supposes, then to miss out on the truth is not to miss out on anything of fundamental importance to my life."

This line of thought struck me as sound before it struck me as Pascalian. I think that coming to conceptualize it as a Pascalian form of argument prevented me, for a while, from appreciating its soundness. For like other philosophers, I knew the stock objections to Pascal's wager, and thought it had been refuted in particular by the "deviant deity" or "many gods" objection. But I eventually realized that the deviant-deity objection succeeds only against the most ambitious versions of Pascal's wager, but not against the modest version of Pascal's wager addressed to my condition. The ambitious version of Pascal's wager aims to show that anyone who assigns a nonzero probability to the truth of Christianity has sufficient practical reason to adopt Christian belief. This version (in its standard formulation, anyway) is a failure, for parallel reasoning could be used to establish the opposite conclusion, given that there is a nonzero probability that

---

[12] Jn 6:68.

there exists a deity who will reward you infinitely if, and only if, you do not adopt Christian beliefs. But there is a more modest version of Pascal's wager that aims to establish only the weaker conclusion that one ought to adopt Christian belief if one thinks Christianity is reasonably likely to be true (say, if one thinks that Christianity is at least 50 percent likely to be true).[13] In my view, this version of Pascal's wager is successful, at least if certain qualifications are made, such as that one is not in abnormal circumstances that would make Christian belief extraordinarily costly—for example, one is not living under a political regime that executes or imprisons Christians. (Whether the argument succeeds without these qualifications was, fortunately, not a question of practical urgency for me.)[14]

Against the backdrop of everything else, this line of thought convinced me to become a Christian. In my conversion to Christianity,

---

[13] Michael Rota develops a version of Pascal's wager along these lines in "A Better Version of Pascal's Wager", *American Catholic Philosophical Quarterly* 90, no. 3 (June 22, 2016): 415–39, https://doi.org/10.5840/acpq20166288.

[14] It might be thought that a deviant-deity objection applies equally to the modest version of Pascal's wager. Given that there is a nonzero probability that there exists a deviant deity who will torture you forever if and only if you adopt Christian beliefs, it would seem to follow that the expected value of adopting Christian beliefs is either negative infinity or undefined. In either case, the expected value of adopting Christian beliefs does not exceed the expected value of the alternative, so (the objection concludes) it's false that you have sufficient practical reason to adopt Christian beliefs. But it's obvious that there's something wrong with this objection, since the same objection can be made against any ordinary piece of practical reasoning. As you lock up your house, you think, "There's a good chance I left the stove on. I should go back in and check. After all, if I left it on, then the cost of not checking would be enormous—my house would likely burn down. And even if I didn't leave the stove on, the cost of playing it safe is negligible—I would lose thirty seconds of my day, and I'm not in much of a hurry anyway." This ordinary piece of practical reasoning is, of course, perfectly acceptable, but it is equally vulnerable to a deviant-deity objection. (There is a nonzero probability that there exists a deviant deity who will torture you forever if, and only if, you go back to check your stove.) Of course, there are technical difficulties with spelling out a formal decision theory that yields the intuitively correct verdict here, a theory that avoids paradox when dealing with infinite utilities. Until we have worked the bugs out of our decision theory, any formal decision-theoretic presentation of Pascalian reasoning will face technical challenges from deviant-deity hypotheses, as would a decision-theoretic presentation of the argument for going back to check your stove. But these challenges are best seen as objections to standard decision theory, not to the reasoning the decision-theoretic apparatus is supposed to be modeling. We don't need a fully worked-out decision theory to know that the practical reasoning in the stove case is sound, any more than we need a formal axiomatization of arithmetic to know that 2 + 7 = 9. In this respect, I see no relevant difference between the "stove" reasoning and the reasoning in the modest Pascalian argument.

there was really no decisive moment of final commitment. The closest thing to a "moment of conversion" occurred during a conversation with two Christian friends of mine, in which I made explicit a certain realization: that I was already a Christian, just not a committed Christian. My new self-conception as an "uncommitted Christian" effectively gave me permission to live the life of a Christian—to pray regularly, go to church, try to live in obedience to Christ, and so forth—without having to make any grand and binding and public commitment, which at the time I was not prepared to do. After carrying on in this way for a few months, without any leaps to mark the transition, the "uncommitted" qualifier gradually faded out of my self-conception.

About nine months after I became a Christian I entered an RCIA (Rite of Christian Initiation of Adults) program and was received into the Catholic Church the following spring, on Easter of 2013. The transition from Christianity to Catholicism involved far less internal conflict and emotional resistance than my conversion to Christianity. I experienced my confirmation into the Catholic Church not as a turning away from a previous life, but a fulfillment of what began at my Christian conversion. At the time of my conversion to Christianity, many of my closest friends were recent Catholic converts, and my wife, through some of the same influences, had begun seriously considering joining the Catholic Church (which she eventually did, a year before me). Conversations with my Catholic convert friends—I am especially indebted to conversations with Jesse Hinde and Keefe Piper—and with my wife, made Catholicism a live possibility for me. I was also influenced by conversations with Robert Koons, a philosophy professor at the University of Texas at Austin, and by his yet-unpublished essay, "A Lutheran's Case for Roman Catholicism", in which he discusses the reasons for his own conversion to the Roman Church.

Once it was a live option, I found Catholicism to be a very natural and attractive option. The reasons for this attraction were too numerous, and in some ways involve too much emotional and aesthetic subtlety, for me to convey adequately, but I shall mention a few of the considerations I found especially compelling. First, I felt that the schism brought about by the Protestant Reformation was such a terrible thing that one should not perpetuate this schism—one should

not be Protestant—without very good reason. And for my part, I had
no serious protests against the Catholic Church. I never saw much
in the standard Protestant objections. I already thought Catholics had
the upper hand on most of the major Reformation-era debates—for
example, the questions of *sola scriptura* and *sola fide*, the relationship
between justification and sanctification, the nature of the sacraments,
the veneration of the saints, and the propriety of art in churches.
With respect to other disagreements between Catholics and (some)
Protestants, such as the issue of infant baptism or the Immaculate
Conception, I had no opinion at all, but I felt no positive resistance
to accepting the Catholic view on these questions. I don't recall any
elements of Catholic doctrine that I found to be significant obstacles.

A second and closely related reason for my attraction to Catholicism was that I thought it was clearly desirable to belong, in a substantial and meaningful way, to the historical Church. Somewhat
more specifically, I thought that Christian practice should take place
within a body that is reasonably continuous with the church of the
apostles. The Catholic Church stands in clear continuity with the
church of the apostles in a way that no Protestant communion does.
It is easy for a Christian to find this idea—that it is desirable to live
in meaningful continuity with the historical Church—intellectually
compelling, but in my case, I also felt a strong emotional and aesthetic connection with the historical Church. The seeds for this
connection were planted years earlier during an extended honeymoon in Europe, during which my wife and I visited many of the
most magnificent churches in Europe. We also spent two months at
L'Abri, a Christian study center in the Netherlands, where I studied medieval Church history and read some of the great literary
works of medieval Christendom. This experience gave me a lasting
affection for the historical Church and the Church of Rome in
particular, an affection that endured at some level even while I was
a nonbeliever. (Even as a nonbeliever, I never had contempt for
Christianity or its historical legacy, and for as long as I have been
historically literate enough to have an opinion on the question, I
have thought that the Church's enduring effects on the world have
been, on the whole, unquestionably positive.)

A third reason for my attraction to Catholicism was the fact that
Jesus evidently intended that there should exist a visible church with

a visible unity, and I thought the Catholic Church was the only visibly unified institution with a credible claim to being the Church established by Christ. And quite apart from Christ's explicitly proclaimed intentions, I was convinced that there is an urgent practical necessity for a magisterium, for a living teaching authority to resolve disputes that threaten the unity of the Church. (We can look to the history of mainline Protestantism over the past few decades for an illustration of this practical necessity.)

A living teaching authority is also, I think, a practical necessity for the spiritual life of the individual believer. In the months following my conversion to Christianity, I became increasingly convinced that if the Catholic Church did not have divine authority, then there was no hope of gaining firm knowledge of much of anything in theology. I felt that if the Church of Rome could not be trusted, then the whole Christian theological project was hopelessly underconstrained. If we go by Scripture alone, then just about every major theological debate in the early centuries of the Church would have to be reopened. The biblical case against Arianism, for example, is not cut-and-dried, nor is the biblical case in favor of Trinitarian dogma or the Chalcedonian definition of Christ's Person. (For me, these are very practical matters. Contemplation of the central dogmas of the Church is no small part of my spiritual nourishment, and my devotional life would be greatly impoverished if the divinity of Christ or Trinitarianism were open questions for me.) Moreover, whatever constraints on theological speculation are provided by the Bible are contingent upon taking the Bible to have special authority, and it is by no means obvious what grounds a non-Catholic Christian has for taking the Bible in this way. And even if we waive this difficulty and grant that the Bible has some kind of authority, it is unclear what *kind* of authority the non-Catholic Christian should take it to have. (Must he regard it as inerrant? Or "inspired" in a sense that does not imply inerrancy? But then what *does* it imply? Would this view ever lead one to accept something on biblical grounds that one would otherwise have rejected?)

I raise these points not for polemical reasons, but only to bring out what I felt to be a practical and personal difficulty. I felt at the time that being a non-Catholic Christian would mean that nearly every theological question would be up for grabs, and that in practice this would mean I would just make up my own theology from scratch. I'm enough of a philosopher that I'm sure I would have a fun time of it. But I also knew that this would be a spiritually destructive pursuit, that on this path I would wander interminably across the fields of philosophical theology and become like the ex-cleric ghost in C. S. Lewis' *Great Divorce*, who tells his old friend:

> For me there is no such thing as a final answer. The free wind of inquiry must always continue to blow through the mind, must it not? ... There is something stifling about the idea of finality.... I am not aware of a thirst for some ready-made truth which puts an end to intellectual activity in the way you seem to be describing. Will it leave me the free play of Mind, Dick? I must insist on that, you know.[15]

The basis for my final decision to make the Catholic Church my spiritual home might be summarized by the friend's response that, on these matters, which touch the spiritual and moral core of life, the intellect is to be "free, as a man is free to drink while he is drinking. He is not free still to be dry.' ... Thirst was made for water; inquiry for truth. What you now call the free play of inquiry has neither more nor less to do with the ends for which intelligence was given you than masturbation has to do with marriage."

---

[15] C. S. Lewis, *The Great Divorce* (New York: HarperCollins, 1973), pp. 40–41.

4

Of Towers and Tongues

Neal Judisch

> But as the old Confusion of tongues was laudable, when men who were of one language in wickedness and impiety, even as some now venture to be, were building the Tower—for by the confusion of their language the unity of their intention was broken up, and their undertaking destroyed—so much more worthy of praise is the present miraculous one. For being poured from One Spirit upon many men, it brings them again into harmony. And there is a diversity of Gifts, which stands in need of yet another Gift to discern which is the best, where all are praiseworthy.
>
> —St. Gregory Nazianzen, *Oration on Pentecost*

Philosophers are normal people with normal concerns. Religious philosophers are no different: they are at bottom religious people who happen to be philosophers by temperament and trade. So suppose a philosopher undergoes religious conversion—in the case of interest, suppose a religious philosopher converts from Protestantism to Catholicism. What is it about such a conversion that commends special attention? Perhaps this: (1) philosophers have the luxury of study and time, and (2) philosophers are trained to reason rigorously and conscientiously. Conversion stories are always of great human interest, but when a philosopher converts, you expect to hear a really *good* conversion story. That's probably because of (1) and (2).

There is a grain of truth here. Philosophers get to think really hard for extended periods of time about whatever excites them, and

they get paid to do it. They also benefit from an academic formation designed to infuse intellectual virtues like clarity of thought and
expression, open-mindedness, and analytical care. All this is true
and relevant. And yet, philosophers remain normal people with normal concerns for all that. A philosopher's conversion story will therefore be a recognizably human story, whenever it is truthfully told.

I belabor this obvious point for two reasons. First, it should be
acknowledged that philosophers are just as susceptible to common
forces of religious conversion as anyone else might be. Here I include
emotional, affective, or other "nonrational" influences; I include as
well individual formative and environmental circumstances, which
are plainly contingent but undeniably impactful.[1] Second, philosophers are supposed to be—and indeed strive to be—aware of these
forces, to hold them at some critical distance, and to "follow the
argument wherever it leads".

The first thing is what makes philosophers human. The second
thing is what makes philosophers philosophers.

But these twin truths expose a real tension. How can a philosopher
be sure that his religious convictions, even when backed by argument,
aren't just reflections of arbitrary circumstances like upbringing, life

---

[1] C. S. Lewis' glancing blow at Freud is at this point worth quoting in full:

"There are of course people in our own day to whom the whole situation seems
altered by the doctrine of the concealed wish. They will admit that men, otherwise
apparently rational, have been deceived by the arguments for religion. But they will
say that they have been deceived first by their own desires and produced these arguments afterwards as a rationalization: that these arguments have never been intrinsically even plausible, but have seemed so because they were secretly weighted by our
wishes. Now I do not doubt that this sort of thing happens in thinking about religion
as in thinking about other things; but as a general explanation of religious assent it
seems to me quite useless. On that issue our wishes may favour either side or both.
The assumption that every man would be pleased, and nothing but pleased, if only
he could conclude that Christianity is true, appears to me to be simply preposterous."
C. S. Lewis, "On Obstinacy in Belief", in *They Asked for a Paper* (London: Geoffery
Bles, 1962), 185–86.

Substitute conversion from atheism to Christianity with conversion from Protestantism to
Catholicism, and there you have my situation. The vaunted "smells and bells", the supposed
appeal of a romanticized ancientness and of mystery, did not draw me but rather put me off.
Thus, the typical and designedly dismissive psychoanalytical explanation of Catholic conversion fails in my case to explain. Still, I do not doubt that "reasons of the heart" supplemented
the historical, biblical, and philosophical evidence that led me to the Church, and I freely
admit that the smells and the bells help keep me there *now*.

history, or intellectual bias? How can a philosopher be sure that his investigations have led to the objective truth? My short answer to this question is, they cannot be sure.[2] My fuller answer is, while they can't be sure, they can at least seek to attenuate error through careful thought and critical evaluation. This is no recipe for infallible certainty, but it is surely the most that religious philosophers (or anyone else) can be asked to do.

Certainty is a rare commodity in religion and philosophy both, and for that reason I view my Catholic faith as simultaneously anchored and dynamic. It is anchored because I find in the Catholic tradition something I can trust and from which I won't easily be dissuaded; it is dynamic because I am fallible.

In what follows I describe my transition from Evangelical Christian to (historically minded) Reformed Christian to Catholic Christian. No one argument took me to that destination, and no one emotional yearning or affective motive led me there, either. The arguments, yearnings, and motives came over time in a jumbled, confused, and ambivalent cluster, and it took me the better part of five years to sort them through. Here I relay them with the benefit of hindsight, but without (I hope) the taint of triumphalism or epistemic hubris.

I cannot remember a time I didn't believe in God or identify as Christian. Brought up in a godly, Evangelical home, I benefitted from the pious example of my parents and the religious formation I received from them and at church. When I asked Jesus into my heart (several times, to make sure it stuck!) and was subsequently baptized by immersion, I meant it. I learned Bible stories and memorized verses, and became adept at answering questions in Sunday school.[3] My childhood was happy.

---

[2] This is not to imply that Catholics cannot possess certainty of faith regarding defined dogma; it is rather to say that "epistemic certainty" of a sort entailing the impossibility of error does not necessarily attach to every argument by which an individual may come to believe in the Catholic faith.

[3] Many years onward, I would read with delight Thomas Howard's book *Evangelical Is Not Enough: Worship of God in Liturgy and Sacrament* (San Francisco: Ignatius Press, 1988), finding in his story a fondly remembered upbringing that mirrored in precise ways my own. If you wish to gain sympathetic insight into the worldview, life, and practice of American Evangelicals, this book is the place to start.

Later, like many adolescents, I lived a period of waywardness during which I continued to identify as Christian but had little interest in being one. It is a credit to my religious formation and the long-suffering of my parents that I was on the whole unhappy and ill at ease throughout those years. My problem was not that I was "limping with two different opinions", as Elijah put it,[4] because if you had asked me then, I would sincerely have told you I was Christian. It was rather that my life belied my belief. I was "double-minded" and "unstable", as James says,[5] which compromised my love of God and (therefore) my love of self and (therefore) my love of others. I felt the virtual force of this contradiction, and it weighed on me.[6]

Not many can live with that kind of dissonance forever; something has got to give. In my own case, for reasons I cannot now remember, I picked up C. S. Lewis' *Mere Christianity* and devoured it. It affected me like an electric surge to a long-dormant system. The religious content of this book was not altogether foreign, but the manner of presentation and quality of argument were new and thrilling. It hit me, too, at just the right time on a personal and emotional plane. I was primed. Probably I would have returned to the fold before long anyhow, but Lewis' book was the actual and energizing catalyst behind my second conversion.

I say "second conversion" advisedly. In the fit of enthusiasm that followed this religious awakening, I decided to get baptized again. My father, in his wisdom, advised against this; and I, in my decidedly superior wisdom, ignored his advice. So I became a Christian twice over. But my thought was this: while a real Christian will experience times of tepidness or of backsliding, the tenor of his life will exhibit a sincere love of God expressed in obedience and continuous spiritual growth. Since these things did not characterize my life, I concluded that my first conversion was faulty, that I never was a true Christian to begin with. And since baptism was an "outward sign of an inward

---

[4] 1 Kings 18:21.

[5] Jas 1:8.

[6] Students of Thomas Aquinas will recognize the results but alter the order: first lacking self-unity (self-love), I lacked union with God and so inevitably with others. I would not learn Aquinas' triadic theory of love or of disunion until much later; this did not stop me from living the reality of it then. For a very useful introduction to St. Thomas' philosophy of love, see Eleonore Stump, *Wandering in Darkness: Narrative and the Problem of Suffering* (Oxford University Press), 2012.

change", where the inward change had to come first, I figured I should get baptized once more to mark the occasion.

That conclusion was in part a product of my own reasoning, but it was shaped as well by the version of Calvinist theology I had begun to imbibe.[7] This is a distinctly American Evangelical variety of Calvinism that can be found in many Southern Baptist churches, including the one I attended then. It's a kind of Calvinism that Calvin himself would not recognize—not, anyway, as a faithful expression of his outlook. It is ahistorical, not particularly covenantal, and (as a result) rather too individualistic to count as Calvinism proper. Its main focus rests on a series of soteriological distinctives (viz., Total Depravity, Unconditional Election, Limited Atonement, Irresistible Grace, and Perseverance of the Saints). If you accept all these, you're a Calvinist; if you deny any one of them, you're not, and you likely do not understand what Protestantism (or the Christian faith) is all about.[8]

People who have not transitioned from mainline Evangelicalism to Evangelical Calvinism may not appreciate its allure. But imagine you were not catechized, did not use a lectionary, and (but for Christmas, Palm Sunday, and Easter) did not mark seasons according to a liturgical calendar. Imagine too that your Bible knowledge consisted of memorable stories and inspirational verses, but not so much in a narrative ordering of the stories or a systematic template relating the verses.

Now enter Evangelical Calvinism. While not particularly steeped in history, it at least gives an air of historical pedigree—we Calvinists knew more Reformation history than other Evangelicals did, and we delighted in it. More than that, such Calvinism is exquisitely systematic, and it has an answer for everything. It pulls together the isolated bits of Scripture in a meticulous, cohesive way, which is almost inexpressibly beautiful to an analytical mind. Perhaps most important, this kind of Calvinism generates a real sense of solidarity

[7] I do not mean to suggest traditional Calvinists would recommend rebaptism. They wouldn't. But it makes some degree of sense from a Southern Baptist-cum-Calvinist point of view.

[8] You might still be a genuine believer, but there would exist in this case a "felicitous inconsistency" between your sincere acceptance of essential truths and your failure to affirm what they imply. For a popular-level introduction expounding the "five points" of Calvinist systematic theology, see R. C. Sproul, *Grace Unknown: The Heart of Reformed Theology* (Grand Rapids, MI: Baker Publishing Group, 1997).

through doctrinal unity or agreement of theological outlook—you know the shibboleths and, by expressing them, you demonstrate belonging to the tribe. Finally, attached to this Calvinism is the keen sense that God's *glory* is at stake in the acceptance or rejection of it. Rejecting it means either that you do not understand the Bible well enough to see its truth (an intellectual problem), or that you *do* understand it but by your "wickedness suppress the truth", as Paul says,[9] because you want some share of God's glory for yourself (a moral, spiritual problem). The idea is easy to grasp: if you believe you are totally depraved and that your salvation results from unmerited divine election, all the glory must go to God. If you reject these doctrines, however, you think you aren't really that sinful and your salvation is a freely willed response to prevenient grace, in which case you must deserve *some* credit for the happy outcome. But only the first theory coheres with *sola gratia*, which is essential to true Christian faith.[10] On this picture, then, the non-Calvinist Christian is either intellectually defective or morally compromised; all thanks to God, the Calvinist is neither.[11]

These factors together exert enormous pressure to conform, and theological disagreements even on seeming minutiae can lead to ruptures in fellowship or (in the limiting case) outright schism. That's one downside of Evangelical Calvinism's robust systematicity. Just as we believed that the five *sola*s of the Reformation and the five points of Calvinism stood or fell together, we traced with ease inferential connections between those dogmas and theological opinions that were *prima facie* matters of Christian liberty—views upon which sincere and informed Christians could agree to disagree. And when Christian unity is primarily a function of doctrinal agreement, even those latter disagreements matter a lot.[12]

---

[9] Rom 1:18.

[10] By "prevenient grace" I mean the general grace God distributes equally to all, as opposed to the efficacious grace God directs only toward the elect. *Sola gratia* is one of the celebrated five *sola*s of the Reformation, which serves as shorthand for the thesis that all glory or credit for any person's salvation accrues to God alone.

[11] Some aspects of Calvinism I still find appealing; they can be absorbed and rightly balanced in the Catholic faith. Here consult Louis Bouyer, *The Spirit and Forms of Protestantism*, new ed. (San Francisco: Ignatius Press, 2017).

[12] I hope this assessment does not sound bitter. While I am able in hindsight to provide it, and in some measure recognized these truths then, I look back on this period of my life with fondness.

Baptism—its nature and meaning—is a case in point. From the Southern Baptist perspective, baptism is not a sacrament but an "ordinance", something Christians do to give public expression to their regenerative faith in God. But the grace by which Christians acquire such faith is *direct*, not mediated through any pretended priestly prerogative. This is why Calvinistic Baptists refrain from baptizing their children and separate themselves from Calvinists who do. Yet most Calvinists do baptize their children. Why?

I studied this question with verve while my wife was pregnant with our first child, and the materials I read exposed me to a richer and more historically authentic version of Calvinism than I had previously known.[13]

According to the authors I read, baptism is the sign and seal of the New Covenant, which supersedes circumcision (the sign and seal of the Old Covenant) as antitype to type. But it still bespeaks covenantal belonging, and covenantal belonging is an *objective* matter passed on via "covenantal succession". As in the Old Covenant, so (all the more) in the New Covenant: the children of believers should be regarded as full-fledged members of the covenant to which their parents belong, because "the promise" is, as St. Peter says, "to you and to your children and to all that are afar off".[14]

Calvinist paedobaptists (those who endorse the practice of baptizing infants) differed among themselves about the sacramental efficacy of baptism—even on whether "sacrament" is the right word for the rite— and they had continually to ward off accusations of "closet Romanism". But it seemed to me that Catholics did not corner the market on baptism, and the mere fact of agreement on infant baptism *as a practice* did not equate to agreement on sacramentology or sacerdotalism[15]

---

[13] In this connection I recommend Peter Leithart, *The Baptized Body* (Moscow, ID: Canon Press, 2007).

[14] Acts 2:39. Without knowing it, I had learned the first lesson of typology—namely, that the thrust is always "from grace to grace", from good to better, in ever-expanding transformative continuity. Thus, whereas circumcision is confined to male members of a particular ethnic group—something narrow, exclusive, and elite—Christian baptism is for Jew and Gentile, male and female, slave and free. It is the inclusive and emancipating grace to which circumcision points as shadow to reality. From this perspective, the idea that children are no longer included makes little sense; the ancient Church therefore had the right of it, and the newfangled ideas of the Anabaptists were wrong.

[15] Sacerdotalism here is understood as the view that sacramental or propitiatory sacrifices are mediated through an ordained priesthood established via apostolic succession.

or anything else Catholic-like. Election and justification were still exclusively divine prerogatives, unmediated by liturgical rite. So while baptism did not *save* you in a final sense, it *did* make you a member of God's covenantal family, and such covenant membership is salvation's context.[16]

Once convinced by these arguments, I segued from Southern Baptist to Presbyterian, the natural home (I believed) of Calvinism unalloyed.

The church belonging to the Presbyterian Church in America (PCA) I joined was just wonderful. It was warm and cerebral and close-knit. Populated heavily by those who made the same transition from Baptist to Presbyterian, we understood each other from top to bottom. In this space, too, I was trained more fully in the confessional standards of the Reformation, particularly in the Westminster Confession and its associated catechisms. I read and reread and memorized them, and began memorizing books of the Bible with a view toward filling my brain with as much Scripture as it could hold. There I also found a sustained emphasis on covenantal theology, which was to us parishioners quite as exciting and crucial as the systematic "five points".

Covenantal theology is the door to Christian history (or Christian historical-biblical theology). It combats the individualistic tendencies of Evangelicalism and sets you thinking about the Body of Christ, extended through time and space. In other words, it gets you thinking of the Church as a *thing*.[17]

---

[16] There are, according to Calvin, two ways of being elect: you can be a recipient of effectual saving grace, or you can belong to the Body of Christ by way of baptism. This is an inclusive disjunction. Not everyone who is elect in the second sense is elect in the first, but being elect in the second sense is still of theological import. Calvinists can thus make sense of the puzzling statements in 1 Peter 3:20–21: "Baptism, which corresponds to this [the situation on Noah's ark] now saves you", where the antitype to the ark is simply covenant membership in the Church via baptism. But this is held to be different from the theory of "baptismal regeneration" as advanced by Catholics.

[17] For an accessible crash course on covenantal theology from a Catholic (convert) perspective, see Scott Hahn, *A Father Who Keeps His Promises: God's Covenant Love in Scripture*, 1st ed. (Cincinnati: Servant, 1998); for a more academic presentation, see his *Kinship by Covenant: A Canonical Approach to the Fulfillment of God's Saving Promises*, 1st ed. (New Haven, CT: Yale University Press, 2009). The incarnational-sacramental ecclesiology born of covenantal theology is well summarized by another Catholic convert, Richard John Neuhaus:

> "The Church participates in nothing less than the very community, or *communio*, of God who is Father, Son, and Holy Spirit. (Although the English word 'community' can hardly bear the full weight and depth of what is intended by *communio*.) This is

This point too may be lost on readers unfamiliar with American Evangelicalism, but it is worth stressing. "The Church" on a typical Evangelical view means either the local body of believers with whom you regularly worship or all genuine believers with whom you have spiritual communion. There are of course many visible, this-worldly institutions called "churches", but *the Church* writ large is an invisible entity made up exclusively of individuals who have a personal relationship with the Lord. This is why the bewildering proliferation of Protestant sects or denominations, not visibly in communion with each other, does not bother Evangelicals over much. It is—and I hope this does not sound harsh—a kind of Gnostic ecclesiology, according to which the "spiritual" overrides and displaces in importance the "bodily". So Christian unity on this picture is a matter of spiritual or invisible unity alone. It has nothing to do with apostolic succession or bishops or sacraments or any earthly institution at all.[18]

Even the Presbyterian tradition to which I belonged may be characterized this way. When now and again we recited the Nicene Creed at service, our pastor would explain that "one, holy, catholic, and apostolic Church" does not mean the Catholic Church or anything like it, but rather the "universal" Church composed of all real Christians whose spiritual unity transcends tangible division.

---

an unabashedly theological, even mystical, way of understanding the Church. It in no way excludes the very human, historical, and even sociological ways of thinking about the Church. After all, we are not ecclesiological docetists. Docetism was an early (and ever recurring) heresy that Christ did not really have a human body, that he did not really suffer and die on the cross. Ecclesiological docetism is to view the Church as a theological abstraction that remains aloof from the very human messiness of history. As important as it is, however, to understand the 'pilgrim Church on earth' in earthly and even earthy terms, she remains always and primarily the temporal *communio* with the eternal life of the triune God; she is that part of history which, by virtue of the incarnation in which God becomes man, guides and impels humanity's pilgrimage toward our transcendent destiny. She is the prolepsis—the present anticipation—of the fulfillment of the story of the world. If that is not, above all, how we understand the Church, it is not evident that the Church has a major claim on our attention, never mind our allegiance, at all." Richard John Neuhaus, *Catholic Matters: Confusion, Controversy, and the Splendor of Truth* (New York: Basic Books, 2006), 173–74.

[18] This is not to say that Evangelicals will not mobilize or make common cause with one another. Evangelical churches do this routinely and to salutary effect, and this is an authentic expression of Christian unity, as John Paul II repeatedly stresses in his encyclical *Ut Unum Sint* (May 25, 1995).

There are definite tensions between this orientation and the otherwise muscular covenantal theology I had absorbed, and still more
tensions between it and the views of the magisterial Protestant
Reformers themselves (to say nothing of theologians hailing from
the Church's first fifteen hundred years). They knew that in his High
Priestly Prayer Christ's dying wish (as it were) was for the Church to
be one as he and the Father were one, so that the world might see
her unity as a sign of divine legitimacy and come also to believe.[19]
So they took schism deadly seriously, in marked contrast to the apa-
thetic, unruffled attitude displayed by most Evangelical Calvinists.
This struck me as odd. No Evangelical would endorse the thought
that a person could possess saving faith, hope, and love but never
act like it—that these virtues are exclusively spiritual and invisible,
without implication for outward behavior. You'll know a tree by its
fruit[20] and a Christian by his love,[21] says Jesus, and Evangelicals generally agree. Again, no Evangelical would find it remotely plausible
that a couple could get divorced, go on to marry others, and create
disjoint families, but still somehow count as exemplars of Christian
marriage.[22] Why then do they accept the ecclesial analogue, that
the Body could be invisibly united whilst visibly rent asunder, and
that invisible union could nevertheless bear meaningful witness to a
watching world? Why doesn't the fruit of ecclesial divorce say something about the tree that generates it too?

I do not intend these as rhetorical questions. For me they were
earnest questions needing answer, and they took on a sense of
urgency while I observed with dismay the "Federal Vision" controversy engulfing confessional Presbyterian communions back
then.[23] The specifics of this controversy do not matter for present

[19] Jn 17.
[20] Mt 7:16, 20.
[21] Jn 13:35.
[22] Evangelicals do not view marriage as a sacrament, but they treat it as such, perhaps more
so than anything else. It is a covenant cut before God and man, mediated by an ordained
minister (in effect, a priest) who pronounces two people "one flesh" by "the power invested"
within him. Those words matter, and so does the liturgical form—by these *God* has joined
something together, and no man can presume to separate what God has joined.
[23] Douglas Wilson's *Reformed Is Not Enough: Recovering the Objectivity of the Covenant* (Moscow, ID: Canon Press, 2002) is a popular-level book that helped transfer this controversy from
the ivory tower to the pew. Everyone was chattering about it, and everyone had a strong
opinion.

purposes, but the form and trajectory of that controversy do. Let me explain.

All sides to this dispute affirmed *sola scriptura* as axiomatic: the Bible alone was our infallible authority, but we looked to our confessions as necessary and trustworthy guides to Scripture's meaning.[24] Our confessions were thus authoritative only to the extent they faithfully expressed essential Christian dogma, which they did either by distilling perspicuous scriptural truths or by demonstrating "good and necessary inference" from those truths to others not quite as perspicuous. Since they were not divinely inspired, however, they were revisable in light of fresh biblical study. Thus the Westminster Confession, as we saw it, (1) was a touchstone of ecclesial unity on which confessional Presbyterians agreed and (2) provided a bulwark against schism arising from contrary private opinions, but which also (3) remained perennially corrigible *in principle*, if ever clear biblical evidence exposed some error within it, and therefore (4) never could supplant the ultimate authority of Scripture itself.

Proponents of Federal Vision argued that their exploratory rethinking of baptism and the sacraments generally—for example, of the nature of justification and its relation to covenant membership—comported with historical Reformed theology and was grounded ultimately in Scripture. They also insisted that the Westminster standards could be reinterpreted conformably to their views, perhaps with minor adjustments in linguistic expression here and there. Opponents saw in these theological explorations elements that looked discomfitingly Catholic,[25] and which conflicted with the plain meaning of the Bible and Westminster standards. They believed the Gospel was at stake and assumed a stalwart Lutheran "Here I Stand" posture against the encroaching tide of Romanism menacing their ranks.

It got ugly.

---

[24] Keith Matthison's *The Shape of Sola Scriptura* (Moscow, ID: Canon Press, 2001) is an accessible introduction to *sola scriptura* as we viewed it. We didn't think this doctrine amounted to "me and my Bible and whatever I happen presently to think"—it was rather that Scripture is the only infallible authority for life and doctrine, but the *regula fidei* (codified in Reformed confessions) and the "true bishops" who transmitted this tradition were fallible but genuinely authoritative as well. It approximates the Anglican triad of Scripture, tradition, and reason, but we were rather gun-shy about the *term* "Tradition" and were somewhat skeptical about the role of "reason" as well.

[25] Echoing the Howard and Wilson book titles, a friend of mine humorously remarked: "Maybe 'Evangelical' or even 'Reformed' is not enough; but 'Catholic' is *way too much*."

The principle of *sola scriptura* and the basic perspicuity of the Bible, the conviction that "Scripture interprets Scripture", even shared allegiance to the Westminster Confession—all this we had. But we could not agree on our interpretation of the Bible and likewise could not agree on our interpretation *of our interpretation* of the Bible (the Westminster standards), and no authority beyond the already fragmented presbyteries could register judgment binding on all. Fresh splits and schisms ensued, whereupon recriminations of heresy hurled in volleys from one trench to the other and back again.

Never before had I doubted *sola scriptura* as a fundamental truth of the Christian faith. But I was now alive to Christian (visible) unity as a nonnegotiable directive of that faith as well, and it seemed to me that *sola scriptura-cum-confessionalism* could not function so as effectually to establish or preserve it. Notoriously, not even the magisterial Protestant Reformers operating from similar principles could avoid bitter internecine division,[26] and in the short span of five hundred years we their progeny had exacerbated the problem exponentially—we had divided not only from "the Protestant church" at large but even (the more remarkably) from our own tiny Presbyterian slice of it. We had again earned our moniker: "The Split-P's".

This was bad, and I didn't know what to think. One nagging worry: perhaps *sola scriptura*—even the sophisticated version—was just wrong.[27] But if so, what then?

To this point I've said nothing of philosophy or of my introduction to the discipline. I'll say something about that now.

---

[26] See Alister McGrath, *Reformation Thought: An Introduction*, 4th ed. (Malden, MA; Oxford: Wiley-Blackwell, 2012), and A. N. S. Lane, "Scripture, Tradition, and Church: An Historical Survey", *Vox Evangelica* 9 (1975).

[27] Maybe the central difficulty is that the sophisticated version of *sola scriptura*, according to which the *regula fidei* and "true bishops" are genuine but fallible authorities, is not so different from the unsophisticated version (which Matthison cleverly dubs "*solo scriptura*"). On the latter approach, each individual interprets the Bible for himself without recourse to the aforementioned authorities, which is a recipe for hermeneutical chaos and ecclesial anarchy. But notice that even on the sophisticated version the individual must decide for himself what the content and meaning of the *regula fidei* is (in order to decide which of the various confessional traditions he ought to adopt) and which bishops are "true", since the class of true bishops is determined not by historico-sacramental succession but by fidelity to Scripture—or rather, to Scripture as the inquirer himself ("solo") interprets it. If this diagnosis is roughly correct, our problem was that while we had Scripture and (interpretive, confessional) tradition, we lacked a recognizable authority to adjudicate dogmatic disagreement (e.g., a magisterium).

I was a college student at the time. And concurrently with the events described, I had changed undergraduate majors from music composition to philosophy. My passion for Christian theology led to a focus on apologetics—the philosophical defense of the faith—that led in turn to fascination with the history and problems of philosophy as such. Behind this transition was the thought that a good apologist must understand in detail philosophical worldviews contrary to Christianity in order the better to defend it, and that the tools of philosophy are indispensable to theological endeavor. In my case, it resulted in a love of philosophy for its own sake as well.

I still view this as a natural progression, especially for those (like me) wishing to attend seminary or pursue postgraduate theological studies. But when graduation approached, I found I was not yet done with philosophy (it wasn't yet done with me?). So I trudged onward toward a Ph.D. at the University of Texas.

There are many admirable Reformed philosophers, highly regarded within the profession. I was proud of them and aspired to join their number. But there is a noticeable qualitative difference between these philosophers and the "Reformed presuppositionalist" philosophers whose works are widely disseminated in Presbyterian pews.[28] These were the philosophical counterparts to our socially sanctioned theologians: just as there are theologians you are supposed to like and others you are expected to dislike, the avowal of "presuppositional" as opposed to "classical" philosophical apologetics[29] establishes your Reformed bona fides.

The guiding idea of presuppositionalism is that "total depravity" is equally a moral-volitional condition and an intellectual-noetic condition, so that the "autonomous reason" of unregenerate persons inevitably runs against (Reformed) Christian truth. Because non-Christians lack the mind of Christ, in other words, their philosophical investigations are necessarily infected with rebellion against God and geared toward falsehood. The task of Christian apologetics, therefore, is not to identify "common ground" with nonbelievers and show forth the reasonableness of Christianity from their point of view—for what

---

[28] Principally, Cornelius Van Til, Greg Bahnsen, and (the best of the lot) John Frame.

[29] "Classical apologetics" refers to the body of work produced by mainstream philosophical theologians in the Western Christian tradition, which encompasses traditional proofs for the existence and various attributes of God from "unaided human reason".

agreement can there be between Christ and Baal?—but instead to begin with (to presuppose) Reformed Christian dogma and lay bare the internal contradictions inherent to every alternative worldview.

As a dialectical procedure, there is nothing especially wrong with this. It can be effective to refuse the burden of proof and set the other guy on his heels. But strategy is one thing and tactics another, and this is where presuppositionalism falls short. Their arguments once joined consist either of "classical" defenses drawn from natural theology (in idiosyncratic verbal dress) or attempts at "transcendental" reasoning,[30] which as far as I could tell were mere bombast.[31]

My foray into presuppositionalist thought did, however, teach me a valuable lesson, even if it was not the one intended. Their core insight was that philosophy does not occur in a theological vacuum, or (more carefully) that philosophical "worldviews" must finally rely on unproven presuppositions—presuppositions that *might* depend for their plausibility on an incipient theism. But they seemed oblivious to the other side of that coin—namely, that theology does not proceed in a philosophical vacuum either. Indeed, the theological system on which they stood and even the biblical exegesis supporting it is shot through with lofty, highly contestable philosophical theories of divine and human nature, of the nature of causation, of the relation of intellect to will, and of many other things besides. This is of course unavoidable—it's just the nature of the beast—but when gone unrecognized and unacknowledged, it is pernicious. The absolute unquestioning trust one has in the Word of God transfers illicitly to human ("presuppositional") theorizing, and critical distance between the two collapses in consequence. Daylight between Scripture and tradition disappears when you think you go by "the Bible alone".[32]

---

[30] "Transcendental" proofs aim to derive conclusions by disclosing the necessary conditions for the possibility of the target phenomenon. Thus a transcendental proof for God's existence may point to the existence of human consciousness, thought, or rationality, or the existence of logical laws, or the existence of reliable laws of nature, and then attempt to demonstrate that these actual phenomena are possible only on the condition that (the Christian) God exists.

[31] It is understandable (indeed, commendable) to extend presuppositionalist authorities a line of credit, but there is a line between *that* and insisting the emperor really does have clothes. Sycophantic devotion to presuppositionalism is harmful.

[32] See Yves Congar, *The Meaning of Tradition* (San Francisco: Ignatius Press, 2004).

Justification—its nature and meaning—is a case in point. Following Luther, we understood this as the article on which the Church stands or falls and identified Catholic repudiation of justification *sola fidei* as schism-inducing apostasy. On their theory, justification (having a right standing before God) was confused with sanctification (personal holiness) and caused formally by Christ's infused righteousness, appropriated in a person through his baptism and maintained by "good works" in synergy with nonefficacious (or resistible) grace. On ours, justification was Christ's "alien" righteousness imputed (*not* infused)[33] by means of a regenerative faith caused monergistically via divine agency, and (progressive) sanctification was something else entirely. Thus we held justification by faith alone and salvation by grace alone, whereas Catholics endorsed salvation by (faith and *mostly*) meritorious works.

There is little historical accuracy and no theological nuance to this dichotomy. It's just how we were conditioned to view the rift. Noteworthy now, however, is that even these caricatures are laden to a breaking point with philosophical theory. Abstruse late medieval debates between realists and nominalists concerning universals, disputes about the concurrence of primary and secondary causes, about the categories of formal and efficient and final and material causation, about virtues and habits—all these made unspoken inroads to disparate theories of justification to salient effect. No doubt, these philosophical theories may be contoured by theology and biblical study as well. The point is that the relation between philosophy and these is one of *reciprocal* influence.[34] No one can pretend to begin with pure, unvarnished Christian "presuppositions" and construct his philosophy or theology from there.

Alister McGrath's *Iustitia Dei*, which I had begun to read during "off-time" in graduate school, forcefully underscored this fact.[35] I had

---

[33] "Imputed righteousness" designates Christ's alien righteousness applied forensically, or legally, to believers, by means of which God "reckons" them righteous or blameless before the divine tribunal. "Infused righteousness" designates by contrast a real ("metaphysical", "vine-branch") sharing in the righteousness of Christ, by means of which the believer is both accounted as and *made* personally holy, by an act of divine grace.

[34] See John Paul II's 1998 encyclical *Fides et Ratio*.

[35] Alister McGrath, *Iustitia Dei: A History of the Christian Doctrine of Justification*, 3rd. ed. (Cambridge: Cambridge University Press, 2005).

embarked on a study of that book and of the primary sources it treats solely for my own gratification; I had no dog in the Federal Vision fight and no position on the "New Perspective on Paul".[36] But I desired to understand classical Protestant construals of *sola fidei* more thoroughly, and McGrath was of tremendous help in that regard. His presentation of Catholic theories was also of peripheral interest, but in truth I did not linger over them long. Apart from the material on Augustine—whom we considered a proto-Protestant despite the clear Catholic shape of his theology[37]—I simply had zero interest in Catholic primary sources. To me they were useful only as foils to the Reformed position, and I figured I could learn what I needed to know of them from critical Protestant texts as opposed to the Romish horse's own mouth.

Yet even this much historical-philosophical inquiry disclosed the profoundly innovative character of classical Protestant theorizing. Theirs was not so much a recovery of ancient dogma on justification as a new way of thinking completely, a clean break from the past fifteen hundred years, and guided by modern (or late medieval) philosophical trends to boot. So as a Protestant I had to accept that justification *sola fidei* was at once (1) central to the Gospel and to the legitimacy of any pretended Christian Church—thus necessitating schism with the apostate Roman See—but (2) unheard of until Luther discovered it in the sixteenth century, in tandem with the emerging modernist philosophy he employed in its development.

This conclusion strained credulity. Again, I was unsure what to think. Still, Catholicism was not so much as on my radar—certainly

---

[36] The New Perspective was associated principally with N. T. Wright, whose groundbreaking work on Pauline theology was considered an inspiration to the Federal Vision movement and (therefore) extremely suspect. For a popular-level introduction to his views over against Reformed traditionalists, see Wright's *Justification: God's Plan and Paul's Vision*, new ed. (Downers Grove, IL: IVP Academic, 2016); for academic purposes see, e.g., his *Climax of the Covenant: Christ and the Law in Pauline Theology* (Minneapolis: Fortress Press, 1993).

[37] It is at once puzzling and understandable that Reformed Christians admire Augustine but dislike (say) Thomas Aquinas. Augustine had done battle with the Pelagians, our sworn enemies; Luther had been an Augustinian monk; Calvin cited in his *Institutes* Augustine more than any other theologian. Aquinas, on the other hand, had been singled out for abuse by Luther and Calvin both; his *Summa Theologica* served as a main reference point at the Council of Trent; he has ever since been enshrined as the Catholic Doctor par excellence. The fact that what we disliked in Aquinas can be found in Augustine, and what we liked in Augustine can be found in Aquinas, was (socially speaking) overshadowed by these historical contingencies.

not as a live possibility. This remained true throughout my undergraduate career and through the entirety of my graduate studies as well. It would change some years down the road, once more through theological-historical and philosophical study combined. But now I was just unmoored from my own theological tradition rather than drawn positively to any other. I remained well outside the gravitational orbit of Rome.

My graduate career spanned over four years, from 2001 to 2005, during which time my wife and I added two more kids to our burgeoning clan. Freshly minted Ph.D. in hand, we girded our loins and pushed off into the wider world.

The advice that mentors had given me at graduate school was to stay aloof from philosophy of religion and specialize in a "core area" instead, which would make the hard task of finding a job on the outside somewhat less daunting. So I focused on metaphysics and the philosophy of mind, while philosophical theology hovered in the wings as a kind of silent partner to my studies. But wouldn't you know—my first professional positions were offered on condition that I could demonstrate teaching competence in philosophy of religion and expertise sufficient to direct dissertations in that area as well(!). Researching, publishing, and teaching in philosophical theology—my first love—had now become professional directives.

Tasked with constructing the courses World Religions and Philosophy and Ancient and Medieval Religious Philosophy, for Texas Tech and the University of Oklahoma, respectively, I took up the jobs with glee. I did not anticipate that developing these courses would eventually (and to disquieting surprise) force scholarly confrontation with the Catholic Church. But finally it did. This occurred in two stages, beginning with World Religions and then with Ancient and Medieval Religious Philosophy.

A bit of backstory: while at graduate school I had become enamored with N. T. Wright, an Anglican theologian respected far and wide for his contributions to New Testament studies, Second Temple Judaism, Pauline studies, and historical-biblical theology generally. Wright was then and now remains among the most influential thinkers in my religious formation, and my unit on Christianity in World Religions bore his imprint. I had there to compress the main

thrust of Christianity into two or so weeks of class; it had to be something deep and meaningful but concise, and I looked to N. T. Wright
for guidance.

Perhaps more than any contemporary, Wright portrays with unique
depth and attention to detail a narrative-covenantal, global-historical
vision of traditional Christianity—one that is both simple and elegant
in outline, but wide-ranging and pregnant in application.[38] From him
I first learned how to read the Old through the New and the New
through the Old; I learned how the breathtaking story of sacred history presents a typologically cohesive narrative of divine and human
interaction, and (in particular) of "the pilgrim Church on earth's"
continuity with Israel on the one hand and her proleptic, sacramental
newness on the other.

Space prohibits many illustrations on this point, but one lesson I
gleaned was of special importance—namely, the narrative-typological
connection between Pentecost and the story of the Tower of Babel.

In Judaism, Pentecost was the occasion—fifty days after Passover—
on which Israel was constituted a nation under divine law. And fifty
days after Easter the Christian Church reiterated Pentecost in its own
constitution, when representatives of "every nation under heaven",[39]
there gathered in Jerusalem, witnessed the apostles speaking in
"tongues" that each one could understand.[40] Both of these Pente-
costs traced a line back to Babel, where the human family had first
been divided and scattered.[41] But the Mosaic Pentecost turned out to
be a penultimate corrective. Through public and heartfelt obedience,
Israel was expected to function as salt and as "a light to the nations"
at large,[42] so as to draw them together again; on Wright's reading,
Jesus saw this mission as compromised by (among other things) ethnic elitism and exclusion. Yet, according to St. Paul, where "works
of the law"[43] had failed, grace and faith would abound. The curse

---

[38] For very accessible books, see the following by Wright: *The Challenge of Jesus: Rediscover-
ing Who Jesus Was and Is* (Downers Grove, IL: InterVarsity Press, 1999), and *Simply Christian:
Why Christianity Makes Sense* (New York: HarperOne, 2010). For more academic treatments,
see (to start with) *The New Testament and the People of God* (Minneapolis: Fortress Press, 1992),
and *Jesus and the Victory of God* (Minneapolis: Fortress Press, 1997).

[39] Acts 2:5.

[40] For the coming of the Holy Spirit at Pentecost, see Acts 2:1–13.

[41] See Gen 11:1–9.

[42] Is 49:6.

[43] Rom 3:20, 28; Gal 2:16; 3:2, 5, 10.

of division, made vivid by the confusion of languages,[44] would be reversed finally by apostolic "tongues" at the second Pentecost— the fulfillment of the first and the ultimate undoing of Babel's curse. Thus, the strange phenomenon of *glossolalia* (speaking in tongues) was not a peculiar exercise in private religious devotion, but a sign of what the Church *is*, what she stands for and how she figures into the long story of God's plan for the world.

Once clued into the broader, historical-typological meaning of Pentecost, it became evident that my previous studies about "tongues" and "gifts" and the cessation of miracles beyond the life of the apostles (i.e.,"cessationism") and so on had missed the forest for the trees. Similar remarks apply to the Gospel writers and to St. Paul, whose applications of Hebrew Scripture to the "Christ Event" seemed embarrassingly fast and loose, implausible, even childish. They seemed that way to me because I did not understand their hermeneutical orientation and didn't appreciate how different it was from mine: my Baptist and Presbyterian traditions made no use of that hermeneutic or of the lectionary that embodies and transmits it, so I had been left somewhat in the dark. Wright changed this for me, and the Bible became new and exciting again.[45]

Fast-forward now to my next academic post.

Developing the course Ancient and Medieval Religious Philosophy for the University of Oklahoma required firsthand study of Christian patristic authors and medieval Christian figures—much more so than the course World Religions had done.[46] But the body of relevant literature in this case is staggering in its enormity. It therefore took several iterations of the course and a couple of further years of study before the "unwelcome conclusion" became impossible to avoid or to ignore.

The unwelcome conclusion: *most* of what I found invigorating in Wright was there already in the Fathers, and in the long (Catholic) history leading up to the Protestant Reformation. What I found

---

[44] See Gen 11:7.

[45] In this connection see also Richard B. Hays, *Echoes of Scripture in the Letters of Paul*, new ed. (New Haven, CT: Yale University Press, 1993).

[46] It also required attention to Greek, Roman, Jewish, and Muslim thinkers, but this does not enter directly into my story. As to the sources germane to "my story", nothing can substitute for reading the patristics and the medievals themselves, but J. N. D. Kelly's *Early Christian Doctrines*, rev. ed. (New York: HarperOne, 1978), is a good place to start.

new and insightful and wonderful in Wright (and in allied Protestant scholars) was to appreciable degree a reinvention of the wheel.[47]
Time and again it seemed the Catholics had already "been there and
done that"—atop every cliff I climbed there were the Catholics at
summit, relaxed and at home. I began to feel like G. K. Chesterton's
adventurer who planted triumphantly the flag in his old hometown,
not realizing the flag had been flying centuries before his arrival.

So Catholics had finally become worth serious attention. I had
of course read "safe" Catholic authors like Chesterton and Peter
Kreeft in the past, but I had now to deal justly with (1) ancient and
medieval Catholics, at least for teaching purposes, and (2) contemporary Catholic scholars for purposes of my own religious study. The
likes of John Henry Newman, Henri de Lubac, and Joseph Cardinal
Ratzinger had thus become required reading—if not for my university courses then at least for *me*. I studied them with an admixture of
trepidation and "forbidden fruit" fascination, looking over my shoulder all the while and keeping my research concealed.[48]

Throughout this period, my family continued to attend Presbyterian churches (the Orthodox Presbyterian Church and the Presbyterian Church in America). We tried to plug in: I taught Sunday
morning classes on the Westminster Shorter Catechism; we befriended
lovely people; we attempted to plant roots in familiar soil. But this
was not to last. My abstract theological fissure with the Reformed
tradition at large coincided with my wife's practical assessment of
the local churches we tried to join. She argued these churches either
did not allow reasoned discussion[49] or did not maintain a standard of
solemnity in worship, and she was right on both counts.

---

[47] Placing to one side his studies on Pauline theology, Wright does not present his biblical-
historical work as original or innovative. *I* thought it was original and innovative because I
had abstained from Catholic and pre-Reformation history. Reading history disabused me of
that notion.

[48] This must sound exaggerated. It isn't. When I finally bought a copy of the *Catechism of
the Catholic Church* from a local bookstore, I did not look the clerk in her eye; I felt as though
I were buying porn, and I hid the *Catechism* from my wife.

[49] We were both taken aback by reaction to my little course on the Shorter Catechism.
My procedure had been to explain the content of that catechism and then to examine with
parishioners how the content was biblically supported; this seemed to some of them sub-
versive or discomfiting, and I was encouraged simply to teach the content without raising
such questions.

Together we decided to migrate to Canterbury. Our stay in the Anglican Communion would prove to be one last pit stop on the long trek to Rome; it was, however, a *necessary* stay for the both of us. We did not yet see the Catholic Church as our home—indeed, our pasts had conditioned us to view her with hostility and suspicion—but we wanted to be catholic (little "c"), and the Episcopal church offered a way. So we tried to be Anglicans.[50]

This too was not to last. Within half a year I had disclosed to her my Catholic studies and my growing unease with Protestantism. My wife helped me navigate these concerns and (in particular) the massive obstacles that lie in wait for any would-be Catholic convert. Many a late-night conversation over relevant books culminated in hesitant agreement: we would attend Mass at a local Catholic parish as uncommitted observers and just see what happened. What "happened", ultimately, was our entry into full communion with the Catholic Church on the feast of Pentecost 2008 (how fitting was *that*!).

Looking back, I suppose the final straw for me concerned the issue of ecclesial authority. Anglicanism's triad of Scripture, Tradition, and reason sounded in abstract a darn sight easier to digest than Rome's triad of Scripture, Tradition, and *magisterium*—now convinced of the legitimacy of apostolic succession, we remained wary of Rome's claims to "primacy" or of its status as "first among equals". At the same time, we could not fail to see that the same fundamental problem afflicting Presbyterian denominations was playing out in the Anglican

---

[50] Some old friends later suggested that our Catholic conversion was a hasty and foolhardy reaction to the dissatisfaction we experienced with local, Reformed communions. If only (they lamented) Presbyterian/Reformed communions of X or Y or Z denomination had been available to us, we never would have "poped". I understood and anticipated the assessment, but it failed seriously to engage with the principled theological motions I have reported here; it was in fact one more example of the armchair psychoanalytic reasoning described in footnote 1. Still, it contained a *measure* of truth. Some years after our reception into the Catholic Church, my wife noted that we might never have moved from Presbyterian to Anglican, or from Anglican to Catholic, if we had found a historically, theologically, and liturgically robust non-Catholic parish. Her evaluation: it is providential that we were disenchanted with local Presbyterian offerings; it is providential that we were habituated to genuinely liturgical worship at the Episcopal parish we attended; it is providential that this otherwise lovely parish was marred by slipshod theological liberalism. Thus, she argued that while this stepwise process eventuating in full communion with the Church was indeed *somewhat* arbitrary, or chock-full of contingencies, it was for us providentially and fortunately arbitrary.

Communion as well. Indeed, the most famous (in some circles, the most infamous) Anglican-Catholic convert, John Henry Cardinal Newman, had anticipated all this with striking prophetic foresight:

> The absolute need of a spiritual supremacy is at present the strongest of the arguments in favour of the fact of its supply. Surely, either an objective revelation has not been given, or it has been provided with means for impressing its objectiveness on the world. If Christianity be a social religion, as it certainly is, and if it be based on certain ideas acknowledged as divine, or a creed, (which shall here be assumed,) and if these ideas have various aspects, and make distinct impressions on different minds, and issue in consequence in a multiplicity of developments, true, or false, or mixed, as has been shown, what power will suffice to meet and to do justice to these conflicting conditions, but a supreme authority ruling and reconciling individual judgments by a divine right and a recognized wisdom? In barbarous times the will is reached through the senses; but in an age in which reason, as it is called, is the standard of truth and right, it is abundantly evident to anyone, who mixes ever so little with the world, that, if things are left to themselves, every individual will have his own view of them, and take his own course; that two or three will agree to-day and part company to-morrow; that Scripture will be read in contrary ways, and history, according to the apologue, will have to different comers its silver shield and its golden; that philosophy, taste, prejudice, passion, party, caprice, will find no common measure, unless there be some supreme power to control the mind and to compel agreement.
>
> There can be no combination on the basis of truth without an organ of truth....
>
> The only general persuasive in matters of conduct is authority; that is, (when truth is in question,) a judgment which we feel to be superior to our own. If Christianity is both social and dogmatic, and indeed intended for all ages, it must humanly speaking have an infallible expounder. Else you will secure unity of form at the loss of unity of doctrine, or unity of doctrine at the loss of unity of form; you will have to choose between a comprehension of opinions and a resolution into parties, between latitudinarian and sectarian error. You may be tolerant or intolerant of contrarieties of thought, but contrarieties you will have. By the Church of England a hollow uniformity is preferred to an infallible chair; and by the sects of England, an interminable division. Germany and Geneva began with persecution, and have ended

in skepticism. The doctrine of infallibility is a less violent hypothesis than this sacrifice either of faith or of charity. It secures the object, while it gives definiteness and force to the matter, of the Revelation.[51]

This critical assessment, perhaps powerful enough on its own, was for me the jab followed by the uppercut.

Just as Pentecost and Babel were situated together, the Petrine passages within the Synoptic and Johannine Gospels each in their ways said the same thing. Jesus—the son of Abraham and son of David, the New Moses and New Adam—was there to fulfill the covenant promises and to restore the kingdom of God "on earth as it is in heaven". For example, in the Gospel of Matthew we have these words of Jesus: "You are Peter, and on this rock I will build my Church, and the gates of Hades shall not prevail against it. I will give you the keys of the kingdom of heaven, and whatever you bind on earth shall be bound in heaven, and whatever you loose on earth shall be loosed in heaven."[52] In the book of the prophet Isaiah, we have these words, which provide typological context: "In that day I will call my servant Eliakim the son of Hilkiah, and I will clothe him with your robe, and will bind your belt on him, and will commit your authority to his hand; and he shall be a father to the inhabitants of Jerusalem and to the house of Judah. And I will place on his shoulder the key of the house of David; he shall open, and none shall shut; and he shall shut, and none shall open. And I will fasten him like a peg in a sure place, and he will become a throne of honor to his father's house."[53]

Jesus had therefore been given the throne of David and initiated the kingdom of heaven on earth. In giving the "keys" of this kingdom to St. Peter, he declared Peter prime minister, "a father to the inhabitants of Jerusalem and to the house of Judah". The name change to "Peter" (*Petros*, "Rock") signified this change in his status before God and man, and Jesus entrusted his prime minister with the symbols of administrative and disciplinary authority over David's house (i.e., the household of God)—the keys of the kingdom and the power to bind and loose with finality.

---

[51] John Henry Cardinal Newman, *An Essay on the Development of Christian Doctrine*, 6th ed. (Notre Dame, IN: Notre Dame Press, 1989), 89–91.

[52] Mt 16:18–19.

[53] Is 22:20–23. For context, see, for example, 2 Sam 7 and Ps 89.

Do not mistake this as an overeasy "proof text" for Petrine primacy and all the Catholic Church has made of it through the years. It is intended here merely to report my initial, surprised discovery that "papism" was *perhaps* not solely a deliverance of an extrabiblical "tradition", designed to clothe what would otherwise have been a naked grab for earthly power. Indeed, volumes of further biblical-historical research would be needed before it came close to a reasonably compelling case, and (in particular) before my own hardwired suspicion of Roman claims to jurisdictional primacy began to weaken. But it was another piece of the Christian puzzle that had now begun taking on a definite Catholic cast. And the recognition that Scripture, Tradition, and magisterium provides a framework that would—if only true—(1) resolve the dilemma of authority and (2) preserve doctrinal truth and ecclesial unity together, began impressing itself upon me with increasing force.[54]

Within another half year, it would prove to be the last piece of the puzzle. In effect I had, without meaning to and certainly without ever *wanting* to, argued my way into the Catholic Church. All that remained was just to admit it, to get over the emotional hang-ups and fears holding me back, and then to pull the trigger.

The largest hang-up of course concerned the putative human usurpation of an authority that belongs to God alone. Pope Emeritus Benedict XVI helped in great degree to see me through and beyond that remaining obstacle, and it seems only fitting the final word on the nature of authority and Petrine primacy should go to him:

> [At] the inmost core of the new commission, which robs the forces of destruction their power, is the grace of forgiveness. It constitutes the Church. The Church is founded upon forgiveness. Peter himself is a personal embodiment of this truth, for he is permitted to be the bearer of the keys after having stumbled, confessed and received the grace of pardon.... She is held together by forgiveness, and Peter is the perpetual living reminder of this reality: she is not a communion of the perfect but a communion of sinners who need and seek

---

[54] The sauce-for-the-gander irony was not lost on me—ultimately, the argument that convinced me of Catholicism was presuppositional in shape: presupposing the Catholic framework resolved in outline the main problems generated by the Protestant frameworks in which I had been formed.

forgiveness. Behind the talk of authority, God's power appears as mercy and thus as the foundation stone of the Church....

The Church can come into being only where man finds his way to the truth about himself, and the truth is that he needs grace. Wherever pride closes him to this insight, man cannot find the way to Jesus. The keys to the Kingdom of Heaven are the words of forgiveness, which man cannot speak of himself but are granted by God's power alone....

But the New Testament shows us more than the formal aspect of a structure; it also reveals to us the inward nature of this structure. It does not merely furnish proof texts, it is a permanent criterion and task. It depicts the tension between *skandalon* and rock; in the very disproportion between man's capacity and God's sovereign disposition, it reveals God to be the one who truly acts and is present. If in the course of history the attribution of such authority to men could repeatedly engender the not entirely unfounded suspicion of human arrogation of power, not only the promise of the New Testament but also the trajectory of that history itself prove the opposite. The men in question are so glaringly, so blatantly unequal to this function that the very empowerment of man to be the rock makes evident how little it is they who sustain the Church but God alone who does so, who does so more in spite of men than through them. The mystery of the Cross is perhaps nowhere so palpably present as in the primacy as a reality of Church history. That its center is forgiveness is both its intrinsic condition and the sign of the distinctive character of God's power. Every single biblical logion about the primacy thus remains from generation to generation a signpost and norm, to which we must ceaselessly resubmit ourselves. When the Church adheres to these words in faith, she is not being triumphalistic but humbly recognizing in wonder and thanksgiving the victory of God over and through human weakness. Whoever deprives these words of their force for fear of triumphalism or of human usurpation of authority does not proclaim that God is greater but diminishes him, since God demonstrates the power of his love, and thus remains faithful to the law of the history of salvation, precisely in the paradox of human impotence. For with the same realism with which we declare today the sins of the popes and their disproportion to the magnitude of their commission, we must also acknowledge that Peter has repeatedly stood as the rock against ideologies, against the dissolution of the word into the plausibilities of a given time, against subjection to the powers of this world.

When we see this in the facts of history, we are not celebrating men but praising the Lord, who does not abandon the Church and who desired to manifest that he is the rock through Peter, the little stumbling stone: "flesh and blood" do not save, but the Lord saves through those who are of flesh and blood. To deny this truth is not a plus of faith, not a plus of humility, but is to shrink from the humility that recognizes God as he is. Therefore the Petrine promise and its historical embodiment in Rome remain at the deepest level an ever-renewed motive for joy: the powers of hell will not prevail against it.[55]

Since entering into full communion with the Catholic Church on Pentecost 2008, our family has grown by three more children, all of whom have been baptized into the Church. Subsequent to our reception, we (my wife and I) experienced the usual honeymoon period, and have since then settled as a family into the ebbs and flows, into the rhythm, of liturgical life. Our decision to trust, to extend a line of credit to the Church, was indeed based on reason—on the "motives of credibility" that must attend any *reasoned* faith—but it was based upon faith and trust all the same. And that's (I surmise) as must be.

The Catholic Church is more akin to a Person than it is to an institution, membership in which is no mere matter of assent to a body of systematic or dogmatic propositions. To be sure, there is dogma, and Church dogma is indeed set forth with authority—it is to be believed. Yet the difference between believing *that* so-and-so is true and believing *in* so-and-so is crucial to the fecundity and reality of Catholic living. Believing *in* "one, holy, catholic, and apostolic Church" takes an act of faith, reasoned though it may be. There is a cost to such believing-in, and that's to be expected: the same is true of belief *in* Christ, as such. But withal, we have learned since our reception that lived experience with and within the Catholic Church is worlds apart from what we thought we knew about the Church in our Protestant days. And I suppose, at this point, it would take a team of wild horses to pull us out.

* * * * *

It is impossible to be just to the Catholic Church. The moment men cease to pull against it they feel a tug towards it. The moment they

---

[55] Joseph Cardinal Ratzinger, *Called to Communion: Understanding the Church Today*, 2nd ed. (San Francisco: Ignatius Press, 1991), 64–65, 72–74.

cease to shout it down they begin to listen to it with pleasure. The moment they try to be fair to it they begin to be fond of it. But when that affection has passed a certain point it begins to take on the tragic and menacing grandeur of a great love affair. The man has exactly the same sense of having committed or compromised himself; of having been in a sense entrapped, even if he is glad to be entrapped. But for a considerable time he is not so much glad as simply terrified. It may be that this real psychological experience has been misunderstood by stupider people and is responsible for all that remains of the legend that Rome is a mere trap. But that legend misses the whole point of the psychology. It is not the Pope who has set the trap or the priests who have baited it. The whole point of the position is that the trap is simply the truth. The whole point is that the man himself has made his way towards the trap of truth, and not the trap that has run after the man. All steps except the last step he has taken eagerly on his own account, out of interest in the truth; and even the last step, or the last stage, only alarms him because it is so very true.[56]

[56] G. K. Chesterton, *The Catholic Church and Conversion*, in *The Collected Works of G. K. Chesterton*, vol. 3 (San Francisco: Ignatius Press, 1990), 92–93.

5

Why?

Peter Kreeft

I have always asked why. As a little kid, I got my jollies asking my
parents that magical question until they gave up. "Why do I have
to learn to tie my shoe laces?" "To keep your shoe on your foot."
"Why do I have to keep my shoe on my foot?" "Because you'll look
silly if you don't." "Why can't I look silly if I want to?" No answer.
But instead of giving up, I kept making myself a pest until I got either
an answer or a brush-off.

I was a member of the RCA, the Reformed Church in America, originally the Dutch Reformed Church. Everyone in my family
had always been Dutch and Reformed, it seemed, for about thirty
thousand years. I could have gone to our denominational college,
Hope College, in Holland, Michigan. But I went to Calvin College in Grand Rapids instead, in 1955, because most of my friends
went there. Calvin was the college of the sister denomination, the
Christian Reformed Church, a younger and breakoff denomination.
(Protestants are continually doing that: protesting and breaking off.
The logical result of this process is that there will eventually be as
many Protestant denominations as there are Protestants. There are
presently tens of thousands of unique sects of Christianity, protesting
and branching off.)

I started out as a preseminary student at Calvin because of a single
sentence that I read somewhere captioning a painting of Jesus on the
Cross. The caption said: "This is what I did for thee; what will you
do for Me?" I did not feel attracted to becoming a preacher, but I

did feel that question as addressed to me personally from my Lord, and I had to respond. That was clear. But how? That was not clear. I did not think I would be a good pastor, for I was always a "loner", not a "people person", for at least four reasons: I was an only child, I was a "thinker", I was a jokester and troublemaker, and I was just plain selfish. But going to seminary and being ordained as a pastor in my church was the only concrete way I could imagine answering that divine "call", except perhaps becoming a missionary. But that probably would mean going to Africa or India, two of the hottest and poorest and therefore least attractive places on earth for me. (Earlier, I had fantasized about becoming an Arctic or Antarctic explorer; my heroes were Byrd, Peary, Scott, and Shackleton. I wanted to get to the top of everything. I think my son inherited this: he climbed trees and roofs, so he became a pilot. But not a Pontius pilot.)

Due to excellent English teachers in both high school and college, I came to love words, their beauty and power. This love made me switch to majoring in English in college, once I asked myself why I was studying for the seminary when I knew I was not personally fit for it. Then, as an English major I found myself asking why again of everything I read, and this made me fall in love with philosophy. So I became a philosophy major, mainly because of the example of William Harry Jellema, the best teacher I ever had. Like Socrates, he never wrote a book. But he made dozens of terrific philosophers out of his students—for example, Nicholas Wolterstorff and Alvin Plantinga.

I never seriously doubted the truth of my Christian faith, but from an early age I loved to question and explore the why of it. I never flirted with atheism or even heresy (why swap a stallion for a donkey?), but I loved to question everything I believed—not as a lawyer would question a hostile witness but as a museumgoer would question a painting. I remember having an ongoing friendly argument with my father for many years about evolution. (My father was a wise and holy man with tons of patience and common sense, and a deacon and then an elder in our local congregation.) I have never understood why Christians were threatened by biological evolution. I also argued about the likelihood of salvation for good pagans, and about good swear words, and about alcohol (my father was a teetotaler). But until college, I never questioned the idea that Catholics were thinly baptized pagans: primitive, sentimental, uneducated, un-American, superstitious, idolatrous, irrational, and dirty. How could a thrifty American Republican Protestant admire a Catholic saint like Francis of Assisi, a poor Italian beggar? If he was a good guy, he must have been the white sheep of the Catholic family. Most of his friends must have been in the Mafia.

Though I never doubted that Christianity was true, I was convinced that the faith "we" had (that is, we Dutch Reformed Protestant Evangelicals) was not the whole truth. Reality had to be more—much more, strikingly, staggeringly more—than "what we had". You could never put God in a box.

This was one of my earliest and most certain religious convictions. I remember a conversation with my father when I was about twelve, which was similar to the following:

"Dad, why are we in the Reformed Church?"

"Because it's true. Because our church teaches the truth." (A good answer. The only honest reason for believing anything is that it's true.)

"So all the other churches get something in their theology wrong?"

"Something, yes. Sometimes big things and sometimes just little things."

"How many other churches are there?"

"I don't know exactly—a couple hundred, maybe a couple thousand."

"And how many Christians are there in our church?"

"About half a million."

"And how many Christians are there in the world?"

"About a billion."

"So why did God let us get it all right and not them? Doesn't he care about them?"

I don't remember his answer, but I remember it wasn't memorable or satisfying. The why remained.

I don't want to give the wrong impression: I did not question *everything*. Far from it. I was not a rebel, but an explorer. To explore, you need a secure home base. To get to a new conclusion you have to have an old premise. The things I believed without questioning them didn't all have reasons attached. Premises seldom do. One's premises are usually deeply dependent on one's early childhood experiences, and are much more unconscious and habitual than we like to admit, and at least in our early years they are deeply tied to one's physical, visual environment—home, family, friends, school, neighborhood—and then, viewed through those lenses, one's larger national, racial, and cultural neighborhood. For me, this cultural neighborhood began in Prospect Park, New Jersey. (Both my house and my church were on its border.) It was a one-mile-square enclave of middle-class Dutch Calvinists. One hundred percent pure. To me Calvinism was not so much a theology as a people—a pious, honest, trustworthy, thrifty, hardworking people who gave me the security and peace and identity from which, years later, I dared to peer out of my rabbit hole to explore the mysterious world outside, the world of otherness. If the rabbit in his hole is insecure, he will not venture far; but if he is secure about his home, he will tend to be adventurous about the world outside it, neither an angry rebel nor a fearful conformist. I think this is a crucial principle of early childhood education in general and therefore also in religion.

In his autobiography *Surprised by Joy*, C.S. Lewis identified the guiding thread of his life as the search for a joy that transcended both definition and attainment in this life. This was a kind of "organ point" or "pedal point", a bass underlying all the treble themes of his life's music, like the drone in bagpipes. Mine was similar: the conviction that "there are more things in heaven and earth than are dreamed of in your philosophy", no matter what that philosophy is. Not fewer things (that's cynicism or reductionism) and not the same number of things (that's arrogant rationalism) but more things (that's idealism, or "romanticism"—call it naiveté if you wish). I was convinced that my favorite question why had to have more answers, not fewer, than we can take in; that even in religion—most especially in religion—no matter what truths, goods, and beauties we know, reality is always more, much more, inconceivably more, than what we know, even if what we know is divine revelation and eternal truth. And this applies to our knowledge of Christ too, for in Scripture we are told that, like us, he too has a new name in heaven.[1] That why is what prompted this rabbit, who was somewhat cowardly and comfortable and conservative by nature, out of his hole to explore

---

[1] See Rev 2:17; 3:12.

the big, bad Catholic thing that I was warned against as "the whore of Babylon".

* * * * *

When I look back now at my "issues" or objections to Catholicism, I see that they were all fears; God responded to my ten biggest fears, my issues, my whys in three ways: with arguments, with experiences, and with helpers, authors, educators. I will summarize the ten most important of each.

The fears were

1. of the Catholic Church as a very big artifact (I didn't realize that the universe itself is a very big artifact);

2. of "authority" and hierarchy (I didn't realize that the universe itself is a hierarchy);

3. of popes, and being poped around by an old Italian celibate who claimed to be the vicar of Christ (I didn't realize that popes were not dictators but servants, the servants of the servants of God);

4. of the "materialism" of sacramentalism (I didn't realize that I was really a Gnostic heretic, and I forgot that the universe itself, God's universe, was material, and so was I);

5. of idolatry (I didn't realize that most idols today are spiritual, not material);

6. of the Catholic idolizing of Church and Tradition at the expense of Scripture (I didn't realize that Scripture itself was written and canonized by the Church and part of her Sacred Tradition);

7. of the gloomy idea of purgatory (I didn't realize that its essence is not suffering but joy: the joy of cleansing from all the vestiges of sin);

8. of what I thought was Catholic Pelagianism and "works righteousness" instead of "salvation by faith alone" (I didn't realize that good works were the works of *love*, which is the other half of faith);

9. of the associated idea of "merit" (I didn't realize that you can't avoid God's justice any more than you can avoid his mercy); and

10. of "Mariolatry" (which I confused with Mariology because I thought it was an alternative to Christocentrism; I didn't realize that Mary was the very essence of Christocentrism).

All Catholic readers will recognize these ten ideas as misunderstandings and know the refutation of them. But it may be of interest to relate how God dealt with my questions and difficulties patiently and reasonably and gently.

1. The first one was more emotional than rational: the fear of the Church's bigness, and strangeness, and foreignness, and Italianness (and perhaps also, subconsciously, a fear of her "she-ness", her mysterious, womanly nature). After all, this was the Church of the Mafia, and the Spanish Inquisition, and of the filthy rich, dissolute, decadent Borgia popes with their mistresses, illegitimate children, and orgies. The Catholic Church was Italian; we were American.

Getting to know and love Maria, my future wife, and her father, who was an Italian immigrant, helped cure my unconscious racism more than any arguments. But God sent me an argument too. My Protestant friends gave me a number of books about how wrong the Church was, and I thought the books were all either dull or dead wrong themselves or both (the very worst and most influential of them was a long tissue of lies by a guy named Lorraine Boettner[2]), but one book about how wicked the Church was I thought was very funny. It was the *Decameron*, a collection of ten cynical but comical short stories by Boccaccio, a Renaissance muckraker and comedian. The story that hooked me took place during the Borgia papacy. Some of those Renaissance popes were probably total hypocrites and not even believers. It was as if the Mafia had controlled the papacy, often by bribery and sometimes even by assassinations, poisonings (Lucretia Borgia was one of the most famous poisoners in history) and stabbings (in the Pazzi conspiracy, two cardinals stabbed each other to death while being hung out the window by their parishioners).

Boccaccio's story was about the pious bishop of Paris and his Jewish businessman friend Abraham. The two of them argue theology in a friendly way, and the bishop thinks Abraham is on the verge of

[2] Loraine Boettner, *Roman Catholicism* (Philadelphia: Presbyterian and Reformed Publishing, 1962).

conversion and baptism. One day Abraham tells the bishop he has to make a business trip to Rome to deal with the Vatican bankers and live with the papal family. The bishop says, "I suspect you're contemplating converting and being baptized; why don't you do that here and now? The air isn't clear down there in Rome." "I can't do that," says Abraham. "A successful businessman first does his work, then his play; first business, then pleasure. We'll see about baptism when I come back." And he goes off to Rome for a few months.

The bishop thinks he's lost him forever, since he'll see the corruption in Rome and run the other way. But when he returns to Paris months later, he says he's ready to be baptized. "What? Didn't you go to Rome?" "I did." "And you lived with the Vatican bankers and the papal family?" "Yes." "So you saw what it's like down there?" "Yes." "And now you want to be baptized? Why?" "Well, I'm not a theologian, I'm a businessman. And here's one thing I know for sure about business: no earthly business that corrupt could possibly last for 14 weeks. Yours has lasted for 14 centuries. It's a miracle. I'm convinced."

I thought that was a serious argument. Legend has it that when Napoleon kidnapped the pope he said to him, "We will destroy your Church." The pope laughed. "If we haven't been able to do that for eighteen centuries, you won't either!" Some popes were positively wicked, but even wicked popes never changed the doctrine. When they had mistresses, and bastard children, and personal fortunes, and hit men, they didn't decree that it was okay for the pope to have them, even when the good cardinals got on their backs for their hypocrisy. They didn't practice what they preached, and they probably didn't even believe it; yet, they kept preaching the truth. Not a single heresy, not a single compromise of doctrine, no matter how insincere and wicked the teachers were. That was indeed a miracle. Has any other institution ever manifested that miracle for two thousand years? Not one. Bocaccio's businessman was right. And I was wrong.

2. I was taught to fear the tyranny of Catholic "authority" and the "hierarchy", and I did for a while. In fact, I won an essay contest in high school for an attack on "Catholic totaliatarianism" based on my misunderstanding of Dostoyevsky's great parable of the Grand Inquisitor. But I soon came to see the beauty of hierarchy, of authority, and of obedience by reading C. S. Lewis, G. K. Chesterton, and

J.R.R. Tolkien. That premodern world was largely a vanished world, but it was a beautiful one. It was full of royal purple; ours was egalitarian gray. It was my heart that educated my head on this one. My imagination was baptized before my intellect was. Not all authority was bad; some was beautiful. The question I had to answer was whether the Church's authority was false and wicked and ugly, or true and good and beautiful. That depended on the facts of history: Did Christ author and authorize the Church that I see in history and around me as the Catholic Church, or not? That was the key question, and it would be addressed later. (See below, point seven in the next list.)

3. Closely connected with the above objection was my fear of the pope. But my fear of "being poped" was countered not only by Church history (even wicked popes never erred in dogma, never changed the dogma) but also by Scripture. Christ did bestow on Peter the name of "Rock", and the keys to the kingdom, and the promise that the church he founded on that rock would conquer hell itself.[3]

4. A fourth big fear was of the Catholic view of the sacraments, especially the Eucharist. The Catholic position seemed very close to magic and materialism. According to Catholic theology, even if a priest was a wicked hypocrite, heretic, and apostate, the sacraments he celebrated "worked", *ex opera operato*, by their own holiness and spiritual power, given by God, not by the holiness and spiritual power of the priest or of the recipients. It sounded mechanical and automatic. It was not "spiritual". How could it be fair that spiritual things depended on physical things—that if on a given day your car broke down and you could not get to Mass, you did not get all the spiritual benefits of receiving Christ's Body and Blood, even if your intentions and desire were greater than that of someone else whose car did not break down and who did get to Mass?

I came to realize (gradually) that I was a heretic—that "I'm not religious but I'm spiritual" was Gnosticism, the oldest and most harmful heresy in Church history. God never told us to be "spiritual"; he told us to be holy. Satan is spiritual—purely spiritual. Christ is incarnate. Socrates and Confucius and Buddha tried to save the world by giving us their minds, but Jesus saved the world by giving us his body.

[3] Mt 16:18–19.

In the Gospel of Matthew, if the woman with the hemorrhage had touched the hem of anyone else's garment, she would not have been healed;[4] her faith and piety alone did not heal her. For *everything* in the world is Christ's mind, as every word in Shakespeare's plays is Shakespeare's mind; but not everything in the world is his Body. You have to go to one place and not another (a Catholic church) and do one thing and not another with your body (open your mouth) in order to get it. In thinking that religion was a matter of "faith alone", I was thinking that religion was a matter of "spirit alone". I was a heretic, a Gnostic, a spiritualist. For when I thought that religion should be "spiritual", I really meant that it should be subjective, that sincerity should be enough, without objective truth. But no one believes that sincerity and subjective piety and good intentions are enough for their surgeon or financial advisor or travel agent—that is, when they are dealing with objective reality. Why then do we expect that in religion? Because we don't see religion as dealing with objective reality. That's a very dangerous heresy. Though I would have vigorously denied it, I was really substituting subjective sincerity for objective truth, spirituality for reality.

5. A fifth why was the accusation of idolatry—that is, giving worship and reverence to creatures that belongs only to the Creator. Catholics had all sorts of idols: Mary, the saints, the Church, Tradition, the sacraments, the Eucharist, statues, formal prayers, good works, free will, artistic beauty, but especially in the liturgy, human efforts and virtues and good works and reason, history, the authority of the pope—just about every difference between Protestants and Catholics took this form.

But there was one key theological doctrine that explained all of them and refuted the charge that they were all examples of "idolatry". That was the doctrine that God is love, and therefore since he loves all that he has made, he does not bypass them or demean them or begrudge them or rival them but perfects them. "Grace perfects nature." It is simply not true that the higher your view of the natural, the lower your view of the supernatural. In fact, it is the opposite. You do not praise God by demeaning man or reason or matter; you insult him. Suppose your mother has knitted you a beautiful sweater,

[4] Mt 9:20–22.

and someone sees you wearing it and praises it, and you try to be humble, so you say, "Oh, it's not really all that beautiful." You are not being humble; you are insulting your mother.

God's new creation will be so much more than we can think, that he can say that "no eye has seen, nor ear heard, nor the heart of man conceived, what God has prepared for those who love him".[5] If this applies to God's new creation, it applies to the old one too, for the character and generosity of God does not change. What God makes and does for us is always more, not less, than we can take in.

6. A sixth issue was Scripture. This seemed to be an exception to the principle above, for Protestants seemed to have a higher view of Scripture than Catholics did. Scripture was the one and only thing that Catholics did not overdo and idolize. In fact they underdid it. This was not simply because there were Catholic theologians who misused the "historical-critical method" and became historical relativists (for Modernism had penetrated Protestantism even more than Catholicism; and the Catholic Church at least had an official magisterium that blocked it), but also because Protestants exalted the Bible more (I thought) because for them it was the whole of divine revelation, *sola scriptura*, not just part of it.

But then I confronted the historical fact that it was the Church (the apostles) that wrote the Bible (the New Testament), and I knew that there could not possibly be more in any effect than in its cause, so if the Church did not have infallibility, as Protestants maintained, then the Bible didn't either! So it was Protestantism, not Catholicism, that led to the undermining of the infallibility of the Bible.

Furthermore, I noticed that the Bible itself calls not itself but the Church "the pillar and bulwark of the truth".[6]

And it is a historical fact that Christ did not write anything, but only spoke and entrusted the Gospel to his apostles, so the first generation of Christians had only the Church, not the New Testament. Did infallibility sleep for a generation?

And how could we be sure that the four Gospels we had were true and the many others (e.g., the Gospel of Thomas, or of Judas) were not? Why were these twenty-seven books infallible divine revelation

[5] I Cor 2:9.
[6] I Tim 3:15.

and no others? There is only one answer to that question: the Church, who canonized (defined) the twenty-seven books of the New Testament. Fallibly or infallibly? If fallibly, we undermine the Bible; if infallibly, she must be infallible. We need an infallible Church to define an infallible Bible infallibly.

Protestants loved to contrast Scripture with tradition and point to Christ's denigration of "the tradition of the elders".[7] But this tradition (1) referred to several traditions, not only one—that is, Sacred Tradition; (2) was clearly labeled as tradition *of the elders*; and (3) was distinguished from the tradition that St. Paul appeals to as authoritative.[8] In the New Testament, the Gospel (Good News) itself is to be treated as tradition—that is, literally, "that which is handed down". Scripture is a part (the most important part) of Sacred Tradition. Here my logical mind had to confess a big "oops" (short Act of Contrition).

7. A seventh question was purgatory. As a Protestant I had thought that (1) it contradicted Scripture's assertion that Christ's death was sufficient to atone for all of our sins ("It is finished"[9]) and implied that we had to finish the job Jesus hadn't finished; that (2) it was "legalistic" (we had to "do time" in God's jail, where the punishments fit the crimes); and (3) that it made a happy, joyful, hopeful death impossible because what the average person had to look forward to for a long time was not heaven but something more like a temporary hell.

My questions were answered (1) by the distinction between justification (which Jesus did finish all by himself) and sanctification (which we had to finish in cooperation with him and his Holy Spirit); (2) by the discovery that the "time" in purgatory was not literal but analogical; and (3) that those in purgatory *want* and even enjoy their spiritual cleansing even though it hurts. I loved the image from C. S. Lewis (who I think would have become a Catholic in a second if God had not prevented him in order to get thousands of Protestants to read him), who said that "our souls *demand* Purgatory",[10] for when we show up at the heavenly mansion full of bugs and dirt, wouldn't

---

[7] Mt 15:2; Mk 7:3; cf. Col 2:8.

[8] 2 Thess 3:6.

[9] Jn 19:30.

[10] C. S. Lewis, *Letters to Malcolm: Chiefly on Prayer* (Orlando, FL: Harcourt, 1992), 108–9 (emphasis in original).

we want to take a hot shower before sitting down to dinner, even though it hurt?

My father and I were arguing about purgatory once, and when we finally shut up for a second, my simple-minded mother intervened:

"John, I think Peter believes the same things we do, really."

"Lucy, how can you say that? We're not Catholics; we don't believe in purgatory. It's not in the Bible."

"But we believe in sin, don't we?"

"Of course."

"And we're sinners right up to the end, aren't we? Doesn't the Bible say: 'If we say we have no sin, we deceive ourselves, and the truth is not in us'[11]?"

"Yes, of course."

"And the difference between sin and holiness is like the difference between darkness and light, right? 'God is light and in him is no darkness at all,'[12] right?"

"Yes."

"So there's a really big difference between sin and holiness, right?"

"Of course."

"And nothing sinful can enter heaven, right? We're not sinners any more in heaven, right?"

"Right."

"Well, then *something* has to happen to us between the time we die as sinners and the time we go to heaven as holy saints. And if Catholics want to call that 'purgatory' and we don't, aren't we fighting over a word?"

"Oh. Well, maybe so; I'll have to think about that more. Let's talk about something else."

I am convinced that Protestants disbelieve in purgatory only for one of three very serious reasons, that are all reasons of size, or seriousness: they underestimate either the size of sin, or the size of holiness, or the size of the difference between them.

8. My fear of Catholic "works righteousness" and Pelagianism was quickly put to rest by finding out what Catholics really taught, by reading Augustine, Aquinas, and the Council of Trent, and, later,

---

[11] I Jn 1:8.
[12] I Jn 1:5.

the 1999 Joint Declaration on the Doctrine of Justification by the Catholic Church and the Lutheran World Federation. Neither "side" said we are saved by works alone, and when Luther said we are saved by faith, not the works of the law, he was only echoing St. Paul in his Letter to the Romans.[13] But "faith alone"? James explicitly denied that.[14] Neither Catholics nor Lutherans believed that faith alone in the sense of mere belief, or intellectual faith, could save us, echoing James;[15] but Catholics, like James and like Paul himself in 1 Corinthians 13, spoke of good works, that is, the works of love, as being included in "salvation" because they meant by "salvation" sanctification as well as justification. Both "sides" believe that both justification and sanctification originate in divine grace, but Catholics add that it is God's grace that turns our free will on, not off.

So when the two sides excommunicated each other in the sixteenth century over the controversy of "justification by faith", they were really two ships that thought they were colliding with each other when in fact they were colliding only with each other's shadows.

9. My fear of Catholic teaching about "merit" was put to rest simply by remembering that "merit" is simply part of the meaning of justice, and justice is as eternal as love; and that if God cannot deny himself, he cannot deny either his justice or his mercy. Since all our merits come from his grace, as both churches insist, it is no excuse for pride; but they do have to come from somewhere. The alternative was God deceiving himself, like a "feel-good" pop psychologist who says "there's nothing to forgive" when there is.

10. A tenth fear was a fear of Catholic devotion to Mary. This is typical for all Evangelical Protestants. As a Protestant, I simply could not understand why Catholics, who seemed so intelligent in other ways, gave such love and attention to Mary. Nearly every Evangelical I know who has crossed the Tiber has (1) begun as a critic of Mariology (theology of Mary), identifying it with Mariolatry (idolatry of Mary), and simply could not understand how Catholics could possibly be so stupid, so pagan; (2) then, while contemplating

---

[13] Rom 3:20: "For no human being will be justified in his sight by works of the law, since through the law comes knowledge of sin."

[14] Jas 2:17: "So faith by itself, if it has no works, is dead."

[15] Jas 2:18.

conversion, has had greater difficulties with this than with any other obstacle, so that it was one of the very last reasons for hesitation; (3) then, as a Catholic, has overtime eventually developed a deep love and devotion to Mary and a gratitude to God and to the Church for the riches of Marian devotion; and (4) now looks back on his own former Protestant *fear* of Mary in exactly the same way as he formerly saw Catholic *devotion* to Mary: as something incomprehensibly stupid.

I have found that this change usually happens only after praying the Rosary daily for years. You learn it only by doing it. You see it after you do it, rather than doing it only after you see it.

I see only two diagnoses of the cause of this strange Protestant fear of Mary and only two prescriptions to overcome it. One is obvious: it is the realization (which always comes gradually, by devotional practice and experience rather than mere thought or theory) that Mary is the exact opposite of what Protestants fear: not a kind of moon goddess eclipsing the sun (the Son) but a beam of light from that very sun (the Son), who gave her to us from the Cross with almost his last words ("Behold, your mother!"[16]). She always points us back beyond herself to him: her last words in Scripture are, "Do whatever he tells you."[17]

The other cause is very politically incorrect to say today: it is the "sexist" point that the typical Protestant, whose religion is more rational, more bookish, more propositional, and distrustful of mysticism and even of the word "mystery", is really spiritual male chauvinism. We all know (whenever we stop listening to the "experts") that Mars and Venus, Adam and Eve, are inherently different and speak "in a different voice", as real feminists like Carol Gilligan say; that men are really superior to women at being men and that women are really superior to men at being women; that men are better than women at knowing conscious, analytical, verbal truths, and women are better than men at knowing unconscious, intuitive, mystical truths. Men are clear; women are profound. A woman's wisdom, like her sex organs, is a garden hidden behind a waterfall, something inside, in the dark; a man's is "out there" in the light and air and public. A

---

[16] Jn 19:27.
[17] Jn 2:5.

hundred years ago we were too sexually repressed to dare to say that; today—well, today we are also too sexually repressed to dare to say it. Unisexism is the new Victorianism.

Many Protestants claim that their objection to the Catholic dogmas about Mary is theological, not psychological, as I have claimed. They argue that the dogma of her Immaculate Conception contradicts Scripture's clear claim that all sons of Adam and daughters of Eve need salvation from sin. But the Church's answer seemed clear to me: Mary too needed salvation by divine grace, but she got it before she sinned rather than after. We all need to be saved from the mortal disease of sin by Christ, who is God's medicine, but Mary got preventative medicine where we got healing medicine. God could certainly do that, and it fits his surprising and unpredictable graciousness and generosity, as it fits him to assume Mary to heaven body and soul, as he did to Enoch[18] and Elijah.[19]

So I had no problems with the dogma of Mary's Assumption, especially because it was so just and fitting that the one mere mortal who had no sin ("our tainted nature's solitary boast"[20]) should not suffer death, the just penalty for sin. But my faith was suddenly shaken very seriously one day, years *after* becoming a Catholic, when I saw some early Eastern Orthodox icons of Mary *in her coffin*. This looked like empirical evidence that the early Church had not believed the ex cathedra Catholic dogma that Mary did not die but was assumed into heaven. I had seen only Western pictures of the Assumption, and I assumed that she had simply "gone up" to heaven as Christ did at the Ascension. I did not know that the more usual version of her Assumption was that she experienced first a "dormition", an apparent death. Once I learned this, my doubts were dispelled. And now I see God allowing this serious doubt as a very good thing, since it taught me how historical, how literal, how realistic, how "materialistic", how refutable the Catholic faith was. It is like science, about real-world data and therefore in principle refutable by real-world data. If science proves that a set of bones in Jerusalem are Jesus' bones, the whole of the Christian faith will

[18] Gen 5:24; Sir 44:16; 49:14; Heb 11:5.
[19] 2 Kings 2:11.
[20] William Wordsworth, "The Virgin", line 4. Published in *Ecclesiastical Sketches*, 1822.

have been disproved as a lie. Christianity is not a philosophy; it is an event.

God dealt kindly and gradually with me, not breaking the bruised reed or quenching the smoking flax but tempering the wind to the shorn lamb. Here are ten crucial experiences he put in my path. All were either my whys or God's answers to them, and all were surprises.

1. The first positive Catholic thought I ever had came when I was about ten or twelve years old, I think. My parents and I often visited New York City (I was an ardent Giants fan, never a Yankees fan), and one day we went into St. Patrick's Cathedral. I had never been in a cathedral. Most Protestant churches used to look like Puritan town meeting halls or large law courts; now most of them look like stages for rock concerts. The shafts of its beauty pierced my heart. This was a different *kind* of beauty, a different genus. Heaven had to look like this. I turned to my father:

"Dad, this is a Catholic church, isn't it?"

"Yes."

"The Catholics are wrong, aren't they?"

"Oh, yes, very wrong."

"Then why are their churches so beautiful?"

It was the first time I ever saw my father simply stumped. I didn't think anything like, "Perhaps someday I shall become a Catholic," but I filed away the why for future reference.

2. The second surprise occurred years later. In college, while already exploring things Catholic that I found intriguing, but from what I thought was a safe Protestant distance, I listened to the sacred music of the Italian Renaissance composer Giovanni Palestrina for the first time. I was alone and without defenses. I had never heard anything like this. Clearly, this could only have come from angels, not mortals. (I meant that literally.) It was the music of heaven. I remember feeling afraid that since I had become this music, I might never be able to get back into my body again. Why don't we have music like that? I loved the old Protestant hymns and still do; they are good water for thirsty souls, but this—this was great wine.

3. A third Catholic surprise was reading my first Catholic saint. It was St. John of the Cross, of all people, and the place I discovered him, of all places, was my favorite place on earth, the beaches of the Jersey shore, where my father taught me the mystical joys of riding

waves. (The only two ways were bodysurfing or on canvas mats; boogie boards were not invented yet, nor were shortboards, and I was too little for longboards.) But one summer there were no waves for many days, so on the beach I read a strange book I had bought out of curiosity, St. John's *Ascent of Mount Carmel*. Like St. Patrick's and Palestrina, it was in another genus, like nothing I had ever read before. I didn't understand most of it, but somehow I just knew it was true—that is, *real*, as massively real as a mountain. I had climbed only anthills; this was an Everest. I followed it up with works by other Catholic saints: Augustine; Bernard of Clairvaux; and Thérèse, the "Little Flower"; as well as the classic Catholic works by Brother Lawrence of the Resurrection (ca. 1614–1691) and by Father Jean-Pierre de Caussade, S.J. (1675–1751)—for example, *The Practice of the Presence of God*, and *Abandonment to Divine Providence*, respectively. However different their styles, they were "into" the same Thing. (The capital letter is not a typo!) Why don't we have saints and believers like that?

4. A fourth surprise was a literal why, a question I couldn't answer. Bill Brown, my new roommate at Calvin College, asked it, in a late-night "bull session" during my first day on campus. (He was not a Catholic, but he was a "thinker" and a good troublemaker, like Socrates.) "Why don't we pray to saints?"

"Because we're Protestants, not Catholics, of course," I answered.

"And why are we Protestants and not Catholics? Because we don't do things like pray to saints, right?"

"Right."

"Isn't that a logical fallacy? Isn't that arguing in a circle?"

"Oh yeah, but there are good reasons not to pray to saints and no good reasons for it."

"Really? I bet you can figure out what my next question is."

"What are the reasons? Well, it's idolatry. We pray to God alone."

"Did you ever read Shakespeare?"

"Sure. What has that got to do with praying to saints?"

"In Shakespearean English, 'pray' means 'please'. Like 'pray' tell me how you feel.' It doesn't mean 'worship'."

"Okay, so what?"

"So maybe that's all they mean by 'praying' to saints: asking them to please do something for you. You ask them to pray to God for you. And what's wrong with that? Is it wrong for me to ask you to pray for me?"

"No, of course not."

"They why is it wrong for us to ask the saints to pray for us?"

"Because they're dead."

"No they're not. They're in heaven. Is heaven a cemetery? They're not dead in heaven; they're alive in heaven, aren't they?"

"Why are you arguing for the Catholic theology?"

"Because I like to argue. Don't you?"

"I do. I think we should do more of it." (And I've been doing it ever since.)

5. A fifth surprise was the contrast between my first two philosophy professors. The first one, a staunch Calvinist named H. Evan Runner, passionately propounded a brilliant but very closed system of "all the answers" from two contemporary Dutch theologians, Hermann Dooyeweerd and D. H. Th. Vollenhoven. There were impressive charts, with squares and columns and diagrams, that enclosed everything in the history of philosophy and everything in human experience. The whole system. All the answers. No more whys. The second professor, William Harry Jellema, though equally committed to Calvinism, set out for his students a much richer table of intellectual foods, from Socrates, Plato, Aristotle, Augustine, Aquinas, Kant, and Hegel, as well as from American philosopher and psychologist William James (1842–1910) and American philosopher Josiah Royce (1855–1916). He encouraged "whys" and offered "mores". I saw in him what I wanted to be. He made me a philosopher. He also introduced me to one of the greatest philosophical and theological minds who ever lived: St. Thomas Aquinas. I became a Thomist long before I became a Catholic. When I told Dr. Jellema that I was thinking of becoming a Catholic, he was not scandalized or even surprised. In fact, he confided that he had had the same thoughts when he was in college.

6. A sixth surprise was discovering the beauty and riches of the Anglican and Eastern Orthodox liturgies. This filled a hunger I did not know I had: the hunger every human heart has for heights, for royalty, for the joy of formality and the celebration of solemn, high beauty. I vividly remember the last time I worshipped in the opposite kind of church, a pious but informal Baptist church. The preacher made me feel a deep joy and love of God, but I could not find any object outside myself to mediate it. I knew that I was not the right object for it (for self-worship is far more dangerous than atheism), and I

knew that God, the only right object for worship, was a pure Spirit, but I was not a pure spirit! I needed the Incarnation, not merely as a past event, like Caesar's coronation, but also somehow as a continuing thing, like the universe. I needed an object that was a symbol. The only symbolic material object in the church was the tiny cross atop the church flag, which was at one end of the platform, opposite the American flag, which had an eagle on top. I absolutely needed that gold cross! My heart *drank* from it for the duration of the service. Afterward, I knew my faith was like a fish whose home was the sea, not a camel whose home was the desert. As a Catholic, I am still an Evangelical—in fact, much more Evangelical than I ever was as a Protestant—but as Tom Howard says in one of his perfect titles, "Evangelical is not enough."[21]

7. A seventh surprise was the most intellectually crucial one of all. I enrolled in a course in Church history at Calvin College, taught by a wise and winsome old Calvinist preacher, Dr. John Weidenaar. The very first day of class, he began by asking us to define the Church. No one answered.

His next question was, "How do we define the Church differently than Roman Catholics do?" Again, no answer. A third question: "Someday, you will meet a Roman Catholic who will have, as you, some questions like these:

'Are you a Christian?'
'Yes.'
'Are you a Catholic?'
'No.'
'What are you?'
'A Calvinist.'

'Oh, you're in the church John Calvin founded five hundred years ago. I'm in the church Jesus Christ founded two thousand years ago. You're in the wrong church.'

What do you say to him?"

Finally, someone answered: "The church Jesus Christ founded is described in the New Testament. It's not the Roman Catholic church."

"Why not?"

[21] Thomas Howard, *Evangelical Is Not Enough: Worship of God in Liturgy and Sacrament* (1984; repr., San Francisco: Ignatius Press, 1988).

"Well ... for one thing, it's not a big organization with a lot of money and power."

"I see. You mean something like what a Jewish friend of mine once said to me, 'I don't understand how twelve smart young Jewish boys let the world's biggest business fall into the hands of the Italians.'"

He had a twinkle in his eye. But only a few students got the joke. He went on: "Seriously, what's the difference between the Catholic Church and the church of the New Testament? It can't be just the size or the external appearance." He then drew two pictures on the blackboard: a little acorn and a big oak tree. "They're the same thing, right? Like a newborn baby and an adult. That's what Catholics say the Church is like: in the New Testament it was small and today it's big, but it's the same church, the thing Christ founded and the thing they have. So what's wrong with that? What's wrong with the picture I just drew on the board?"

No one had an answer. So he drew another picture: Noah's ark, with bumps under its hull. "Anybody know what those bumps are?"

"Barnacles," answered a student who knew something about fishing.

"Right. And what are barnacles?"

"Hard little organisms."

"And where do they come from? Are they from the boat?"

"No, they come from the water."

"And what do we do with them?"

"We scrape them off."

"Why?"

"Because if we don't, they'll sink the boat."

"Right! Now all these things that Catholics believe and we don't believe—the Mass and praying to saints and the pope and purgatory and the seven sacraments—Catholics say those are just good leaves on the tree that Jesus planted, but we say they're bad barnacles from outside, and after they had accumulated for centuries, some of the sailors on the ark, Luther and Calvin especially, said it's time to scrape them off. So that's what we did. In other words, Catholics accuse us of being the new kids on the block, but really they're the new kids on the block. The Reformation didn't create a new church; the Catholics did. We just restored the old one, the one Christ founded."

This was exactly what I was looking for. One of the reasons I enrolled in this class was to deal with what I thought were temptations to Catholicism. Now I had my justification for remaining Protestant. I translated my insight into a question: I raised my hand and asked, "Professor, do you mean to say that if my Catholic friend and I both got into a time machine and went back to the first century, I'd be more at home as a Protestant than he would as a Catholic?"

I still remember his wry smile. "That's a very strange way to put my point—a time machine—but yes, that's the point. All those Catholic additions to the New Testament—they're barnacles, not leaves."

Good, I thought: it's a matter of historical facts, not just theological arguments. I don't have to figure out each theological issue separately as to who's right; all I have to do is read the earliest Christian writings, the "Church Fathers", and I'll see how Protestant they are rather than Catholic.

You know the rest of the story. It was exactly John Henry Cardinal Newman's path to Rome (though I knew nothing about Newman at the time). As Newman said, "To be deep in history is to cease to be a Protestant."[22]

The doctrine that blew me away the most was the Real Presence of Christ in the Eucharist. Not a single Christian denied it for one thousand years; and the very few who did in the next five hundred years (Berengar of Tours in the eleventh century and the Albigensians in the thirteenth century) were all immediately, strongly, and clearly labeled heretics and were excommunicated. How could the Holy Spirit have fallen asleep so badly for fifteen hundred years that he let all Christians commit this ridiculous and egregious idolatry?

If Catholics are right about that—that the thing that looks like bread and wine is not really bread and wine after the Consecration, but Christ's real, literal Body and Blood, and Soul and Divinity, the whole Christ, worthy of worship and adoration—if Catholics are right about that, then we Protestants, who reduce that presence to something symbolic or spiritual or subjective, are missing out on the most perfect and real and complete relationship with Christ that is possible in this life. It was like reducing marriage to friendship. And if the

[22] John Henry Cardinal Newman, *Essay on the Development of Christian Doctrine*, 6th ed. (South Bend, IN: University of Notre Dame Press, 1989), 8.

Catholics are wrong, then they've invented the most idiotic idolatry in history, worshipping wine and bowing down to bread as if it was God! That's an either-or as stark as Christ's claim to divinity: if it's false, it's fantastically false, and if it's true, it's terribly true. It's also like the Church's claim about herself: a tremendous truth if it's true and blatantly blasphemous if it's false. No other Christian church claims the infallibility and authority she does, just as no other religious founder claims the divinity Christ did. The Catholic dogma about the Eucharist fit the same pattern.

The reason is that it is the same reality: the Incarnation, the Church, and the Eucharist are simply three aspects or outreaches of the very same objective reality, which is Christ's own Body. His Body in the Eucharist is the very same reality as his Mystical Body that is the Church and his human body on the Cross. He doesn't have three bodies; he has only one, but he gives it to us in three ways, three places.

8. Here is my eighth surprise from God. I was increasingly feeling both fear and desire about becoming a Catholic. Fear, because I'm conservative by nature: I didn't *want* Catholicism to be true; I didn't want to change. I also didn't want to hurt my parents, and I knew I would, inevitably and deeply. But at the same time as I felt fear, I also felt a desire, because if this strange new thing was true, and good, and beautiful, I did want it, with my whole heart.

But like Augustine, I was weak-willed and procrastinating. I would have sat on the far bank of the Tiber contemplating Rome's towers for years if divine grace had not given me an eighth surprise. It was an image that appeared suddenly as I prayed alone in my room at Calvin: a huge image of Noah's ark, sailing down the seas of history, with Augustine and Aquinas and all the other Catholic saints calling out to me out of its windows, "Come aboard! Join us!" I was in a spiffy little new motorboat following in the wake of the rickety old ark, and probably going to the same heaven she was, but why was I not with the others, including all those great sailors and all those weird animals? What was calling me was not just an idea, but persons: the saints, and their Captain. If he was my Captain too, I had to let myself be dragooned aboard his ship. It was as simple as that. And it still is, for everybody.

9. Here is my ninth surprise. My "dragooned aboard the ark" moment had come in the spring of my senior year at Calvin, and I

planned to join the Church, by baptism (they required Protestants to receive what was called "conditional rebaptism" in those days), as soon as I was away from home and in graduate school at Yale in the fall. So on the first day on campus I rang the door of the local Catholic rectory early in the morning, all bright-eyed and bushy-tailed. The priest who came down the stairs to answer the bell was Father Quinlan, a fat little Irishman from Brooklyn. He was utterly humble, practical, and nonintellectual, and had a permanent twinkle in his eye. He was still in his bathrobe.

"Good morning. So what can I do for you?"

"Father, I want to become a Catholic."

"Oh, that's nice. So who's the girl?"

Father Quinlan was the perfect providential choice to give me instructions in the faith. Instead of learning more theology from Aquinas or Newman, I had to learn practicality and humility. I had to memorize the first two questions and answers to the Penny Catechism, the one they gave little kids.

1. Q: Who made you?
   A: God made me.
2. Q: Why did God make you?
   A: God made me to know him, to love him, and to serve him in this world and to be happy with him forever in the next.

I would come with questions from St. Thomas Aquinas or St. John of the Cross, and Father Quinlan would always say, "Well, let's see what the catechism says first. You have to crawl before you walk, and walk before you run." I absolutely needed that lesson in humility and simplicity. No "double truth" theory in the Catholic Church! The Ivy League philosopher gets the same truth little kids get, because truth is truth.

As for "who's the girl", there actually was a girl, but Maria was not my girlfriend (I thought I was going to be a priest), but she was the only Catholic girl I knew, so I asked her to be my godmother. At my baptism, she asked the priest, jokingly, "Hey, Father, what if I fall in love with this guy?" He replied, "Oh, then you're in deep doo-doo. Marriage between godparent and godchild is spiritual incest. You'd have to get a special dispensation from the pope."

A year later, Maria and I were back at the rectory asking Father Quinlan if he could get that dispensation for us.

The three most important choices in your life are the choice of a church, a spouse, and a career. God gave me the best of all possible worlds three times: the Catholic Church, Maria, and philosophy. And because I decided to become the other kind of father, my six best books will be in heaven forever: the ones who were coauthored by myself and Maria (two miscarriages, four pregnancies). My other eighty or so books are ephemeral and trivial by comparison.

10. The tenth surprise was what happened at my First Communion. It was the best thing that could possibly have happened: nothing. No visions, no voices, no tears, no mystical experiences. Just the absolute certainty of sheer, stubborn faith (which is a knowing, not a feeling) that this thing that looked and felt and tasted exactly like bread was in fact the infinite, eternal, omnipotent Word of God, who created the universe. Nothing else. No events. Time stopped or simply ceased to matter. Questions also ceased. No more whys. They were not solved but dissolved. All my boats sank, baptized in a sea of silence.

I thank God for that silence, that simplicity, that absence of all "sensible consolations", as the saints put it. I am by nature a naively idealistic Romantic, and an experience addict: the poetry of Wordsworth and Keats and the symphonies of Sibelius, Beethoven, Tchaikovsky, and Wagner make me weep. But God did not indulge my spiritual sweet tooth. He gave me instead the Eucharist as a spiritual exercise machine to build up the muscles of my faith so that I could walk on the ground of facts, not on the crutches of feelings. God is very simple and practical, and I learned that faith is also very simple and practical. Here is my favorite definition of faith: God said it, and I believe it, and that settles it. And here is my favorite sermon of all time: God's four-word summary of all of divine revelation to St. Catherine, in a vision—"I'm God; you're not."[23]

[23] God also put the books I needed into my life at the right time. "Loners" need books especially, because books are a way of making many wise friends. The most useful to me were Leslie Rumble and Charles M. Carty, *Radio Replies* (Rockford, IL: TAN Books, 1979); Frank Sheed and Maisie Ward, *Catholic Evidence Training Outlines* (Steubenville, OH: Franciscan University Press, 1993); St. Augustine, *Confessions*, trans. Henry Chadwick (Oxford: Oxford University Press, 2009); G. K. Chesterton, *Orthodoxy*, repr. ed. (San Francisco: Ignatius

My earliest whys were about "mere Christianity"—why do we believe what we do?—and I got good answers to those questions. My next whys were about Catholicism—why Catholics believe what they do—and I got good answers to those questions too. But there is a third why that I will never, this side of heaven, get an adequate answer to—that is, why God loved me so much as to give me all those graces, why he played the providentially perfect gambit of these particular chess moves with his white pieces to conquer my black ones (i.e., the many forces of darkness: sin, stupidity, selfishness, and shallowness).

A student in one of my Philosophy in Literature classes once asked me a similar why, which I thought was the ultimate unanswerable question. We had just gone through one of the world's most profoundly Christian novels, Fyodor Mikhailovich Dostoevsky's *The Brothers Karamazov* (1880), and she said,

---

Press, 1995); G. K. Chesterton, *The Everlasting Man*, repr. ed. (San Francisco: Ignatius Press, 1993); Fulton J. Sheen, *God and Intelligence in Modern Philosophy: A Critical Study in the Light of the Philosophy of Saint Thomas*, repr. ed. (Eugene, OR: Wipf & Stock Publishers, 2009); Archbishop Fulton J. Sheen, *The World's First Love: Mary, Mother of God*, 2nd ed. (San Francisco: Ignatius Press, 2010); Fulton J. Sheen, *Three to Get Married* (Princeton, NJ: Scepter Publishers, 1996); Etienne Gilson, *The Unity of Philosophical Experience*, rev. ed. (San Francisco: Ignatius Press, 1999); Mortimer J. Adler, *Ten Philosophical Mistakes*, repr. ed. (New York: Touchstone, 1997). The earliest writer who gave me a big shove across the Tiber was St. Justin Martyr, the first Christian philosopher. Compared with Augustine and Aquinas his philosophy seemed simple and "primitive", but his Catholicism was clear: his description of the worship of the second-century Church centered on the Mass and the Real Presence. If the Church went bad (i.e., Catholic) that early, the Holy Spirit must have taken a sleeping pill. Reading St. Thomas Aquinas also refuted the typical Protestant critique of Catholic theology that I had been taught—that it was Pelagian self-salvation by accumulating merit. I discovered that Aquinas, and the decrees of the Council of Trent, which used him, was as strong on the absolute priority and necessity of grace as Luther and Calvin were, but his vision of salvation did not ignore or deny human free will and the works of love, as theirs did. C. S. Lewis, though he was a Protestant (Anglican) all his life, also showed me an essentially Catholic theology that included hierarchy, purgatory, the Real Presence, tradition, and authority. He explicitly contradicted two very basic Protestant doctrines: Luther's antimetaphysical, nominalist "federal" or legal theory of atonement, in part 4 of *Mere Christianity*, and Calvin's doctrine of "total depravity" in *The Problem of Pain*. The only consistent and intellectually admirable Protestant alternative to the Catholic philosophy that I found was Søren Kierkegaard. His irrationalism was not only brilliant, but even rational (consistent). I still admire him as the greatest Protestant mind of all time, but I just could not embrace his fideism. The book that was to me a Rubicon to cross was Ronald Knox's *The Belief of Catholics* (San Francisco: Ignatius Press, 2000). It read a bit like Augustine: passionate and eloquent as well as clear and rational. I also was impressed by his *Difficulties*, a dialogue with Sir Arnold Lunn, a brilliant Protestant controversialist who eventually became Catholic due to Knox's replies.

"Do you believe what Dostoyevsky believes?"

"About what?" I asked.

"About God's love. Because that's what this long, dark novel is about in the end, isn't it?"

"Yes, it is," I said, impressed with her wisdom.

"Well, why?" she asked. "Why does God love us so much?"

I was literally stunned by the gap between the size of the question and the size of any answer I could put into words. I said, jokingly, "I don't know. Ask me next year, maybe I'll know then." Exactly a year from that day she came to my office.

"Remember me?"

"Yes."

"Do you remember the question I asked you at the end of your Philosophy in Literature course?"

"Yes. I'll never forget it."

"You said to come back in a year. Did you find the answer?"

This time I was more honest. "No, and I don't think I'll find it next year either. I think that's why we have to go to heaven: that's the only place we'll get the answer to that one."

That's why God gave us the Catholic Church: so I could say to all of my friends, "Hope to see you there."

6

A Pastor's Kid Finds the Catholic Church

Logan Paul Gage

> I loved to choose and see my path; but now
> Lead Thou me on!...
>
> So long Thy power hath blest me, sure it still
> Will lead me on.
>
> —John Henry Newman, "Lead, Kindly Light"

Introduction

More than once when people have asked about my decision to become Catholic, I've responded naively, like one who tries to retell a *Saturday Night Live* sketch. If you've ever done this, you've realized that your rendition isn't very funny to one who hasn't already seen the original. Similarly, to one who hasn't had some of the experiences and thoughts that converts typically have, or to one who is looking to knock down Catholic arguments, my reasons may not be helpful. Whether one finds an argument convincing depends greatly on one's experiences, dispositions, and background information.

Our reasons for belief are far more complex than popular, rationalistic apologetics admits. Looking for *the* reason I became Catholic, as though there is one reason (or simply a handful) that could be easily repeated in syllogistic form, is misguided. Even trained philosophers—perhaps especially, trained philosophers—make this mistake. We are often trained to look for killer arguments. Initially I evaluated Catholicism like this: "That's not a knockdown argument, nor is that one, nor that; therefore, Catholicism is false or unjustified." But this stance fails to appreciate the nature of so-called cumulative cases; we usually have multiple, converging reasons for belief. If you look only for stand-alone arguments and set the bar for success too high, nothing will satisfy. This isn't special pleading for Catholicism. When was the last time you reversed deeply held religious or political views because of a syllogism? Human beings don't typically work that way. We accumulate reasons from many sources and form an overall impression of the world.

But arguments are not worthless. With a realistic view of human reason we can charitably and empathetically entertain others' worldviews. We can hear their stories, think about their reasons in context, and perhaps come to see that they are not unreasonable. Over time we might even see that their vision of life is more winsome than our own; it suddenly rings true. Large-scale changes of belief are more like Gestalt shifts than the acquisition of a single new argument. Conversion commonly consists, not in the overthrowing of all past belief, but in seeing old things in a new way.[1]

So I caution the reader: the search for killer arguments that vanquish all foes is in vain. I don't expect the reasons adduced in this book to bowl over trenchant non-Catholic readers. But remember, neither would their arguments bowl us over. We've carefully considered them and found them so wanting that, in some cases, we left friends and family to follow Christ alone. It is in this spirit that I share some glimpses into my own life. I am Catholic because Catholicism seems true to me. Explaining *why* it seems true is much more difficult to summarize.

Early Life

When I first read Augustine's *Confessions* with an Evangelical outlook, I saw it as a conversion story. Everything comes together at the end of book 8, when Augustine hears "Tolle lege! Tolle lege!"

---

[1] If evidence consists in experience, as my Ph.D. dissertation argued, then it is easy to see how one's evidence isn't easily summarized and packaged for others' consumption.

("Take and read! Take and read!"); he opens the Scriptures, sees in them the truth against which he has rebelled, and yields his heart to God. But as I read the story again and again, I began to notice something different—something that changed how I viewed my own story. The drama of Augustine's life, as I first saw it, was in his radical conversion. In fact, I would feel anxious as I read, wanting Augustine to hurry up and convert. I began to sense that while the conversion at the end of book 8 was pivotal, the backstory was just as important. Augustine's story is more one of a gradual awakening to truth than a one-time conversion. He has to see the intellectual and moral errors that are clouding his vision; they must be uprooted and supplanted one by one before he can find rest in God.

As a young Evangelical, I told my story as one of conversion—the single truly important event for understanding me, I thought, was the moment (at age fourteen) in which I determined to give my entire life to Christ Jesus. Augustine helped me bring balance to the story: God's hand had been over my life from the beginning. In hindsight I see that my life was shaped by God through my parents and his other provisions—not just through my own autonomous choice. My self-understanding, at this time, was filtered through the lens of the all-important, one-time-choice-for-God framework. While neither Augustine nor I want to downplay the momentous nature of such decisions, this emphasis can obscure God's continual providence over our lives and minimize our daily decisions for Christ. So I'll start at the beginning.

I was born the son of a preacher man in San Diego in 1981. In Evangelical lingo, I'm a "P.K.", or pastor's kid. While I had to take ownership of my own faith when I grew up, the faith is something I received—more like a precious family inheritance than an item chosen off the shelf. This is God's generosity, provided for me at the request of four praying grandparents (another grace). I've lived in a dozen states. We moved around a lot as my father ministered to various congregations, but most of my childhood was spent near Flint, Michigan. My parents grew up in the Assemblies of God and met at a Bible college. My dad received his M.Div. from Trinity Evangelical Divinity School in the 1970s. While he initially ministered in the Assemblies of God, doctrinal differences developed after years of Bible study, and he was dually ordained with the American Baptist

Churches USA (basically, the Northern Baptists) and the Southern
Baptist Convention.

People often ask me if I had trouble with the priesthood before
converting. I didn't. If the Old Covenant contained a priesthood, it
certainly isn't crazy that the New Covenant would. Moreover, the
New Testament is full of talk about bishops and priests. But I never
noticed it—despite beginning to read through the Bible for the first
time around age eight—because my NIV (New International Version) Bible translated *episkopos* (the word for "bishop") as "overseer"[2]
and *presbyter* (the word from which we derive the English word
"priest") as "elder".[3] The job of most Evangelical ministers is part
scholar, part preacher, part committee organizer, part staff adminis-
trator, part accountant, part counselor—basically part *everything*. This
is hard on family. The Church's decision, in its wisdom and long
experience, that such ministry calls for total service to Christ made
sense to me.

I had a typical Evangelical upbringing. I played on church playgrounds; attended Sunday school, Vacation Bible School (VBS), and
Christian summer camps; and went to church nearly every Sunday,
Sunday night, and Wednesday evening. I recall taking Matthew 6:6
literally ("When you pray, go into your room and shut the door")
and praying the sinner's prayer in my closet at age four or five. It was
so early that I didn't see much transformation from this event. I had
the privilege of being both baptized and married by my father, but I
don't even remember the name of the church where I was baptized at
age twelve. We viewed baptism as a milestone and a public profession
of faith. But I wasn't very concerned with the faith at that point, and
we didn't see baptism as a sacrament that transforms. So I didn't give
it much thought. My youth was spent playing sports and wandering
the woods all day doing boy things—building forts, playing army,
exploring nature.

Because our lives were so centered on our church, I don't recall
having a single pious Catholic friend. A neighborhood acquaintance
once took me to a Byzantine Catholic Mass. It struck me as very
strange. Mostly I remember finding a beer tap in the basement rec

[2] E.g., 1 Tim 3:1.
[3] E.g., Jas 5:14.

hall. This confirmed my suspicion that they were heathens, since no Christians I knew drank. My impression as a kid was that perhaps *some* Catholics are "saved", but these few were saved in spite of their strange superstitions. This wasn't serious anti-Catholicism but simply condescension. Given the number of nominal Catholics, perhaps this attitude was sometimes warranted—but surely not as often as we assumed. My impression was simply that all the energy and vitality of the Gospel was in Evangelicalism. So Catholicism was never a live option. Our subculture spoke "Evangelicalese", and those who didn't we failed to recognize as our own. As a boy I recall asking my dad about the Reformation. He told me it was about getting back to the beliefs and practices of the early Church. I think I've had a desire to do just that ever since.

Choosing Christ

I experienced two transformative years—ones that have shaped the course of my entire life—between the ages of fourteen and sixteen. Living on the north side of Indianapolis, I wound up at the youth group of a large nondenominational church in Carmel, Indiana. There, for the first time, the faith came alive. Following Jesus suddenly didn't seem like a parochial thing but a serious and passionate way of life. My ears were opened, and Jesus' words struck me to the core. God's presence was palpable in worship and Bible study. I made a very serious commitment to Christ at a student conference—one that I've stuck to ever since. I began carrying my Bible to school. I couldn't get enough of it and wanted to give outward witness to others as to how much my heart was changing. I started to move away from friends I loved but who didn't place the same priority upon living for Christ as I knew I must and toward those that did.

I don't think I could overstate the importance of the formation I received during those two years. I tremble at who I might have become without these people—I tremble at what I might value and the meaningless, worldly things that might have consumed my life. C. S. Lewis' poem "Nearly They Stood" (1933), stanza 2, often echoes in my mind:

Nearly they fell who stand.
These with cold after-fear
Look back and note how near
They grazed the Siren's land
Wondering to think that fate
By threads so spidery-fine
The choice of ways so small, the event so great
Should thus entwine.

That community shaped the person I am and want to be, showing
me that it isn't impossible to love God with everything you have and
winsomely live the faith in today's world.

In high school my family moved to the northwest corner of Washington State. In the small Dutch American community of Lynden,
Washington, I met new Christian friends who encouraged me (and
still encourage me) in the faith. They watered the seed sown in
Indiana (and indeed the seedling given by my parents). With only
minimal talent, I threw myself into music ministry. At one point, I
simultaneously led worship at seven different services across a variety
of churches and youth groups—Reformed, Baptist, nondenominational, etc. Often when people ask me why so many Evangelicals
are converting to Catholicism, I point to the fact that so many of
us lack ethnic or nationalistic denominational ties. Unlike previous
generations, we've experienced many good churches and won't be
Lutheran just because of Swedish ancestry. During this time, I went
on mission trips to West Africa, Haiti, and Mexico that both enriched
my faith and gave me a larger view of the world. I assumed I would
become a missionary.

At age sixteen my intellectual curiosity exploded. I quit playing
sports because I wanted more time to read and think. I listened to
Plato's dialogues while washing carts at a local golf course. I read
almost everything C. S. Lewis ever wrote. And I decided that I
wanted to study philosophy and theology in college. As I matured,
and as my personality and temperament developed, I became a little
uneasy with Evangelicalism's tendencies toward emotionalism, celeb-
rities, and fads. I didn't (and don't) have any ill will toward Evangelicalism; I was just looking for more meat. I wasn't interested in
the Evangelical books of that time: *I Kissed Dating Goodbye*, *Wild at*

Heart, and the *Left Behind* series. I wanted a girlfriend, thought my masculinity was just fine even though I prefer the indoors, and didn't have much use for pretribulationist speculation.[4]

Young Adulthood

I wanted head and heart to meet and find a balance. So when I arrived at Whitworth College in Spokane, Washington, in the fall of 2000, I stopped all the busyness to drink in books and ideas. I decided not to become involved in the Evangelical music and leadership scene. College became in many ways a spiritual and intellectual retreat. It wasn't wasted on me that I had an incredibly privileged opportunity to spend four years reading and gaining all kinds of knowledge. I read as widely as possible and committed loads of poetry to memory with cigar smoke wafting up from public benches on campus. Whitworth is affiliated with the Presbyterian Church (U.S.A.). I attended the Presbyterian church on campus, as it had a somewhat Evangelical character and never emphasized the rougher edges of Calvinism. Objectively speaking, the church wasn't very liturgical; but it sure was to me. Theology wasn't much on my mind, because as an Evangelical I thought that only essential doctrines could be known with assurance. Everything else seemed like intermural debate. So I gravitated toward philosophy.

After college I helped a think tank establish an office in Washington, D.C. I wrote newspaper and magazine articles, set up book events for C-SPAN, and did liaison work on Capitol Hill. At first I lived with my colleague Mark and his family in northern Virginia while I searched for an apartment in the city. Mark and his wife, Katy, have nine children. I had never seen (or even heard of) such a thing. I thought it was peculiar, but wonderful. These people were *definitely* Catholic. From my first day with them it was clear to me that they were engaged in a difficult but beautiful project. Mealtime was amazing. The table was huge, and the conversation energetic and engaging.

---

[4] Pretribulationism holds that God removes his followers from earth before an intense period of judgment or tribulation.

As Mark and I commuted along the Potomac River, we would discuss our theological differences. He cleared up many of my misunderstandings of Catholicism. Because his father was a Protestant-minister-turned-Catholic priest, Mark had respect for the good things in Protestantism and spoke both languages. During our friendly arguments I was struck by our different styles. I would get excited about defending some point of doctrine or biblical interpretation, but Mark would show me another, not unreasonable way to look at things. When Mark didn't have an answer for some jab of mine, he would say something like, "Huh, I don't know. That's a good question." He was so calm, and his theology didn't hang on the latest scholarly arguments about some passage of Scripture. His confidence unnerved me because it seemed like he *knew* Catholicism was true.

Mark gave me some books on Catholicism. I read them but wasn't yet in a place where they could speak to me. My walls were still up. I was still in battle mode. After all, these were the only serious Catholics I had ever known. My entire circle of trust was Evangelical— friends, family, favorite academics. In the end, though, the witness of Mark's family and other good Catholics I met in D.C. changed me. It let me put my guard down long enough to consider their arguments honestly. I started to see that while I had spent my life in church and even attended a Christian college, I really didn't know that much about Church history. If Protestantism was about getting back to the early Church, why did we spend so little time studying the early Church and the Church Fathers?

When I moved to downtown D.C., I had to "find a church home", as Evangelicals say. I was always told to find a "Bible-preaching church". For the first time I wondered if this just meant a church whose reading of the Bible I agreed with. At any rate, I wound up at a Presbyterian church (Presbyterian Church in America) in the heart of the city. I found that the more liturgical service allowed for contemplation and worship in a way that the increasingly rock-concert style of Evangelicalism could not. Most importantly I met my future wife there in 2005. She was raised in a large Evangelical nondenominational church in Charlotte, North Carolina, that taught her to love God and memorize Scripture. She met my Catholic friends from work, and we had occasional conversations about Catholicism. But neither of us took it too seriously.

"The Catholic question" increasingly bothered me, however. My best friend in D.C. as well as some of my think-tank colleagues converted. These were big surprises. Knowing their deep faith and serious intellectual gifts, I found it was no longer possible to bury my head in the sand. At a party I got distracted by a bookcase—as you can tell, I'm *real* fun at parties—and chanced upon David Currie's *Born Fundamentalist, Born Again Catholic.*[5] I devoured it. I didn't like the title, as I never would have identified as a fundamentalist. But as I read I recognized his description of my childhood Evangelical culture. The book gave voice to my worries about the canon of Scripture, the Eucharist, justification, and more. It made me feel like I wasn't crazy, like someone had already discovered the problems in Evangelicalism and their possible resolution in Catholicism.

I knew I couldn't figure out every issue for myself. They're too complex, and I'm simply not smart enough. For a time I was under the illusion that I could. But I have too many friends with relevant linguistic and theological training who still disagree on baptism, the Eucharist, and more. I increasingly sensed that *if* Jesus desired true doctrine to be known, then he would have left us something more solid than a book. In fact, it struck me for the first time that Jesus *didn't* leave us a book before his Ascension; he didn't even write anything. My wife too had been under the illusion that she could sort everything out. Having encountered substantial theological disagreement in Evangelicalism, she took lessons in Greek and planned to study Hebrew in Israel. But the more we considered it, the more it just seemed that it couldn't be God's plan to give us a book and leave us to our own interpretations (or those of historically recent denominations). After all, even at the turn of the twentieth century the world illiteracy rate was around 80 percent.[6] Most Christians *had* to rely on tradition.[7] Here we were in the early twenty-first century, extraordinarily educated by historical standards (my wife is a lawyer

---

[5] David Currie, *Born Fundamentalist, Born Again Catholic* (San Francisco: Ignatius Press, 1996).

[6] Max Roser and Esteban Ortiz-Ospina, "Literacy", *Our World in Data*, accessed August 17, 2018, https://ourworldindata.org/literacy.

[7] I was instinctively negative toward tradition. I later discovered that my 1984 NIV Bible translated the same word (*paradosis*) as "tradition" in negative contexts (e.g., Mt 15:3) but as "teachings" in positive contexts (e.g., 1 Cor 11:2).

by training), and we knew that we couldn't figure it all out ourselves no matter how much we studied. We began to see the need
for authority. Catholics had the best claim to authority, but we still
thought them mistaken on too many doctrines.

I decided to investigate the two issues that bothered me most: the
nature of the Eucharist and the canon of Scripture. By then I could
see that Catholicism taught a lot of truth. If Catholics got these two
key doctrines correct, I was going to give them much more trust.
At first, I found the Real Presence of Christ in the Eucharist totally
bizarre. Why would Jesus want me to eat his literal body? But if
I looked historically and Christians had always believed something
like this, then I would stop protesting and yield to the wisdom of
the early Church. I figured, though, that it was a superstitious late-
medieval invention. More importantly, if Protestants couldn't adequately ground their sixty-six-book canon, then *sola scriptura* seemed
irrelevant. It makes little sense to claim that the Bible alone is the final
doctrinal authority without the right Bible. How can you know *what*
it teaches unless you know what it *is*?[8]

Protestantism and the Canon of Scripture

I revered the Bible I knew, and so when Catholics seemed to have
seven more Old Testament books (called "apocrypha" by Protestants and "deuterocanonicals" by Catholics), I assumed they were
added at some late date. Scholars I trusted claimed they "were never
included in the Hebrew canon of the Old Testament".[9] I began
reading everything I could about the canon, sticking only to non-
Catholic authors out of suspicion. I quickly learned that the disputed
books were present in the Septuagint manuscript tradition (the early
Greek translation of the Old Testament).[10] This shocked me, since

[8] Amazingly, the influential Protestant theologian Wayne Grudem rejects the deuterocanonicals, in part, because they contain supposedly unbiblical doctrines. See his quotation
of E.J. Young in Wayne Grudem, *Systematic Theology* (Grand Rapids, MI: Zondervan,
1994), 59.

[9] Neil R. Lightfoot, *How We Got the Bible*, 3rd ed. (Grand Rapids, MI: Baker Books,
2003), 167.

[10] Jaroslav Pelikan, *Whose Bible Is It?* (New York: Penguin, 2005), appendix 1.

I knew the Septuagint was the Old Testament of the apostles and early Christians—in fact, the entire Greek-speaking world including the Jewish diaspora (the majority of Jews at the time).[11] "For most early Christians," one Protestant scholar writes, "the Greek Bible was their only Bible from the very beginning of the Christian movement."[12] And, another adds, "In the first two centuries at any rate the Church seems to have accepted all, or most of, these additional books as inspired and to have treated them without question as Scripture."[13] The Septuagint was in use by the Jews for three centuries prior to Christ. The vast majority of New Testament quotations of the Old Testament are from the Septuagint;[14] it was used in early Christian liturgy;[15] it (including the deuterocanonical books) is quoted *as Scripture* by the Church Fathers;[16] and the view that the Septuagint was divinely inspired was "common among many of the early church fathers"[17]—the leaders of those who discerned the correct New Testament canon.[18] Clearly, the default Old Testament canon should follow the Septuagint manuscript tradition.

Numerous Protestants claimed, however, that the official Jewish canon, settled by the so-called Council of Jamnia (A.D. 90), did not include the disputed books. But I could never see how this was

---

[11] Sometimes it is argued that first-century Jews *in Palestine* had a unified canon identical to the current Protestant Old Testament. Yet sects like the Samaritans and Essenes differed, and even the Sadducees held a different canon than the Pharisees. This is why it is problematic to point to an author like Josephus—a Pharisee—and claim that he describes the *true* Hebrew canon in *Against Apion* 1.8.38–42. Note too that Josephus accepts the additional material from 1 Esdras and Greek Esther. See Roger Beckwith, *The Old Testament Canon of the New Testament Church* (London: SPCK, 1985), 405.

[12] Lee Martin McDonald, *The Biblical Canon* (Grand Rapids, MI: Baker Academic, 2007), 102.

[13] J. N. D. Kelly, *Early Christian Doctrines*, 5th ed. (London: Continuum, 1977), 54.

[14] Ibid., 53.

[15] Timothy Michael Law, *When God Spoke Greek* (New York: Oxford University Press, 2013), 139.

[16] Craig D. Allert, *A High View of Scripture?* (Grand Rapids, MI: Baker Academic, 2007), appendix.

[17] Craig A. Evans, introduction to *Exploring the Origins of the Bible*, ed. Craig A. Evans and Emanuel Tov (Grand Rapids, MI: Baker Academic, 2008), 18. In fact, many Jews may have thought the Septuagint inspired as well. See Philo, *On the Life of Moses* 2.37–40, and Jennifer M. Dines, *The Septuagint* (New York: T&T Clark, 2004), 63–78.

[18] It seems inconsistent to hold, as does Beckwith (*Old Testament Canon*), that fourth-century Christians botched the Old Testament canon because their memory of the first century had faded but flawlessly discerned the first-century New Testament.

supposed to help the Protestant case, since (1) I couldn't see what authority the rabbis at Jamnia had to settle the canon for all Jews let alone for Christians (especially after the destruction of the temple and the death of nearly all the apostles),[19] (2) surely, these rabbis would reject the New Testament books as canonical,[20] and (3) numerous scholars suggest that the increased Jewish reliance on the Hebrew text was a reaction to the Christian adoption of the Septuagint.[21] Regardless, the nineteenth-century Jamnia hypothesis—and that's all it is, a late nineteenth-century hypothesis by German scholar Heinrich Graetz—has been discredited by more recent scholarship.[22] There simply is no good evidence for the occurrence of a council at Jamnia. Historical records show rabbis debating Ecclesiastes and Song of Songs but no council rejecting the deuterocanonical books. Further complicating the Protestants-simply-follow-the-first-century-Jewish-canon narrative, the rabbinical literature also records disputes among rabbis regarding other books Protestants deem canonical (Ezekiel, Proverbs, and Esther) occurring in the early centuries after Jesus.[23] In fact, "Debates over some books continued in Judaism until the sixth century CE."[24]

---

[19] Tom Brown comments: "A major problem with this canon theory is that it grants to the Jewish leaders of Jesus' day an authority which, it claims, if possessed by the Church, would undermine the authority of Scripture." Tom Brown, "The Canon Question", Called to Communion, January 23, 2010, http://www.calledtocommunion.com/2010/01/the-canon-question.

[20] Bruce Metzger amazingly says that "the Assembly at Jamnia merely ratified what the most spiritually sensitive souls in Judaism had been accustomed to regard as holy Scripture." Bruce Metzger, An Introduction to the Apocrypha (New York: Oxford University Press, 1957), 8. This is amazing, not only because one wonders how he discerns which Jews are most spiritually sensitive, but because these very rabbis also rejected Christianity. As Brown asks, "Why ... is the opinion of the non-converting Jews more reliable than the opinion of those who converted to Christ and widely used the Greek Septuagint?" Brown, "Canon Question".

[21] E.g., R. Laird Harris, Inspiration and Canonicity of the Scriptures (Eugene, OR: Wipf & Stock Publishers, 2008), 182–83, and F. F. Bruce, The Canon of Scripture (Downers Grove, IL: IVP Academic, 1988), 50. Tertullian (On Women's Dress 1.3) thought that the Jews rejected books that witnessed to Christ. Justin Martyr (Dialogue with Trypho 71–73, 120) and Origin (Letter to Africanus 2, 5) say something similar about the additions to Daniel and Jeremiah.

[22] See Jack P. Lewis, "Jamnia Revisited", in The Canon Debate, ed. Lee Martin McDonald and James A. Sanders (Peabody, MA: Hendrickson Publishers, 2002), 146–62.

[23] R. T. Beckwith, "The Canon of the Old Testament", in The Origin of the Bible, ed. Philip Wesley Comfort (Carol Stream, IL: Tyndale House, 2003), 51.

[24] James H. Charlesworth, "Writings Ostensibly outside the Canon", in Evans and Tov, Exploring Origins of the Bible, 58. Cf. McDonald, Biblical Canon, 175–89.

"So why did so many Protestant scholars look to Jewish *tradition* (supposedly from Jamnia) at all?", I began to wonder. The answer became obvious: they needed a closed Jewish canon, because the Reformers rejected the widespread and long-standing Christian acceptance of the deuterocanonicals. As one Protestant scholar writes:

> A Jamnia council decision is attractive, since no other prior time can be identified when a significant decision was made about the scope of the Hebrew biblical canon by the rabbinic teachers. No evidence, however, supports any formal action taken at Jamnia, and this view is largely abandoned today. The scope of the Hebrew biblical canon within Judaism was more likely settled in the second century C.E., and possibly even later than that.[25]

Indeed, the second century seems to be the scholarly consensus.[26] Agreeing that there was no Jewish conciliar decision, the director of the Princeton Dead Sea Scrolls Project notes that "the texts of the so-called Old Testament were fluid" before A.D. 70.[27] The "Christian Scriptures were larger [i.e., contained the deuterocanonicals] because the Jews at an earlier time included more writings than they did later under the influence of rabbinic Judaism."[28]

Beyond the deuterocanonicals, the big question is, what determines the canon, so that we can confidently know all the writings that have divine authority over our lives? The question isn't what *makes* a book authoritative; all Christians think the reason some books are authoritative is because they are "God-breathed" (i.e., inspired).[29] What we are looking for is a reliable *epistemic criterion* by which we can know that these are the God-breathed books. We aren't just looking to invent a criterion, either. If our criterion wasn't used historically, then it seems arbitrary, ad hoc—invented to fit our presuppositions rather than reality. Further, the criterion must be consonant with our theology. The Protestant holding to *sola scriptura* shouldn't appeal to a theological authority they wouldn't normally accept.

[25] McDonald, *Biblical Canon*, 174.
[26] E.g., Law, *When God Spoke Greek*, 19–32.
[27] Charlesworth, "Writings Ostensibly outside the Canon", 63. Cf. McDonald, *Biblical Canon*, 169.
[28] McDonald, *Biblical Canon*, 102.
[29] Cf. *Catechism of the Catholic Church*, nos. 105–8.

Initially, I thought I could hold that God instrumentally used the early Church to give us the right canon.[30] This is not incorrect, but for a Protestant it is a bad strategy. The early Church canon wasn't the Protestant one. One can point to Catholics through the ages who questioned the Catholic canon—just as some Protestants have questioned the Protestant canon—but there seem to be *no* Church Fathers or Church councils holding to the Protestant canon as it presently stands. Not one.[31] Moreover, this position is clearly ad hoc. How could I trust the early Church on *this*—even invoking the guidance of the Holy Spirit—but not on any other matter of doctrine? As one Protestant rightly asks, "By the later fourth century ... many features of the church that evangelical ... Protestants find questionable are already functioning. Does it make sense to say that the fourth-century church was making very good decisions about the Bible but mostly poor ones about everything else?"[32]

How then could I avoid this ad hoc move? In a bootstrapping maneuver, many Christians claim that the Bible establishes its own canon. They note that biblical books often claim divine authority, quote other biblical books, and (with regard to the New Testament) are written by apostles. But these criteria threaten to truncate the sixty-six-book canon: not all of those books claim divine authority, are written by apostles, or are quoted by other biblical books. In other cases, these criteria threaten to expand the canon: there are numerous New Testament parallels and allusions to the deuterocanonicals,[33] and Jude even quotes from 1 Enoch (a book neither Protestants nor Catholics deem canonical). If maneuvers like this fail, it seemed to me that the canon must be determined by something outside of itself.

---

[30] Cf. James R. White, *Scripture Alone* (Grand Rapids, MI: Bethany House, 2004), 106–9.

[31] Often Protestants point to Jerome and Origen. But this is a mistake. See, for instance, Jerome's prologues in the Vulgate and his *Against Rufinus* 2.33. See also Origen's list in Eusebius' *Church History* 6.25, and his letters to Julius Africanus. Even if I'm mistaken and *one or two* Fathers advanced the current Protestant canon, this would only prove the point that a sixty-six-book canon was uncommon in the early Church.

[32] Frederick W. Norris, "The Canon of Scripture in the Church", in *The Free Church and the Early Church*, ed. D. H. Williams (Grand Rapids, MI: Eerdmans, 2002), 15.

[33] See McDonald, *Biblical Canon*, appendix D, and Metzger, *Introduction to the Apocrypha*, 158–70; see also p. 188, where Metzger notes that even the 1611 King James Bible contained 113 margin references to the deuterocanonicals.

Because they held that the Bible is the ultimate doctrinal authority, however, the classical Reformers I encountered proclaimed an external determinant of the canon unacceptable. It would place something above the Scriptures, a rule to which they must conform. They were forced to the incredible position that the Scriptures all but determine themselves. As Dutch theologian Herman Ridderbos explains:

> Calvin appealed not only to the witness of the Holy Spirit in the hearts of believers but above all to the self-attestation of the Scriptures. The divine character of the Bible itself gives it its authority. This divine character is so evident that anyone who has eyes to see is directly convinced and does not need the mediation of the church.... [As] Karl Barth wrote, "the Bible makes itself to be canon."[34]

Michael J. Kruger similarly maintains that "the church did not choose the canon, but the canon, in a sense, chose itself."[35] Just as many hold to the "perspicuity" of Scripture despite educated, sincere, and widespread disagreement, many hold that Scripture's divine qualities are simply obvious when compared to any noncanonical document—despite centuries of disagreement. The "corporate church, as a whole, would naturally recognize the canonical books."[36]

The classical Reformed confessions (e.g., Belgic, Westminster) adopt the view that Christians discern Scripture by the testimony of the Holy Spirit in their hearts. It struck me as wildly implausible, however, that two new, Spirit-filled believers (or churches) would automatically agree on the canon.[37] Early Christians didn't possess universal agreement at all times and places. Anyone who has attended Bible studies knows that possessing the Holy Spirit is insufficient for determining the Scriptures' meaning. Why then think this "test" sufficient for determining its contents? "It is unlikely," one of the greatest Protestant scholars of the last century notes, "that the Spirit's witness would enable a reader to discern that Ecclesiastes is the word of God while Ecclesiasticus is not."[38] Unless you are willing to say

---

[34] Herman Ridderbos, *Redemptive History and the New Testament Scriptures*, 2nd ed. (Phillipsburg, NJ: P&R, 1988), 9.

[35] Michael J. Kruger, *Canon Revisited* (Wheaton, IL: Crossway, 2012), 106.

[36] Ibid., 107.

[37] See Brown, "Canon Question".

[38] Bruce, *Canon of Scripture*, 281–82.

that Catholics and the Orthodox just don't have the Holy Spirit, centuries of Christian debate prove this criterion too subjective. And by the time I encountered this classical Reformed reasoning, I knew too many such Spirit-filled people. Even if you are willing to bite that bullet,[39] you'd also have to conclude that neither Augustine nor Luther (who will be discussed below) was guided by the Holy Spirit, since neither advocated the current Protestant canon.

This view is a muddle, but what else can a Protestant following the Reformation say? They can't use anything outside of the canon itself lest they imply that it has authority over the canon (thus violating *sola scriptura*).[40] It struck me that Calvin offers a false dilemma: either each believer using the Holy Spirit recognizes the canon, or else the canon rests on mere human authority.[41] Why can't the Holy Spirit guide corporately or institutionally rather than individually? If the canon was determined by men given authority by God, then we do not set these men above God or his Word. They have delegated, but real, authority. If the claim that "human Church leaders with the Holy Spirit discern the canon" places men over God, why doesn't the claim that "individual human beings with the Holy Spirit discern the canon" do so as well? Regardless, this view is ahistorical: the canon was not individualistically determined.

The Catholic View of the Canon

I began to think the Catholic position more congruent with the historical evidence. Jesus left us an institution—people filling offices with derived authority—rather than a book. He singled out Peter first and then gave power to the others. Even taken as just a historical document, the Gospel of Matthew shows Jesus changing Simon Peter's name (a biblical sign of a new mission reminiscent of Abraham

---

[39] Kruger seems willing: Catholics either didn't (don't?) have the Spirit, or else they were (are?) blinded by sin. *Canon Revisited*, 200–201n11. Collins and Walls heavily rely on Kruger's work to defend the current Protestant canon. Given their commitment to ecumenism, however, it is unclear whether they too are willing to accept the implications of Kruger's work. Kenneth J. Collins and Jerry L. Walls, *Roman but Not Catholic* (Grand Rapids, MI: Baker Academic, 2017), 64–70.

[40] Ridderbos, *Redemptive History*, 35. Cf. Herman Bavinck, *Reformed Dogmatics*, ed. John Bolt, trans. John Vriend, 4 vols. (Grand Rapids, MI: Baker Academic, 2003–2008).

[41] John Calvin, *Institutes of the Christian Religion* 1.7.

and Jacob), telling him that he will build his Church "on this rock" (he just changed Simon's name to "Rock"),[42] and giving him special divine authority signaled in (1) the "keys of the kingdom of heaven" and (2) the power to "bind" and "loose".[43] This parallels Isaiah 22:22, where we see keys given to a prime minister or steward who has charge over a house, with the king's full authority, while the king is away.[44] Later in Matthew's Gospel, we see a similar authority given by Jesus to his disciples; he gives them the power to bind and loose.[45] In first-century Judaism, binding and loosing were rabbinical terms conveying the power to make religious law for the community. Binding prohibits, while loosing permits.

Reading this, it struck me for the first time how Peter was singled out first, the only one to receive a new name—how he alone received the keys and was told that Christ himself would build the Church on him, but not the others. I started to study Peter in the Bible more closely and found all sorts of things to which I had previously been blind. I found he was mentioned around two hundred times—more than all the other disciples combined. As a prominent Oxford New Testament scholar remarks, "It is surely significant that Peter is, after Jesus, the most frequently mentioned individual both in the Gospels and in the NT as a whole."[46] I then noticed the *way* the disciples were listed: Peter was constantly first.[47] I thought this a coincidence until I saw Judas constantly last. Even when only the inner circle is mentioned, Peter is consistently first.[48] In fact, Peter is *the first* to witness the Resurrection,[49] to receive Paul,[50] to preach the Gospel,[51] and to perform miracles.[52] He speaks for the apostles[53] so often that even Protestant authors refer to him as the "spokesman for

---

[42] Mt 16:18.

[43] Mt 16:19.

[44] See especially Stephen K. Ray, *Upon This Rock* (San Francisco: Ignatius Press, 1999), 32–41.

[45] Mt 18:18.

[46] Markus Bockmuehl, *Simon Peter in Scripture and Memory* (Grand Rapids, MI: Baker Academic, 2012), 4.

[47] Mt 10:2–4; Mk 3:16–19; Lk 6:14–16; Acts 1:13.

[48] E.g., Mk 5:37.

[49] 1 Cor 15:5. Notice how even John waits for Peter to go into the tomb first (Jn 20:1–10).

[50] Gal 1:18.

[51] Acts 2:14–42.

[52] Acts 3:1–10.

[53] E.g., Mt 16:16; 17:1–8; Mk 10:28; Jn 6:68–69.

the Twelve".[54] And shortly before his Ascension, Jesus again singles out Peter to shepherd his flock.[55] Outside the Bible, Peter's reputation seems so well known that he is commonly listed first in other Christian literature.[56] As Evangelical apologist Sean McDowell notes, knowledge of Peter's preeminence is further confirmed by the voluminous apocryphal works claiming Petrine authorship (Acts of Peter and the Twelve Apostles, the Apocalypse of Peter, the Gospel of Peter, etc.).[57]

I still thought, though, that apostolic authority—along with Peter's preeminence—ended with the apostles. So I studied more. What struck me most was Acts 1. Having seen so much moral and theological disagreement within Protestantism, it seemed to me that it would be great if we had God's ongoing guidance. If anything, we need it more than the first generation of Christians. Acts 1 is crucial, because it shows that the apostles held an *office*. After Judas dies, the remaining apostles replace him. This doesn't make much sense unless there was to be an ongoing lineage—that is, successors of the apostles. I thought this was all made up later, but there it was in the Scriptures. Quoting the psalmist, Peter speaks for them all, saying, "His office let another take."[58] An office is a position multiple people hold over time. So Jesus gave divine authority to his disciples, and they understood this authority as part of an office needing to be filled after death. Matthias was to "take the place in this ministry and apostleship".[59] This all signals ongoing rather than temporary apostolic ministry.

If this is right, then despite the messiness and length of the process, Catholics can have assurance that the texts declared canonical via the continuing apostolic ministry—ultimately the ministry of the Holy Spirit—possess divine authority. The Church discerned the correct list over time because she retained authentic apostolic tradition. She sifted writings according to essential Christian doctrine referred to as

---

[54] E.g., Sean McDowell, *The Fate of the Apostles* (New York: Routledge, 2015), 55.

[55] Jn 21:15–19.

[56] Paul Foster, "Peter in Non-Canonical Traditions", in *Peter in Early Christianity*, ed. Helen K. Bond and Larry W. Hurtado (Grand Rapids, MI: Eerdmans, 2015), 228.

[57] McDowell, *Fate of the Apostles*, 55n3.

[58] Acts 1:20. Peter was quoting Ps 109:8.

[59] Acts 1:25.

"the rule of faith". As even Protestant scholar Bruce Metzger notes, the fundamental prerequisite for canonicity was "congruity of a given document with the basic Christian tradition recognized as normative by the Church".[60] "It was this Rule of Faith against which everything was measured in the second century—even the writings of the developing New Testament," writes another Protestant scholar.[61] Christians were a people with doctrinal unity *long* before any sort of unified Bible emerged. This unity didn't depend solely on the written words of the apostles.[62] In fact, early Church Fathers (Clement of Rome, Irenaeus, and Clement of Alexandria) used "canon" (*kanōn*) to refer to the rule of faith rather than an authoritative collection of Scriptures.[63] The earliest reference to "the new testament" (*he kaine diatheke*) isn't to Scripture but to the covenant expressed in the Eucharist.[64] Christians were a covenant people with orthodox beliefs and practices (baptism, Eucharist, etc.) long before the Bible. The collection of books now known as "the New Testament" were selected by the covenant people, the Church. Evangelical Craig Allert is utterly candid:

> No matter how one looks at the history, it is difficult to maintain that the church had a closed New Testament canon for the first four hundred years of its existence. This means that an appeal to the "Bible" as the early church's sole rule for faith and life is anachronistic.
>
> ... The assertion that these documents forced their way into the canon by virtue of their unique inspiration has little historical support. In our desire to avoid the corrupting influence of tradition, we have often missed the fact that the very Bible we claim to accept as our only guide is itself a product of the very tradition we avoid.[65]

With the discovery that the Church's existence, authority, and basic beliefs preexisted the canon—and that the Church tested books against these preexisting orthodox beliefs to form the canon—holding that

[60] See Bruce M. Metzger, *The Canon of the New Testament* (New York: Oxford University Press, 1987), 251. Cf. Bruce, *Canon of Scripture*, 255, 260.

[61] Allert, *High View of Scripture?*, 125.

[62] Cf. Acts 2:42; 2 Thess 2:15; 3:6; 2 Tim 2:2.

[63] *1 Clement* 7.2, *Against Heresies* 1.22.1, and *Stromata* 4.15.98, respectively.

[64] 1 Cor 11:25.

[65] Allert, *High View of Scripture?*, 144–45.

only the Bible is the rule or measure of orthodoxy no longer seemed tenable.

The Catholic view began to make sense of why differing canonical lists didn't rip the early Church apart. If the apostles left only writings, and we are to be a People of the Book Alone, it is imperative to get the canon right. But Christians weren't in a hurry to settle the canon. "The earliest Christians did not," F. F. Bruce writes, "trouble themselves about criteria of canonicity."[66] Proposed lists were slow in arriving and weren't uniform. Athanasius' *Festal Letter 39* (A.D. 367) is the first to list the full Christian New Testament as canonical.[67] Yet the Church had a way to settle disagreements about the canon while maintaining unity instead of splintering into endless new churches and denominations. The Church's canon begins to be standardized by the late fourth-century councils—Rome (A.D. 382), Hippo (A.D. 393), and Carthage (A.D. 397)—which include the deuterocanonicals. Lest this seem too far after the books were written, note that it took the Jews centuries to deem the various parts of the Old Testament canonical as well.[68] History records no swaths of fourth-century proto-Protestants decrying the supposedly obvious addition of the deuterocanonicals to the sixty-six-book canon. The Orthodox split with the Western Church in 1054 and accept these books. One can find occasional disagreements about the canon, and so the same list was affirmed by the Council of Florence in 1442 (before the Reformation) and by the Council of Trent in 1546 (after the Reformation).[69]

---

[66] Bruce, *Canon of Scripture*, 255.

[67] Allert writes: "Evangelicals generally use Athanasius's New Testament list for support on canonical issues but tend to ignore his Old Testament list, which includes apocryphal books. If he is authoritative for one, why is he not authoritative for the other?" *High View of Scripture?*, 51n39. Allert worries that Evangelicals too quickly paper over the messy history in an attempt to push the date of the canon back as early as possible. Ibid., 74.

[68] Metzger, *Introduction to the Apocrypha*, 7–8. Note well: in some sense there was a canon before 382. Augustine, after all, advocates the Catholic list not because of his private judgment but because of the *sensus fidelium* (the acceptance of the churches). See Augustine, *On Christian Doctrine* 2.8. This is why it is a mistake to claim that Augustine and Jerome were at odds over the canon and Augustine's outsized influence simply won the day over Jerome (the better biblical scholar). See Norman L. Geisler and Ralph E. MacKenzie, *Roman Catholics and Evangelicals* (Grand Rapids, MI: Baker Books, 1995), 169–70.

[69] The Second Council of Nicaea in 787 also technically affirmed it since it acknowledged the conclusions of the Council of Carthage.

Despite all this, Luther, the Reformer I somehow found myself following, placed these seven books in an appendix at the end of his German translation of the Bible. He also segregated Hebrews, James, Jude, and Revelation from what was in his view the real, authoritative New Testament. These books contained doctrines Luther rejected (2 Maccabees 12:38–45 speaks of prayers for the dead and hints at purgatory; James 2:24 says that we are *not* justified by faith alone). So he literally reformed the canon. Realizing that I implicitly followed someone who would do this terrified me. Others later restored the four New Testament books but not the deuterocanonicals (which remained in an appendix).[70] This was the situation for centuries among Protestants. The 1611 King James Bible included the deuterocanonicals, as did other Protestant Bibles, in various languages, for years. I had been completely unaware that "the Apocrypha were included in every major Protestant version of the English Bible from Coverdale [1535] to the Revised Standard Version"[71] in the 1950s and simply faded away—not with a bang but with a whimper. Less than two hundred years ago the British and Foreign Bible Society in London and the American Bible Society, after much debate, began dropping the deuterocanonicals from their printed Bibles.[72] They weren't in my NIV or ESV (English Standard Version). I became irate: What *authority* did Luther, the American Bible Society, or the NIV committee possess?

All this shook me. If Protestantism was mistaken about such a foundational doctrine, what else did it get wrong? History seemed to reveal that the canon neither determined nor preserved itself. Furthermore, having the right Scriptures is only half the battle. My experience in countless Bible-believing churches as well as seeing the way early Church heretics quoted the Scriptures in their defense indicated that even where there is agreement on what Scripture *is*,

---

[70] Luther's canon seems driven not only by doctrinal presuppositions but by a historical mistake: influenced by the Renaissance impulse to get back to the original texts, Luther (mistakenly) assumed that the thirty-nine-book Jewish Masoretic Text available in his day was representative of the Jewish understanding of a closed canon at the time of Christ. Cf. R. Glenn Wooden, "The Role of the 'Septuagint' in the Formation of the Biblical Canons", in Evans and Tov, *Exploring Origins of the Bible*, 136–37.

[71] Bruce, *Canon of Scripture*, 114n32.

[72] Metzger, *Introduction to the Apocrypha*, 201–2.

there need not be agreement on what Scripture *says*. I came to think we need authentic apostolic tradition and living apostolic authority, both to have the right Bible and to read the Bible aright.

The Eucharist

While I was exploring all this, we migrated to a wonderful Evangelical Anglican church in our Alexandria, Virginia, neighborhood. The liturgy moved me. But I began to feel uneasy about communion. It took me a while to figure out the source of unease, but finally I realized that the liturgy seemed parasitic to me (only later did I realize it was based on Roman Catholic liturgy). It seemed like exactly the kind of thing you'd do if you believed that the Eucharist was truly the Body and Blood of Jesus Christ. But Anglicans seemed to allow a variety of opinions on the matter, signaling that they don't think we've received revelation on the matter. I started to worry that, given my Baptist view of communion, I was eating and drinking "without discerning the body".[73] So I refrained for a time and studied more. Many Catholic friends told me to read John 6. I was so stuck in the Evangelical paradigm, however, that I couldn't see it as implying the Real Presence of Christ. I read the chapter over, and over, and over. Then suddenly something clicked, like when you finally see the picture in a Magic Eye drawing. Certain features of the text stood out like never before. In John 6:50–53, Jesus claims we must eat (*phago*) his Flesh. When hearers balked, he could have—but didn't— explained that it was a mere metaphor. Instead, he doubles down, makes it even more graphic, and says in verses 54–58 that we must chew (*trogo*) on his Flesh to have eternal life.

Beyond lending credibility to Catholic doctrine, this experience confirmed for me that we always read Scripture in light of our tradition. So it is imperative to have the right one. I desired to read the Bible with the Church of the ages rather than with a historically young American Evangelical subculture. Reading the Church Fathers on the Eucharist, it was apparent that they would not attend any of the churches of which I had been a part. They struck me as thoroughly

---

[73] I Cor 11:29.

Catholic and committed to the Real Presence of Christ in the Eucharist.[74] I initially dismissed them as already corrupt. But I soon realized that this was to adopt something like the Mormon view of history: anyone can say that at some unspecified time Christianity went astray because it doesn't believe what they teach. Reading the apostolic Fathers confirmed that there isn't some gap where the Church suddenly changed doctrine. Ignatius of Antioch—whose ministry overlaps the apostolic age—could not be clearer that the Eucharist is the true Flesh and Blood of Jesus Christ.[75] In the next century one finds the same teaching from Justin Martyr, Irenaeus, Clement of Alexandria, and Tertullian. Such teachings aren't explained by the accretions of the centuries; they are too early. If Ignatius had radically altered Church teaching, surely he would be rebuffed by the Christian community, who had recently been informed by the apostles themselves. But no such thing happened. And if the disciples' disciples didn't understand Jesus' teachings, what hope do we have?

Reception into the Catholic Church

After much prayer and consideration, my wife and I were increasingly confident that the Catholic Church was founded by Jesus himself. But we had only been to Mass a few times. When we arrived in Waco, Texas, where I would pursue my doctoral studies in philosophy at Baylor University, we met a wonderful priest (who wrote a doctoral dissertation on Baptist theology). When we began to participate in Catholic life, our remaining fears and prejudices dissolved. There we stood; we could do no other. We completed RCIA (Rite of Christian Initiation of Adults) and were joyfully received into the Catholic Church just before Easter of 2010.

This has been the biggest blessing of our Christian lives. While some personal relationships suffered, we have never regretted the decision. Finding not just Jesus but his visible Church has given us

---

[74] For a good summary of what I found, see Tim A. Troutman, "The Church Fathers on Transubstantiation", Called to Communion, December 13, 2010, http://www.calledto communion.com/2010/12/church-fathers-on-transubstantiation/.

[75] *Epistle to the Smyrnaeans* 7.

the radical life for Christ that I wanted so long ago when I thought I had to be a missionary. Life lived according to its ancient wisdom is demanding but rewarding. The consistent ethical teachings on what I previously saw as "nonessentials" (e.g., contraception) are, in hindsight, fundamental to the cruciform life. By the Church's light we are slowly but surely conformed to Christ through the Eucharist, prayer, repentance, and self-sacrifice in our vocations as mother and father of five small boys. *Soli Deo gloria.*

7

A Lutheran's Path to Catholicism

Robert C. Koons

Author's Preface

I wrote the following essay in early 2006 while still a member of the Lutheran Church–Missouri Synod. On the Vigil of Pentecost in 2007 I was formally received into the fellowship of the Roman Catholic Church at the parish of St. Louis the King of France in Austin, Texas. These notes were written with an audience of one (myself) in mind. In writing them, I gave no thought to being diplomatic or irenic. I have decided not to add or revise my comments now that I have joined the Church of Rome. I have left the essay as written by my earlier, Lutheran self.

The essay began as a set of private notes written as a purely intellectual exercise: an attempt to exorcise my doubts about Lutheranism by putting them to paper and exposing them to critique (both on my part and on that of others). As it turned out, the more I wrote, the more reasons I found for changing my outlook. John Henry Newman's book *An Essay on the Development of Doctrine* (1845) is essential background reading, because he provides the decisive rebuttal to the argument that the supremacy of the pope and other contemporary, distinctively Roman Catholic doctrines constitute objectionable "innovations". Newman convincingly argues that the recognition of genuine development in Christian doctrine is inescapable, as anyone who knows the history of the doctrines of the Trinity and the two natures of Christ must recognize.

By the time I wrote the essay in 2006, the other controversial issues (*sola scriptura* vs. the authority of tradition, intercession of the saints, Marian doctrines, the number of sacraments, purgatory) had all resolved themselves in my mind in favor of the Catholic position. *Sola scriptura* never had much attraction for me, because of the obvious logical contradiction at its heart: the Scriptures themselves did not teach *sola scriptura* and never even defined what counts as Scripture. I saw the clear advantages in tradition and in the unity of the Church as anchored in a social institution, the succession of apostolic authority through the bishops. God clearly intended the goal of Church unity,[1] and so he must have intended a means that was proportionate and appropriate to the social nature of human beings, and this must be a continuing institution, and not merely a text or set of abstract propositions. The Protestant principle in the end required each believer to perform a theological task beyond the capacities of any one individual—namely, discerning which church body had correctly interpreted the Bible and established true theological continuity with Jesus and the apostles.

The whole question, therefore, turned for me on the issue of *justification*: the question of how we are made right in our relationship to God, fulfilling the conditions of obtaining eternal life. If the Church of Rome was in error on this central point of the Gospel, then her claim to apostolic authority could not be sustained. If it wasn't in error, then the whole Reformation, with its wrenching destruction of the Church's unity and continuity, was built on a mistake.

The essay should be of relevance to all Protestants, even non-Lutherans. If the original, Lutheran Reformation was predicated upon an error about the nature of justification, this error infected all subsequent reformations, including the Calvinist, Anglican, and Arminian movements, all of which rely heavily on Luther's faith-only doctrine to justify their break with Rome.

Introduction

I have always thought that the doctrine of justification is the crux of the controversy between Lutheranism and Catholicism. If the Roman Church has been in error on this point, even condemning the true

[1] E.g., see Jn 15:1–17; 17:20–25.

understanding of the basis of our righteousness before God, then the Reformation was fully justified. Conversely, if Rome has not been in error, if her position can be charitably interpreted as a faithful exposition of the Gospel and her condemnations (at the Council of Trent) interpreted as the rejection of genuine errors, then the Reformation, which destroyed the visible unity of the Church and broke ancient bonds of fellowship, could not be justified. I take all other issues as secondary: *sola scriptura*, the role of the papacy, purgatory, the veneration and invocation of the saints, and so on.

My rethinking of the issue of justification has been a long process, begun nearly thirty years ago, when I was an undergraduate student. This reflection was intensified in more recent years by the Joint Declaration on the Doctrine of Justification, issued by Lutheran and Roman Catholic theologians in 1999, in which it was argued that the two churches are in agreement on the essential points of this doctrine. In my view, the joint declaration was flawed, relying in places on equivocation and euphemism in place of clarity, but it did help to highlight the fact that the difference on this issue is much subtler than had been generally recognized by Lutherans.

I used to be confident that the teachings of Paul in Romans, Galatians, and Ephesians made it quite clear that the Roman position on justification was fundamentally wrong. I've come to have serious doubts about this, however, based in part on recent scholarship about Paul's writings (including especially the work of N. T. Wright[2]), and partly on a better understanding of exactly what the Roman Church teaches. In addition, I've come to the conclusion that the Lutheran position on justification is an unstable one, incorporating at least one fatal self-contradiction.

1. The Burden of Proof

When I was a college student, a friend of mine invited me to join a group that was reading together some of the works of the Church

[2] N. T. Wright, *Paul: In Fresh Perspective* (Minneapolis: Fortress Press, 2005); Magnus Zetterholm, *Approaches to Paul: A Student's Guide to Recent Scholarship* (Minneapolis: Fortress Press, Minneapolis, 2009).

Fathers—they were reading Cyprian when I joined them. This was a deeply disturbing experience for me, one from which I have never fully recovered. For I found that, contrary to my expectations, the early Fathers sounded much more Roman than proto-Lutheran. Further reading of the Patristics when at Oxford and more recently has only confirmed this impression. It is clear beyond all reasonable doubt to me that Luther's, and by extension all of Protestantism's, teaching on justification, insofar as it differs from Roman Catholic theology, was truly novel. It was not simply the recovery of the Augustinian or pre-Scholastic doctrine of the Church; it was an unprecedented innovation. If correct, Luther was the first major theologian to recover the true meaning of Paul's epistles.

Many Lutherans have disputed this charge of innovation. This raises an issue of fundamental importance. Can the Lutheran doctrine of justification be found in the Fathers? Here we must resist the temptation to engage in what scientists call "cherry-picking" the data—citing proof texts in which Church Fathers insist that we are saved by faith and by the merits of Christ. These points aren't the ones in dispute. The crucial issue is this: Is the righteousness by which the justified are justified an "alien" righteousness—as Luther and many subsequent Protestants would have it—the righteousness of Christ entirely outside of us (*extra nos*) and apart from regeneration and the new kind of life that results? I cannot find this idea defended anywhere before Luther. If we look at the corpus of Fathers who are typically cited by Lutherans—Clement of Rome, Ambrose, Basil, John Chrysostom, Augustine—we find that they all give to regeneration and to the fruits of the Spirit a role to play in our justification. In short, we find the Fathers affirming what Lutherans affirm, but not denying what Lutherans deny, and it is the denials rather than the affirmations that are in dispute in the conflict between Rome and the Lutherans. This point is admitted by both second-generation Lutheran Reformer and theologian Martin Chemnitz (1522–1586) and by Robert Preus, in Preus' more recent book, *Justification and Rome*.[3]

---

[3] Martin Chemnitz, *Justification: The Chief Article of Christian Doctrine as Expounded in Loci Theologici*, trans. J. A. O. Preus (St. Louis: Concordia Publishing House, 1985); and Robert D. Preus, *Justification and Rome* (St. Louis: Concordia Publishing House, 1997).

An egregious example of cherry-picking from the Fathers is found in German Lutheran Reformer Philipp Melanchthon's (1497–1560) quotations from St. Augustine's *On the Spirit and the Letter*.[4] Melanchthon, in his *Apology of the Augsburg Confession* (one of the official Lutheran confessions), picks out a few, brief excerpts from this text, arguing that they establish that the Lutheran doctrine of justification by faith alone (apart from love) is no innovation but is wholly continuous with Augustinian theology. To read the entirety of Augustine's *On the Spirit and the Letter* after reading Melanchthon is shocking: in that work, Augustine explicitly rejects the very doctrine that Melanchthon claims to find there. For example, in chapter 18, St. Augustine writes:

> It is called the righteousness of God, because *by His bestowal of it He makes us righteous*, just as we read that "salvation is the Lord's," because He makes us safe.... By this faith of Jesus Christ—that is, the faith which Christ has given us—we believe it is from God that we now have, and shall have more and more, *the ability of living righteously*; wherefore we give Him thanks. (emphasis added)[5]

By grace through faith, God makes us righteous, enabling us to live righteously and thereby to stand in a right relationship with God. As St. Augustine explains in chapter 46, "Belonging to the new testament means having the law of God not written on tables, but on the heart,—that is, *embracing the righteousness of the law with innermost affection, where faith works by love* (Gal. 5:6)" (emphasis added). In contrast, Melanchthon interprets Augustine (in article 2 of the *Apology*) as *denying* that justification is the product of a "formed faith" that includes the love of God infused in us by grace. The gap between the plain sense of Augustine's text and Melanchthon's construction of it is so great that I found my confidence in Melanchthon's good faith as a scholar and teacher badly shaken.

The early Church (e.g., St. Ignatius and St. Ireneaus) taught that orthodox teaching is built on three pillars: the apostolic succession,

---

[4] Philipp Melanchthon, "The Apology of the Augsburg Confession", in *Concordia or Book of Concord: The Symbols of the Evangelical Lutheran Church*, trans. W. H. T. Dau and F. Bente (St. Louis: Concordia Publishing House, 1922), 40–41.

[5] St. Augustine, *On the Spirit and the Letter*, www.newadvent.org/fathers/1502.htm.

the consistent rule of faith, and the Holy Scriptures. Lutherans have intentionally set aside at least one of the three pillars of orthodoxy (the consensus of the apostolic bishops) and effectively disregarded the second (the rule of faith, reflected in the unanimous testimony of the Fathers), in favor of the third alone, the Scriptures. This can be defended only if the testimony of the Scriptures on the disputed points is unambiguous and unmistakable.

There is a real tension in the Lutheran position, which holds, on the one hand, that the doctrine of justification is the "article on which the Church stands or falls", and which also asserts, in defending infant baptism, that the Church has existed continuously from the time of the apostles. Given that we cannot find the Lutheran doctrine of justification among the pre-Reformation Church Fathers, we must conclude either that this doctrine is not essential to the Gospel or that the Church literally ceased to exist until revived at the time of the Reformation. The latter thesis is both in conflict with the Lutheran Confessions (especially Luther's defense of infant baptism in the Large Catechism[6]) and in conflict with Jesus' promise to be with the Church until the very end.[7]

This tension could be put in another way. The Lutheran church accepts the New Testament canon—that is, the selection of books that the New Testament contains, in accordance with the consensus of the Church as it developed over the first four centuries. Although Luther had some doubt about the epistle of James, this doubt was explicitly rejected by the authoritative confessions of the Lutheran church. Both Lutherans and Roman Catholics agree that it is not the authority of the Church that makes an inspired text canonical; both also agree that the testimony of the Church is a reliable guide to which books were in fact inspired. At the same time, however, Lutherans must hold that the early Church during this period was hopelessly confused about the central doctrine contained in the canonical books (from the Lutheran perspective)—namely, the doctrine of justification by faith alone. Thus, Lutherans are in the awkward position of holding that the early Church was wholly reliable in recognizing

---

[6] See Martin Luther, *Luther's Large Catechism*, trans. J. N. Lender (Minneapolis: Augsburg, 1967), 132.

[7] Mt 28:20.

which books were inspired and yet wholly unreliable in understanding what those books were saying. This seems inconsistent: How could the Church reliably recognize a book as God's Word without accurately understanding its meaning?

The Gospel of John gives us good reason to expect the Church to be both thoroughly orthodox and visibly united. The members of the Church are commanded to "love one another",[8] which presupposes a kind of visible unity (in particular, in the form of Eucharistic unity, i.e., fellowship in what the early Church called the *agape* meal). Jesus prays that the Father would sanctify them (plural) in the truth of his Word,[9] and he prays that all who believe in him "may become perfectly one"—visibly one, so that the world might believe in Christ.[10] It is only through the apostolic succession, centered in the successor of Peter in Rome, that the Church has been able to maintain both doctrinal discipline and global Eucharistic unity. History demonstrates that churches following the Protestant principle must sacrifice either one or the other: either choosing doctrinal purity over unity (conservatives) or choosing unity over purity (liberals and latitudinarians). Only through a visible authority (popes and councils) able to bring controversies to a decisive conclusion can the Church realize both of Christ's stated intentions for her.

2. The Question of Justification

2.1 What exactly is at issue

The greatest difficulty in understanding the controversy over justification is sorting out the different meanings that the two sides attach to the words "justification", "grace", and "faith". All three words are understood in two fundamentally different ways.

This variation in meaning greatly complicates the discussion, making it seem that the two sides agree when they do not, and that they do not agree when they do. Thus, both sides will affirm that we are

[8] Jn 15:17.
[9] Jn 17:19.
[10] Jn 17:23; see 17:21–22.

"justified by grace alone", but they mean quite different things. Similarly, Lutherans affirm that we are justified through faith alone, while Catholics deny this, but this superficial disagreement fails entirely to capture the substance of the issue, since the two sides are not affirming and denying the same thing by the phrase "justification through faith alone".

Rome teaches that final salvation is by infused virtue (including charity), and not through full doctrinal assent (i.e., "faith") alone. Lutherans teach that reconciliation and acceptance by God are by undeserved favor through personal trust alone. Is there a disagreement here? As I understand it, Rome does not deny what Lutherans teach. Nor do Lutherans teach that our final salvation is by means of doctrinal assent alone. So far, no disagreement.

In addition, Rome teaches that salvation is the normally expected result of faith (understood in the narrow sense of doctrinal assent). In the Council of Trent, faith is described as the root and foundation of justification. Consequently, Rome has no difficulty with passages that describe salvation or justification as the result of faith.[11] Nor is there any real disagreement on the question of whether all believers (understood by both Catholics and Lutherans to mean all who persevere in faith until death) will be saved. Rome teaches that sanctification is the natural result of persistence in faith (assuming a regular participation in the sacraments, the means of grace), and Lutherans agree that saving faith is always accompanied by good works. Thus, "he who believes and is baptized will be saved",[12] "he who endures to the end will be saved",[13] and God "will render to every man according to his works".[14] The disagreement lies, as we shall see, not in a dispute about which class of people will be saved, but about what the basis or ultimate reason for their justification consists in.

Rome teaches that we must "merit" eternal life, but that we can do so only by means of the infused virtue of grace, not by means of our own unaided efforts. Lutherans teach that we obtain eternal life only by having Christ's righteousness applied to us through an

[11] E.g., Jn 3:16; Rom 10:10; Eph 2:8.
[12] Mk 16:16.
[13] Mt 24:13.
[14] Rom 2:6.

external justification. For Lutherans, our own inherent qualities and
the actions that flow from them are completely irrelevant to our right
standing before God, even when those qualities in us are the direct
result of divine help.

When Roman theologians speak of our supernatural virtues or
our supernaturally inspired works as "meriting" eternal life and other
blessings, they do not mean to imply that eternal life is earned. In fact,
traditional Catholic theology, following the Scholastics, has insisted
that an action or attribute's merit need not have anything to do with
its inherent moral or ethical quality. Rather, a human act or attribute
"merits" reward when God, out of his gracious mercy, has promised
freely to provide a reward to actions or attributes of that type.[15] As
Alister McGrath notes, the later Scholastic theologians understood
merit in an ontological or causal sense (as that which acts as a means
of God's grace), rather than in an ethical, forensic, or judicial sense.[16]
So if we translate Lutheran theology into Catholic language, we could
legitimately say that our faith in Christ "merits" justification, and that
the means of grace (the Word and sacraments) "merit" the remission of
sins. Baptism merits regeneration, the remission of sins and the gift
of the Spirit, not because there is any inherent quality in the event of
being baptized, but solely because of God's promise.

Here's another attempt at isolating the issue: Lutherans insist that
Christ's righteousness is "imputed" to us forensically, in such a way
that we are deemed to be righteous before God despite our inherent
sinfulness, and that it is this merely imputed righteousness, and nothing inherent in us, that justifies us before God. To this, the obvious
question is, if an omnipotent God "imputes" Christ's righteousness
to us, must this not make us really (i.e., inherently) righteous? When
God said, "Let there be light," there was light. Similarly, if God says,
"Let this Christian be righteous," must not this declaration make the
Christian really righteous? To this, orthodox Lutherans answer, in

---

[15] This is a point on which the otherwise very reliable Norman Geisler and Ralph Mac-
Kenzie fall into error. They consistently interpret "merit" as meaning "partially earns", without providing any evidence for the correctness of this interpretation. Norman L. Geisler and
Ralph E. MacKenzie, *Roman Catholics and Evangelicals* (Grand Rapids, MI: Baker Academic,
1995).

[16] Alister McGrath, *Iustitia Dei: A History of the Christian Doctrine of Justification*, 3rd ed.
(Cambridge: Cambridge University Press, 2005), 143.

one voice, Yes! So, there is a real righteousness in us that is effected by God's imputation to believers of Christ's own righteousness, and this inherent righteousness is something distinct from Christ's righteousness (since it is in us, and not in Christ). However, Lutherans insist that we are not *justified* by this inherent righteousness, but only (objectively speaking) by Christ's righteousness and (subjectively speaking) by our faith in Christ. And on the latter point Catholics differ, insisting that the subjective side of our right standing before God is a genuine, internal righteousness that is the effect of infused grace. This is the heart of the issue. Who is right? Let's look first at the case for the Lutheran side (in sections 2.2 through 2.6).

2.2 Justification as forensic

Lutherans commonly appeal to the fact that the word "justify" in the Greek is primarily forensic in character—that is, it means to be declared or considered righteous, not to be made intrinsically righteous.

However, Rome does not deny that we are, at our conversion, forensically declared righteous (and thereby adopted as God's children and incorporated into Christ) through our faith alone. Our initial justification (which the Council of Trent refers to as "the justification of the impious"[17]) results in a new status, a new standing before God, as well as the infusion into our hearts of the Holy Spirit and his gifts of grace. What Roman Catholics deny is that the whole process of salvation ends with this forensic declaration and new status.

In fact, Lutherans don't really deny this, since Lutherans agree that all the saints in heaven will be intrinsically sinless. More importantly, Lutherans agree that the imputed righteousness given to faith in this life is not a mere fiction or supposition. When God declares someone righteous, the object of his declaration becomes, immediately, truly righteous as a result. In his *Disputation concerning Justification* (1536), Luther writes, "This imputation is not a thing of no consequence"; it is not a "game or delusion".[18] As the seventeenth-century Lutheran theologian Johannes Andreas Quenstedt put it,

---

[17] Council of Trent, Sixth Session, Decree on Justification, chaps. 4, 7, and 8.

[18] Martin Luther, "Disputation on Justification", in *Luther's Works*, vol. 34 of *Career of the Reformer*, trans. and ed. Lewis W. Smith (Philadelphia: Muhlenberg Press, 1960), 167.

the imputation is "most real" (*realissima*), because it is an exercise of God's infallible word.[19] Lutherans deny, however, that this real righteousness involves a "grafting or indwelling"[20]—that is, that the righteousness dwells in us "formally and intrinsically".[21] This aspect of Lutheran teaching is one that is difficult to make sense of, accounting for the fact that Lutherans are often misrepresented as teaching that imputed righteousness is merely a fiction. If God's declaration of our righteousness is necessarily effective, with the result that we are really righteous, how can it be that the righteousness does not in any sense dwell "within" us? If I really have an attribute (of righteousness), it is standard practice to say that that attribute is "in" me. What do Lutherans mean by denying this?

I think there are two closely related possibilities. First, let us look closely at what Luther writes in his 1535 *Commentary on Galatians*:

> Christ and my conscience become one body. Turning to myself and looking into myself, into what I am and ought to be and do, I lose sight of Christ, who alone is my righteousness and my life ... works, which only compel us to look to ourselves again, and turn our eyes from that brazen serpent, Christ crucified.[22]

Similarly, in a sermon in 1532, Luther writes:

> I feel in myself nothing but sin; and yet I am righteous and holy, not in myself, but in Christ Jesus who of God is made for me wisdom and righteousness and sanctification and redemption.[23]

In describing the righteousness we have in Christ as "alien" and "outside of us" (*extra nos*), Luther is pointing to the fact that this imputed

---

[19] *Systema*, Par I, Cap 8, 5, 2, q5. See Preus, *Justification and Rome*, 71–76, for more examples.

[20] Friedrich Balduin, *Commentarius in omnis Epistulas Beati Apostoli Pauli* (Frankfurt am Main: Ex officina Zumnneriana, typis Johannis Philippi Andreae, 1710), 78.

[21] Johann Andreas Quenstedt, *Theologia Didactico-Polemica Sive Systema Theologicum*, Par I, Cap 8, 5, q1 (Keipzig: Thomam Fritsch, 1715).

[22] Martin Luther, *Commentary on the Epistle to the Galatians*, in *Luther's Works*, ed. J. Pelikan (St. Louis: Concordia Publishing, 1963), 166.

[23] Martin Luther, "Sermon for the Feast of the Beheading of John the Baptist", 1532, in *Dr. M. Luthers Sämmtliche Werke*, vol. 6 (Frankfurt am Main und Erlangen: Verlag Heyder und Zimmer, 1826–1857), 281–82 (my translation).

righteousness is not introspectible or internally "feelable". We do not find it by looking within, by examining our own consciousness or our works, but only by looking to Christ. Thus, it is "in" us in one sense, ontologically and metaphysically speaking, but it is "outside of" of us in another sense, epistemologically and phenomenologically (that is, in terms of our knowledge and conscious experience, respectively). That Luther takes the righteousness of Christ to be in us ontologically is clear from his reference to the "inseparable union and conjunction I have with Him through faith ... through faith you are so closely joined together with Christ that you and He are made one person."[24] If my reader will indulge me in the use of a little philosophical jargon, I would say that Luther and his followers made the understandable error of *ontologizing the phenomenology of faith*—that is, of inferring that what is true of our experience is necessarily true of the underlying reality. It is true that we experience Christ's righteousness as something external to us, aware as we are of our own failings. Nonetheless, we ought to believe that we are really united to Christ in such a way that his righteousness is now internal to us and not merely externally imputed (as Luther thought).

A second related reason that Lutherans deny that imputed righteousness is not wholly intrinsic to the believer is that, on this model, righteousness essentially involves an extrinsic relationship to Christ. It is only because faith relates us to Christ that we are really righteous. Whatever state is internal to us counts as righteousness only because of this external connection to Christ. This answer is connected to the first, since it explains why the imputed righteousness can't be seen by introspection, but only by looking outward toward Christ.

What differences there are between the Catholic and Lutheran views on justification are subtle, as the preceding discussion should make clear. So it may be useful to make an equally subtle distinction—namely, between righteousness as an *internal* reality and as an *intrinsic* fact. Since we become really righteous as a result of God's imputation to us of Christ's righteousness, this righteousness is (ontologically speaking) an internal reality. However, it is not (wholly) an intrinsic fact about us, as though the internal reality would constitute righteousness before God on its own, apart from any connection to

[24] Luther, *Commentary on the Epistle to the Galatians*, 166f.

Christ. Given this distinction, the position of Lutherans and Catholics can be fully reconciled: both can agree that there is an internal righteousness that results from the imputation of Christ's righteousness to us, but that we are not thereby intrinsically righteous (autonomously, apart from our union to Christ).[25] Here is how the *Catechism of the Catholic Church* puts it:

> *The charity of Christ is the source in us of all our merits* (emphasis in original) before God. Grace, by *uniting us to Christ* (emphasis added) in active love, ensures the supernatural quality of our acts and consequently their merit before God and before men.[26]

The distinction between internal and intrinsic is not mere hairsplitting. Consider, for example, the fact of being married. One cannot be married without an appropriate internal state: one must know what is happening during the marriage ceremony and intend to be married in order for marriage to take place. For example, if someone participates in a marriage ceremony, thinking that he is merely rehearsing a play, a valid marriage does not result. At the same time, a marriage is not a *wholly intrinsic* fact: merely intending to be married or believing that one is married is not enough to constitute a true marriage. Marriage is partly constituted by external facts: a relation to one's spouse and to a valid public ceremony. In the same way, justification is constituted by an extrinsic relationship to Christ and his righteousness, but this state of justification must also correspond to a genuine internal reality.

Fiat currency provides another analogy. What makes a piece of paper hold the value of one dollar? Unlike a bar of gold, the value of a dollar bill is extrinsic: it possesses the value it does by virtue of its relation to external facts, including the fact that it was printed by a press authorized for this purpose by the Federal Reserve. At the same time, its value also depends on certain internal characteristics. A bill that has been reduced to ashes or pulp is no longer legal tender.

The only dispute between Roman Catholics and Lutherans concerns the exact nature of this internal reality: Does it consist at all

---

[25] See also the excellent work Christopher Malloy, *Engrafted into Christ: A Critique of the Joint Declaration* (New York: Peter Lang, 2005).

[26] *Catechism of the Catholic Church*, no. 2011.

times of a mere attitude of "faith" alone (understood as confidence in God's mercy) that could not be considered to be in itself a form of righteous living at all, as Lutherans have typically taught, or does it consist of a grace-propelled progression into a condition of active love, as suggested by Roman Catholicism?

Both sides agree that some internal state (whether faith alone, or love and the acts that flow from it) constitutes righteousness before God only because it unites us with Christ. Of course, an obvious difference remains: Is it our faith alone that unites us with Christ (Lutherans), or does the love that is poured into our hearts and the resulting works of love also play some role (Roman Catholics)?

Lutherans argue that Roman Catholics have confused justification itself from the fruits of justification. Lutherans identify our regeneration (including our new capacity to love God and neighbor) as a *fruit* or result of justification. On the Lutheran view, our regeneration does not unite us with Christ: regeneration is rather the result of justification, and the latter—a consequence of faith by itself—unites us with Christ.[27] However, there are strong grounds for thinking that it is really the Lutherans who are confused here. We should distinguish between that which God's imputation *effects* and that which it *causes*. Employing this language, I would say that Oswald's killing of JFK *effected* JFK's death; it did not *cause* it. Why not? Oswald's killing of JFK (as opposed, say, to Oswald's shooting of him) *includes* JFK's death as an essential part: Oswald's killing of JFK was not complete until JFK had actually died. The effects of Oswald's killing of JFK (the things that it caused) include, not JFK's death, but the ramifications of that death, including the escalation of the Vietnam War. In a similar way, imputation effects our regeneration; it does not cause it. Our new birth is not some remote consequence of our justifying faith. Rather, our regeneration is an *essential part* of God's imputation of Christ's righteousness to us; it is not merely the fruit of that imputation.

Both sides also agree that justification is inseparable from regeneration and the gift of the Holy Spirit. On the Catholic view, regeneration and justification are one and the same action, described from the point

---

[27] Strictly speaking, this language choice only fits later Lutheran thought. In both the *Augsburg Confession* and in Melanchthon's *Apology*, the terms "justification" and "regeneration" are often used interchangeably. For example, in article 4 of the *Apology*, Melanchthon explicitly identifies justification with the effecting of regeneration.

of view of the patient—namely, a person (regeneration) or the agent: namely, God (justification). Lutherans came to insist (at the time of the Formula of Concord in 1577) that justification and regeneration are separate actions (Formula of Concord, *Solid Declaration* 3.19), the latter being merely the fruit of the former (although this distinction is not drawn in the Augsburg Confession or in Melanchthon's *Apology*). I don't find this separation taught anywhere in the Scriptures or in the Fathers. It's a Lutheran innovation. Ironically, the Lutheran insistence that regeneration follows justification by faith commits Lutherans to a kind of Pelagianism, since they ignore the fact that only the regenerate can trust God—that is, the official Lutheran doctrine (of the 1577 *Solid Declaration*) implies that one who is unregenerate (and so living without the benefit of grace) can attain a saving faith in God by his own, unaided efforts, with the infusion of grace that constitute regeneration occurring only as a consequence of one's autonomous act of faith. This is analogous to the heresy of Pelagius, who taught that unregenerate human beings could, without grace, attain a condition of righteousness on their own. The Council of Trent teaches, in contrast, that conversion is impossible apart from grace, a thesis also vigorously affirmed by earlier Reformers, including Luther.

However, isn't it through *faith alone* that regeneration occurs in the first place? In a sense, yes, and the Roman Catholic Church agrees: the Council of Trent taught that faith is the "beginning", "root", and "foundation" of our justification. Moreover, since nothing else is described in this way, Trent taught that faith alone is the root and foundation of justification: it is that *one* juncture with Christ through which all of the blessings of his life, death, and Resurrection flow to the believer. Thus, there is one sense in which the Council of Trent, like the Lutheran Book of Concord, teaches that we are justified by faith alone: faith plays a unique, foundational role in our justification. However, once conversion has taken place, the "imputation" of Christ's righteousness through faith essentially includes the *infusion* of the charity of God in our hearts, which then plays a causal role in maintaining our union with Christ. Consider, for example, Ephesians 2:8–9:

> For by grace you have been saved [*note*: past perfect tense] through faith; and this is not your own doing, it is the gift of God—not because of works, lest any man should boast.

This passage from Ephesians refers to a past event that is already fully completed: our conversion, introduction to grace, what I referred to earlier as our "first justification". This first justification is through faith alone. However, the state of justification does not *consist* solely of our faith in Christ: it includes essentially the regeneration of the heart that is effected by God's imputation of righteousness to the believer. That this is so was conceded by Melanchthon's identification of *justification* and *regeneration* in the *Apology*, and by Luther's identification of justification with that *union* and *conjunction* of the believer with Christ that faith effects.

The righteousness that is both imputed to us and infused into us is Christ's own righteousness. Christ's righteousness was not an extrinsic matter: it surely included Christ's love for God and for people, his willing obedience to God, and his patient acceptance of suffering. If this very righteousness is imputed to us by God's declaration, then the righteousness we thereby acquire must be (at least in part) an internal affair—that is, we must have some share in Christ's love for God and for people. And thus our justification must include our regeneration, the gift of the Spirit, and the indwelling of Christ himself,[28] since it is only by our regeneration that we might have a genuine, internal sharing in Christ's righteousness.

Moreover, if purely extrinsic righteousness were enough, why do we not remain both saints and sinners in heaven? Surely it is because there is something incompatible between sin and eternal blessedness. In order to enjoy the gift of heaven, we must at some point be purged of our sin, made fit for God's presence. Even on the Lutheran view, the "imputation" of Christ's righteousness gives all the actual resources (most crucially, the gift of the Holy Spirit) needed to complete the process of sanctification. This is why, in Hebrews 10:14, we are told that Christ has already perfected us (past tense) who are being sanctified (present tense).

The core of the Lutheran position, then, seems to be that this internal transformation (i.e., our final glorification) must be deferred and occur instantaneously and willy-nilly only at the death of the believer—with no active cooperation by us being involved at any point in the process. Lutherans in effect insist that sanctification has nothing to do with glorification—we are all equally and immediately

---

[28] Gal 2:20.

glorified at death, regardless of how far our sanctification has progressed, and this final step requires no cooperation or suffering on our part. What is the scriptural basis for this claim? The only passage that comes close is Jesus' word to the thief in the cross: "Today you will be with me in Paradise."[29] However, it is dangerous to generalize from one example. It may be that the thief completed the process of sanctification through patiently enduring his torturous death on the cross. Moreover, this verse doesn't teach that the thief will be instantly perfected at the moment of death: the "today" of Christ's promise is consistent with an interval of time. Additionally, in opposition to the Lutheran notion of instantaneous glorification at death, there is the passage in 1 Corinthians 3, in which Paul teaches that those who have built with straw will enter eternal life "as through fire" (v. 15), certainly suggesting something like a purgative process.

The Lutheran conception of glorification embodies a kind of Manichaeanism, wrongly identifying our sinfulness with our physical bodies (as did the Persian prophet Mani and his followers in the early centuries A.D.). Lutheran theologians assume that the death of our mortal bodies will, all by itself, free us forever from the propensity to sin, as though sin's reality in our lives is grounded entirely in our physical aspects. In fact, Paul uses the word "flesh" (*sarx*) to refer to aspects of our lives that are entirely mental, intellectual, and spiritual in nature (such as envy or pride).[30] If our soul is still "fleshly" at death, the mere separation of that soul from our bodies will not suffice to correct its disordered state: a process of purification after death will be required.

The Lutheran position depends on a strict distinction between justification (a change in status) and sanctification (a gradual, internal change). However, Lutherans read this distinction into, rather than out of, the Scriptures. In many places, the words "sanctify" and "renew" are used interchangeably with "justify" and "save".[31]

2.3 Grace as favor vs. grace as gift

Lutherans insist that the grace by which we are saved is the undeserved favor of God, granted to us for Christ's sake, while Roman

[29] Lk 23:43.
[30] See Rom 7:25; 8:1–13; Gal 3:3; 5:16–25; 6:8.
[31] E.g., Acts 26:17–18; 1 Cor 6:11; 2 Thess 2:13; Heb 10:10, 13–14; 13:12; 1 Pet 1:1–2.

Catholics insist that grace is primarily a gift: the gift of the Holy Spirit, and of the "habitual grace" that the Spirit produces in the believer's life, especially the supernatural virtues of faith, hope, and love.

The word "grace" (*charis*) in the New Testament seems to carry both meanings.[32] Thus the repeated emphasis in Paul's letters that we are "saved by grace" does not clearly support the Lutheran position.

2.4 Faith, not works or human merit

Lutherans appeal to Paul's teaching that there is a contradiction between being saved by faith and being saved by "works of the law".[33] The main problem here is that Luther's interpretation seems to involve an extrapolation from the text. The "works of the law" that Paul most clearly has in mind is circumcision, an external sign required by the Old Covenant. Read strictly, Paul is saying that we are not justified by any works of the Torah (the law of the Sinai covenant), including (but not limited to) works related to the ceremonial aspects of that law. Luther extrapolates this Pauline doctrine to exclude from our justification any human actions whatsoever. Paul's central concern (as N. T. Wright has argued[34]) throughout Romans 3 and 4 and the book of Galatians is to secure the equality of Jews and Gentiles by insisting that fulfilling the law of Moses, which effected the complete separation of the Jews from the Gentile world through circumcision and the kosher regulations, is not in any sense a prerequisite for introduction into the grace of Christ.[35]

The standard Lutheran response[36] is to point to Romans 7:7, in which the commandment against coveting is given as an example of what the law demands. This is certainly a moral, and not merely a ceremonial or ritual, requirement. Here, Lutherans follow Augustine's interpretation of Paul and reject St. Jerome's suggestion that the

---

[32] Meaning favor: Rom 3:24; 4:4; 5:20, 21; 6:1, 14, 15; 11:5, 6; Gal 1:6; 2:21; Eph 1:7; 2:7–8; 2 Thess 2:16; 2 Tim 1:9; Tit 3:7; 1 Pet 1:13; 2:20; Jude 1:4. Meaning help: Acts 14:26; 20:32; Rom 1:5; 12:3, 6; 2 Cor 1:15; 8:4, 6–7; 12:9; Gal 2:9; Eph 3:8; 4:7, 29; 2 Tim 2:1; Heb 4:16; 12:15; 13:9; Jas 4:6; 1 Pet 4:10; 5:5; 2 Pet 3:18.

[33] Rom 3:20; Gal 2:16; 3:10.

[34] N. T. Wright, *What St. Paul Really Said* (Grand Rapids, MI: Eerdmans, 1997). See also E. P. Sanders, *Paul and Palestinian Judaism* (Minneapolis: Fortress Press, 1977), and James D. G. Dunn, *The New Perspective on Paul* (Minneapolis: Fortress Press, 2005).

[35] See Rom 3:28–31; Gal 3:17.

[36] Found already in Melanchthon's *Apology*, for example.

phrase "works of the law" be understood in Paul's writings as limited to the ceremonial law of Sinai.

Lutherans and Roman Catholics agree that it was Augustine, and not Jerome, who had the better interpretation. Paul certainly meant to include the moral law, and not merely the ceremonial law, in insisting that we are justified by faith, apart from the works of the law. However, we must pay close attention to Paul's use of "work" and "law" in these passages. It is significant that Paul uses the word "work" (*ergon*) here. Paul consistently talks of the "works of the flesh"[37] as opposed to the "fruit [*karpos*] of the Spirit".[38] A "work" of the law would seem to be more than just acting in accordance with or fulfilling the law. By associating "work" and "law" with "flesh",[39] Paul seems to be defining a "work of the law" as something that is

1. an autonomous act of an independent self,
2. natural,
3. entirely under one's own exclusive control,
4. having a self-contained value that places God under an obligation to repay one,[40]
5. a value that is obvious and measurable in human terms, and
6. a finite value, unable to compensate for the guilt of sin (and so entailing the necessity of perfect compliance with the law).

The fruit of the Spirit, in contrast, is

1. wholly the work of God in us,
2. supernatural in quality,
3. a matter of cooperation between the individual and the Spirit,
4. having a value that depends on its connection to Christ and his merits, with the result that any reward it receives is the result of a free promise, not a natural debt,
5. a value that is hidden and mysterious, beyond human judgment, and
6. a value that is infinite, overwhelming, and negating the guilt of our daily sins.

[37] Gal 5:19.
[38] Gal 5:22.
[39] Rom 3:20; 8:3; Gal 2:16; 3:2–3.
[40] Rom 4:4.

This distinction corresponds roughly, but not perfectly, to a temporal distinction: before and after conversion. All of our attempts to justify ourselves prior to conversion to Christ will fall into the first category, works of the law. In general, the good we do after conversion, when moved by the Holy Spirit and regenerated by Christ's own life, will fall into the second category. However, as Paul's Letter to the Galatians demonstrates, it is possible for Christians to fall back into a purely law-based system, seeking to replace self-effort and the letter of the law for God's grace and the leading of the Spirit.

Roman Catholics interpret these passages as teaching that we are justified, not by our outward actions, but by the fruit of the Spirit, including the inner quality of our heart (which is certainly a theme of Jesus and of the later prophets). Moreover, this inner quality is not something we have created ourselves—it is an unearned gift infused into us by God's grace for Christ's sake. In addition, the quality and its value cannot be separated from Christ and his merits: the inner quality is the very life of Christ within us, and the quality merits salvation only by uniting us to Christ and his merits, not by virtue of any natural or intrinsic power or virtue in them. This inner quality is, in the first instance, the virtue of faith, but it also encompasses hope (trust) and love or charity. As Paul himself teaches, we are justified by "faith working through love".[41]

The Roman Catholic language of "merit" can lend itself to confusion here, especially to those raised in a Lutheran environment. Roman theologians distinguish two kinds of "merit": condign and congruous. There is, theoretically, a third kind of merit, which I will call "absolute" or "strict" merit. "Absolute" merit would be the kind of righteousness that would compel God, by virtue of strict justice and apart from any economy of gracious promises, to accept us as worthy of eternal life. Roman theologians, following Aquinas, simply deny that human creatures can claim any such absolute merit.[42] As absolutely sovereign, God cannot be bound in strict justice to any of his creatures, so no one can claim absolute merit before God. For this reason, Roman Catholics do not speak of our "earning"

---

[41] Gal 5:6.

[42] See *Catechism of the Catholic Church*, no. 2007. See also McGrath, *Iustitia Dei*, 143–44, and St. Thomas Aquinas, *Summa Theologiae* I–II, q. 114, a. 1.

our salvation, and they can agree with Paul that salvation cannot be thought of as wages earned by work done: for the "one who works, his wages are not reckoned as a gift but as his due."[43]

Condign merit presupposes the order of grace but implies, within that order, a correspondence between the work done and the reward received, due to God's explicit promise. *Congruous* merit refers to a kind of value that God chooses to reward in ad hoc fashion, apart from any promise to do so. This distinction corresponds to another difference between the two forms of merit: condign merit attaches to the fruits of divine grace in the already-being-justified Christian, while congruous merit pertains to acts performed outside the scope of grace. There is a certain fitness or appropriateness to God's respecting acts of congruous merit, but he is not bound to do so by the promises inherent in the Gospel itself. The notion of contiguous merit is of great importance, since it exonerates God from the charge of being utterly arbitrary and capricious in the distribution of justifying grace.

Correcting the errors of some of the nominalists (like Ockham and Biel) to whom the Reformers had rightly objected, the Council of Trent clearly denied that human beings are able to merit in the strict sense (condignly) their own conversion to faith (which I have called "first justification").[44] According to Trent, we are able (after regeneration) to merit condignly further increases in grace, and ultimately eternal life itself. However, the equality between merit and reward depends ultimately on the fact that we are cooperating with God's own grace, so that "it is no longer I who live, but Christ who lives in me."[45] As Augustine put it, God is simply crowning his own gifts to us.

Lutherans insist that we are saved by faith alone, apart from human merit, because we are, even after regeneration, unable to keep the law *perfectly*. For Lutherans, the law's primary function is as a mirror, revealing to us our sinfulness and our need for a Savior. The Roman Catholic Church does not deny that believers stand in daily need of forgiveness through the merits of Christ. Our works that merit eternal

---

[43] Rom 4:4.
[44] Council of Trent, Sixth Session, chap. 8.
[45] Gal 2:20.

life fulfill the law,[46] not by achieving a perfect, unbroken conformity to the law's requirements, but by being the fruit of the Spirit—the result of the supernatural renewal of our lives in Christ, connecting us to Christ, who alone perfectly fulfilled the law's demands. Both sides agree that forgiveness is an aspect to justification, one that renders perfect conformity to the law unnecessary for salvation.

Some Lutherans argue that the crux of the difference between Lutheranism and Rome lies in the question of the assurance of salvation. Although Roman theologians deny that the believer can be absolutely certain of their salvation, Catholics can have confidence in their own salvation, even a moral certainty, based on God's love and mercy and the abundance of grace available in the sacraments.

There is, in addition, a problem of terminology. When Lutherans speak of assurance of salvation, they mean the assurance that the believer is now in a state of grace, not the assurance that one will persevere until death. However, when Catholics deny the assurance of salvation, it is primarily the latter that they have in mind. Since Lutherans agree with Catholics that we can lose our salvation (by losing our saving faith), the assurance of salvation that Lutheranism provides is a highly qualified one.

In fact, what Luther himself sought in the form of assurance was simply the belief that there was at least a bare *possibility* that he should persevere and be saved. For Luther, even this minimal assurance of the possibility of salvation depended on believing that his perseverance depended solely on God's sovereign election, and not at all on himself. This seems to rely on a non sequitur—namely, that if something is 100 percent God's work, then it is 0 percent ours. But Paul teaches that it can be both ours and God's at once: "Work out your own salvation with fear and trembling; for God is at work in you, both to will and to work".[47]

The weakness of the Lutheran position lies in its one-sidedness. Even in the texts most central to Lutheran theology (the epistles to

---

[46] Rom 8:4.

[47] Phil 2:12-13. There is one respect in which Lutheran assurance is decidedly inferior to its Roman counterpart. Lutherans deny that the sacraments (of baptism and of penance) are effective unless the individual exercises saving faith, while Romans stipulate that the sacraments are effective unless the individual actively intends to use them for base purposes. The technical term for this dispute is *ex opere operata* (Romans affirm this and Lutherans deny it).

the Romans and the Galatians), there are many passages that indicate that our renewed life in the Spirit is essential to salvation:

- God will render "to those who by patience in well-doing seek for glory and honor and immortality, he will give eternal life".[48]
- "Glory and honor and peace for every one who does good.... For God shows no partiality."[49]
- "Through him we have obtained access to this grace in which we stand".[50]
- "If by the Spirit you put to death the deeds of the body you will live."[51]
- "He who sows to the Spirit will from the Spirit reap eternal life."[52]

2.5 Faith as "passive" and "merely receptive"

Lutheran theology includes the claim that faith is purely "passive", a mere "organ of receptivity".[53] In other words, faith is something we have (a condition) rather than something we do. This is obviously an attempt to maintain the consistency between the claim that we are justified solely by grace, without any dependence on any contribution from us, and the claim that only believers are justified in fact. If faith is a subjective condition of justification, how can it be claimed that we make no contribution? Only by asserting that in believing we contribute nothing to our justification: faith is merely the means by which we receive God's contribution.

The logical consequence of the Lutheran position is that I cannot be sure that I am now in a state of grace, reconciled to God, unless I am sure that I have saving faith. In contrast, the Catholic can be assured that his sins are forgiven, so long as he has not intentionally created some inner obstacle to the efficacy of the sacrament. This means that when the Catholic exercises faith or trust, the object of the trust is simply the grace and mercy of God, whereas when the Lutheran does so, he must to a certain degree rely on the quality of his own trust. This subjective, self-referential character of the Lutheran conception of trust can place a serious obstacle to one's assurance of one's present state of grace.

[48] Rom 2:7.
[49] Rom 2:10–11.
[50] Rom 5:2.
[51] Rom 8:13.
[52] Gal 6:8.
[53] Formula of Concord, *Thorough Declaration* 2.249.

However, it is not at all clear what could be meant by saying that faith is a state of "pure passivity" and "receptivity". If it means that faith is a gift of God, that we are unable to believe by exercising our unaided capacity, then by the same token hope and love, and even the works that flow from a regenerate heart, could be described as purely passive and receptive in nature. "God's love has been poured into our hearts through the Holy Spirit";[54] what could be more passive than that?

Lutherans insist that faith is a mere channel by which we receive Christ's righteousness, with no autonomous value of its own. This forces the question, why must this channel of receptivity be identified with faith alone, and not with "faith working in love", or even with the combination of faith, regeneration, and the fruit that naturally flows from these? For example, Robert Preus writes, "If justification is declared freely (*dorean, gratis*) over the sinner by God's grace (Romans 3:24), then only faith is left to justify."[55] This is a non sequitur. If justification is free, how can anything be "left to justify"? If faith can justify despite our being justified "freely", then why is it impossible that it is faith and love together that do the justifying, so long as both are free gifts of God for Christ's sake? As long as Rome is willing to admit—as it does—that our righteousness in Christ is partly an extrinsic matter, a matter of our being united to Christ and his righteousness, then the subjective basis of justification within us could be any condition that sustains our union with Christ. There is no reason given why only faith could play this receptive role. A life of Christian charity, so long as it is produced in us by God's grace, could equally well count as a channel of pure receptivity.

Now, let's turn, in the final two sections, to the case for the Roman Catholic view of justification.

2.6 Salvation as a reward

Lutherans claim that the idea of human merit (apart from the merits of Christ) is utterly alien to the Scriptures, yet the Bible often speaks of works as meriting eternal life: Revelation 20:12–15; Matthew 25:31–46; Romans 2:6, 9–11; 8:13; Galatians 6:7–8; and 2 Corinthians 5:10.

---

[54] Rom 5:5.
[55] Preus, *Justification and Rome*, 97.

These Scriptures teach not merely that all who are saved (through their faith alone) also do good works, but that they are judged by the quality of the works they do. This can be reconciled with Paul's formula of "grace through faith, not works",[56] by supposing that these good works are not merely external works in conformity to the ceremonial law, that the works count as meriting eternal life only for the sake of Christ's merits, and that the works are meritorious only because they are the fruits of the Holy Spirit at work within the believer. Moreover, these passages do not deny that the believers' sins are freely forgiven for Christ's sake.

The Scriptures also speak of eternal life as a *reward*: Colossians 3:24; Hebrews 10:35;11:6; Revelation 11:18; 22:12; and as a prize: Philippians 3:14; 1 Corinthians 9:24; 2 Timothy 4:8; James 1:12.

Phillip Melanchthon discusses these passages in article 3 of his *Apology of the Augsburg Confession*. He claims that Rome teaches that good works "are worthy of grace and life eternal, and do not stand in need of mercy, or of Christ as mediator". This is inaccurate, for two reasons. First, it overlooks the fact that believers rely on the forgiveness of sins, which is freely offered on a daily basis to believers and, for more serious sins, in the sacrament of penance on the basis of Christ's merit alone.[57] Second, it fails to take into account the fact that the works merit eternal life only because they are the fruit of God's work within us for Christ's sake.[58] Melanchthon writes:

We do not contend concerning the term "reward". We dispute concerning the matter, namely, whether good works are themselves worthy of grace and of eternal life, or whether they please only on account of faith, which apprehends Christ as mediator.... If the adversaries will concede that we are accounted righteous by faith because of Christ, and that good works please God because of faith, we will not afterwards contend much concerning the term "reward". We confess that eternal life is a reward, because it is something due on account

[56] See Eph 2:8–9.

[57] Council of Trent, Sixth Session, chap. 14.

[58] "Jesus Christ Himself continually infuses his virtue into the said justified—as the head into the members, and the vine into the branches—and this virtue always precedes and accompanies and follows their good works, which without it could not in any wise be pleasing and meritorious before God". Ibid., chap. 16.

of the promise, not on account of our merits.... Now if passages which treat of works are understood in such a manner as to comprise faith, they are not opposed to our doctrine.... Therefore it is a sufficient reason why eternal life is called a reward, because thereby the tribulations which we suffer, and the works of love which we do, are compensated, although we have not deserved it.[59]

Melanchthon seems here to be conceding, on behalf of the Lutheran church, that it is not objectionable to speak of eternal life as a reward for our good works, so long as it is conceded that these good works are meritorious only because of our faith in Christ as the mediator. He later seems to admit that eternal life is a kind of "compensation" given to us for our good works and our suffering for Christ's sake: "Therefore it is a sufficient reason why eternal life is called a reward, because thereby the tribulations which we suffer, and the works of love which we do, are *compensated*, although we have not deserved it."[60] If this is correct, these are devastating concessions on Melanchthon's part, since Rome readily agrees with the point Melanchthon insists on. Our works are meritorious only insofar as they are the fruit of Christ's work within us, a grace merited entirely by Christ's own death and Passion. The Council of Trent stated that faith is the "root" and "foundation" of justification, without which it is impossible to please God[61] and to come into the fellowship of his sons.[62] Moreover, it asserts that works cannot justify apart from Christ as mediator, since "no one can be just, but he to whom the merits of the Passion of our Lord Jesus Christ are communicated."[63]

2.7 The fatal contradiction in the Lutheran position

Lutherans affirm what seem to be three mutually inconsistent theses: (1) that we can lose our faith, and thereby our salvation, (2) that our faith is strengthened through the external means of grace (Word and sacrament), which require our diligent use, and (3) that our

---

[59] Melanchthon, "Apology of the Augsburg Confession", article 3, p. 67 (emphasis added).
[60] Ibid.
[61] Heb 11:6.
[62] Council of Trent, Sixth Session, chap. 8.
[63] Ibid., chap. 7.

works have absolutely no role in securing our final salvation. If our persistence in faith depends on our actions (claim 2), and our ultimate salvation depends on our persistence in faith (claim 1), then our actions do contribute causally to our salvation (in contradiction to claim 3). Calvinists, with their doctrine of the perseverance of the saints, and modern Evangelicals, who embrace the theory of "once saved, always saved", have the virtue of logical consistency. On their view, once we have received the free gift of salvation through faith, there is absolutely nothing we can do or fail to do that would entail the loss of our salvation. The Lutheran Confessions (the *Apology of the Augsburg Confession* and the *Formula of Concord*) rightly reject this position as offering a merely "carnal assurance". For example, Melanchthon writes in the *Apology*:

> For Peter speaks of works following the remission of sins, and teaches why they should be done, namely, that the calling may be sure, i.e., lest they may fall from their calling if they sin again. Do good works that you may persevere in your calling, that you do not fall away again, grow cold and may not noise the gifts of your calling, which were given you before, and not on account of works that follow, and which now are retained by faith; for faith does not remain in those who lose the Holy Ghost, who reject repentance."[64]

Similarly, the *Formula of Concord* insists that grace can be lost through serious sin:

> The false Epicurean delusion is to be earnestly censured and rejected, namely, that some imagine that faith and righteousness and salvation which they have received can be lost through no sins or wicked deeds, not even through willful and intentional ones, but that a Christian, although he indulges his wicked lusts without fear, resists the Holy Ghost, and purposely engages in sin against conscience, yet none the less retains faith, God's grace, righteousness and salvation.[65]

There are two ways to make the Lutheran position consistent. First, a Lutheran might assert that our continuing in faith, and our

---

[64] Melanchthon, "Apology of the Augsburg Confession", article 20, p. 104.
[65] Formula of Concord, *Thorough Declaration* 4.

avoidance of a kind of carnal sin that is incompatible with saving faith, has nothing whatsoever to do with our own efforts or our active cooperation with the Holy Spirit. This sort of "quietist" view can be found in Luther, but later Lutherans explicitly reject it (as in the Formula of Concord, which insists that believers can and must cooperate with the Holy Spirit). The quietist view seems inconsistent with the many exhortations to avoid the occasions of sin and to remain faithful in worship and the study of the Scriptures to be found throughout the New Testament.

Alternatively, a Lutheran could admit that we can cooperate in our own sanctification but deny that progress in sanctification has any effect on our persistence in saving faith. This not only flies in the face of common sense and Christian experience; it is also difficult to square with scriptural injunctions to avoid a fall into sin and unrepentance.[66]

Thus, it seems that Lutherans must admit that our works do contribute to our final salvation, so speaking of "salvation through faith alone" is an exaggeration.

Afterword

I was in 2006 one of history's slowest and most reluctant converts to Catholicism. I entered the Church not out of any dissatisfaction with Lutheranism nor out of any special attraction to the spirituality, aesthetics, or sanctity of Catholics. My decision was driven purely by an intellectual conviction that the Reformation was founded upon a number of theological errors. I felt that my commitment to Christ and to the Church demanded that I bring my life into conformity with my theological discoveries.

Frankly, I expected my life as a Catholic to be little different from my life as a sincere and fervent Protestant. In fact, I feared that much would be lost on a practical and aesthetic level. I loved, and still love, the traditional hymns and liturgical music of the Lutheran tradition, and I worried that I would find few Catholics with an interest in the study of the Bible, and many (perhaps an overwhelming majority)

---

[66] I Cor 10:12; Heb 3:12; I Pet 3:17.

whose faith and practice were lukewarm at best. I'm happy to report that all of this pessimism has proved utterly unfounded.

The one great thing I didn't anticipate is what a profound difference the reception of the full range of Catholic sacraments would have on my spiritual development. The sacrament of penance and reconciliation and, of course, that of the Eucharist have freed me from many self-destructive vices that I had come to think of as inevitable features of human life, and I have seen a renewal of spiritual growth and development in my fifties and sixties that I would have thought impossible for someone so fixed in habits and character. I've also enjoyed a richness of fellowship in the Church with people from many different lands and backgrounds. I entered the forbidding gates with great fear and trembling, but I've found my true home on the other side.

8

A Marriage of Faith and Reason:
One Couple's Journey to the Catholic Church

W. Scott and Lindsay K. Cleveland

We married one another before becoming philosophers or Catholics. We're now both. Scott was first to find philosophy, and Lindsay was first to find the Catholic Church. Our journeys followed different, although overlapping, roads and ended at the same destination. Lindsay's journey may be characterized as one of a search for the true meaning of Jesus' radical call to discipleship, for the truth regarding the relationship of faith and reason, and, ultimately, for a reliable guide for interpreting Scripture and understanding and living out the Christian faith. Scott's journey may be characterized as one of a search for truth in focused areas of biblical studies, theology, and philosophy, which, quite unexpectedly, developed into a direct investigation of whether or not all those truths fit together in the way expressed by the Catholic faith and intellectual tradition.

Lindsay's Background

I, Lindsay, grew up in a Christian home. My parents had me baptized as an infant in the Lutheran church. My brother and I were raised by our single mother, who, following the example of her parents, taught us of God's love for us, took us to church on Sundays, and led us in praying before meals. For as long as I can remember, I believed God to be our loving and good Creator. I understood that God wanted me to be good and I desired to be so. For much of my childhood I took such goodness to consist in a sort of basic Christian morality, including following the Ten Commandments. I was taught to believe that God became human in the Person of Jesus and died for our sakes, but I don't remember having any significant understanding of what that meant or how it should inform my life. As I grew, I adopted many of the typical concerns of adolescents: to be accepted by others and to succeed in schoolwork, leadership roles, and sports.

When I was a junior in high school, I attended a retreat where, for the first time, the Gospel message that humans were created to live in intimate relationship with God and that such a relationship is possible through the Person of Jesus Christ struck a chord in me that has been resounding ever since. A light went on that was cast on my entire life. I began to realize that I was missing the heart of what it is to be a Christian—to be a friend of God. Soon all the other concerns and activities of my life seemed less important in one sense, because their significance paled in comparison with the significance of being a friend of God. But they also acquired new significance as the practical ways in which I could live my life in service of God. I began praying and reading the Bible daily and had a hunger to learn more about God. My newfound understanding of my life's purpose and activities and my commitment to prayer enabled me, by God's grace, to stay afloat and remain largely at peace amid some storms in my life that I had been weathering and others that soon followed.

The chord of faith in and love for God that was struck in me while I was in high school became part of the tune of the Evangelical campus ministry that I was actively involved with throughout college. Through this ministry, I met some of my best friends and I grew in prayer, my knowledge of the Bible, and my service of God through sharing my faith with others. I found motivating this ministry's interpretation of Jesus' radical call to discipleship as primarily involving evangelism in the form of inviting others to a personal relationship with Jesus. I also came to view my relationship with God through the lens with which that ministry viewed Christianity, which emphasized the individual's assenting to certain beliefs about God's plan of salvation for humans and making a decision to accept Jesus as one's personal Lord and Savior. There was a strong emphasis placed on the Reformation themes of faith alone as necessary for eternal salvation and Scripture as the only authority with respect to matters of faith.

Having already tacitly accepted these themes through the Protestant culture in which I was raised, I easily accepted them when they were made more explicit. And as a high achiever with perfectionist tendencies, I found the message that faith alone is what matters for eternal salvation to help liberate me from the pressures I put on myself.

By the end of college, my academic interests were largely in ethics and political theory. I was especially interested in the relationship between religion and politics. Having been encouraged by my advisor to pursue a career as a university professor, I was considering applying for graduate school. But I was experiencing a gap between the faith to which I was firmly committed and what I was learning in the classroom. It wasn't so much that I thought there was a conflict between the two; rather, I thought my faith should be relevant to my studies, but I didn't have the resources to relate them. At this point, I learned about a unique Christian learning community, called the Trinity Forum Academy,[1] intended for recent college graduates to spend an academic year living, praying, and serving together and reading and reflecting on the relationship between Christian faith and the rest of life. I eagerly applied, was accepted, and became part of that community during the year after I graduated from college. It was there that my path overlapped with Scott's.

Scott's Background

I, Scott, was raised in a devout Evangelical home, and my family were active members in a variety of Protestant communities on the military bases where my father was stationed. My parents began teaching me about God's love for me early in my childhood, and at a young age I desired to love God in return. A youth-group trip to Holland and a mission trip to Albania catalyzed my desire for a wholehearted friendship with God. I was soon baptized as a young teenager. My faith was earnest and I was inquisitive, but I was not formed in a denomination with a tradition of systematic reflection on faith. My mother's homeschooling provided me significant opportunity to read, and she directed me toward some of my important early

[1] It is now called the Trinity Fellows Academy.

intellectual influences: George Macdonald and C. S. Lewis. These, as well as a few key role models, helped me to avoid the anti-intellectual tendencies of some of my well-meaning pastors. I attended Taylor University, where I studied philosophy and biblical literature.

I came to college with unsettled theological questions, especially pertaining to the scope of God's (salvific) love (i.e., whether God desires all people or only some to be saved) and the relation of God's providence and human freedom. While these questions are intellectual, they were primarily motivated by my love for God and desire to understand how his goodness was compatible with certain answers to my questions that restricted God's love and human freedom. I wondered, how could God be perfectly loving if he did not desire to save all people, and how could he be perfectly good if he determined all human actions, even those whereby people reject him? I was burning for answers. I did not know what philosophy was, but I found philosophy faculty and students who were deeply wrestling with such questions and seeking to give careful answers. In my first philosophy class, I felt like I had arrived at a home I didn't know existed. I was also attracted to the study of biblical literature. For I sought answers to my theological and philosophical questions concerning God that were grounded in an accurate understanding of God's revelation in Scripture. I was seeking the truth using both the reason of Athens and the faith of Jerusalem.

My studies in philosophy and biblical literature both strengthened my faith, through increased understanding, and raised objections to my faith (especially, in philosophy, from the objection to God's existence from evil and, in biblical studies, from challenges to the infallibility of Scripture advanced by scholars I read who were committed to the modern historical-critical method). In reading Christian philosophers, I found compelling responses to the problem of evil and illuminating reflection on the rationality of Christian belief, the Atonement, the attributes of God, and other issues.[2] This, together with conversations with friends and faculty, increased my desire to do philosophical theology and philosophy of religion. Because these fields of study often focus on beliefs that almost all Christians share, I

[2] Especially helpful were Alvin Plantinga, Eleonore Stump, Richard Swinburne, and Nicholas Wolterstorff.

did not delve much into interdenominational debates including questions about the nature of the Church.

Two topics in biblical studies that were significant for me, and eventually for my openness to considering Catholicism, were Palestinian Judaism in the centuries preceding Christ and the so-called New Perspective on Paul (NPP).[3] The former, along with studying the parables of Jesus with a Jewish scholar, helped me to understand and appreciate the Jewishness of Jesus and his fulfillment of the law rather than its abolishment. The latter helped me to appreciate even more the continuity (despite significant differences) between God's covenant with Israel and his covenant with the New Testament People of God.

As my studies increased my desire for understanding, graduate school was my natural next step. I loved biblical studies but I loved philosophical theology more. I was unsure of whether to pursue graduate work in philosophy or theology, and so I applied to Yale Divinity School, which I thought would give me an opportunity to test both waters. I deferred enrollment to Yale to attend the Trinity Forum Academy—the opportunity to integrate study, work, and spiritual disciplines in an intentional community was unique and attractive. There I met Lindsay.

Growing in Faith and Friendship

Going to the Trinity Forum Academy (TFA) was, for me, Lindsay, like discovering that within the metaphorical house I inhabited (as a Christian), there were passageways and rooms I didn't know existed. I was introduced to a new manner of reflection on human life and the relevance of the substance of Christian faith to it that I found exhilarating. I encountered literature, such as Dante's *Divine Comedy* and C. S. Lewis' *The Great Divorce*, which expressed the Christian faith in ways I had never considered. I read works of theology and biblical interpretation that explored issues that were broader and deeper than the ones I had come upon before. Though Scott came to the TFA

---

[3] Especially helpful were Krister Stendahl, E. P. Sanders, James Dunn, and N. T. Wright. I say "so-called" because the NPP is not a single perspective nor is it always new.

with more exposure to such works and issues from his college experience, he too encountered new ways of understanding the substance, practice, and relevance of the Christian faith. Through the unique experience of living in Christian community, we developed significant friendships and a deeper understanding of and appreciation for the role of community in the Christian life. The two of us especially enjoyed discussing ideas and other mutual interests with one another, and just over two months into our nine months at the TFA, we began dating.

While the focal point of our readings and discussions was the salvation of humans to a relationship with God through the Person of Jesus Christ, they offered to both of us a broader and deeper understanding than we previously had and that we found better supported by Scripture. We both came to the TFA thinking of salvation as going to heaven after death in virtue of one's sins being forgiven wholly because of a private act of placing one's faith in Christ's atoning death. We came to recognize that such a wholly otherworldly conception of salvation effected wholly by an individual, private act of faith was both different from the conception of salvation depicted in the Bible taken as a whole and strikingly similar to the post-Enlightenment view of religion as a mere matter of private judgment.

The New Testament conception of salvation makes central the forgiveness of sins and eternal life in heaven in virtue of Christ's atoning sacrifice on the Cross, but it includes more. It includes not just what happens after death, but a distinctive way of life here and now that engages our whole embodied selves[4] and that includes membership in the People of God. Given this understanding of the biblical conception of salvation, we came to recognize the centrality to the Christian faith of our commitment to a particular local church and spiritual disciplines such as silence, solitude, fasting, feasting, and service, in addition to prayer and Scripture study. We also developed a deeper appreciation for the view of God as a Trinity of Persons— Father, Son, and Holy Spirit—whose relationships to one another are characterized by self-giving love and in whose communion we are invited to participate.

---

[4] Significant for our understanding of this was Dallas Willard, *The Spirit of the Disciplines* (San Francisco: HarperOne, 1999).

What we gained from our experience at the TFA in terms of our understanding of the Christian faith may be characterized as a deeper understanding of the story of Scripture as well as of the core Christian beliefs expressed by the Nicene Creed. The TFA itself is not affiliated with any denomination, and the participants in our group came from a variety of Christian backgrounds. Our readings and discussions largely focused on the big themes in Scripture rather than on denominationally divisive ones. When our group considered various Christian denominations, our focus was largely on identifying both strengths and weaknesses within each with respect to their faithfulness to the biblical view of salvation we discussed. So, we left the TFA with the intention to commit to a local church wherever we went, but without a sense of commitment to any particular denomination. We also left committed to one another and to seeking confirmation that our desire to marry one another was God's will.

Diversity, Disagreement, and Development

After the TFA, we both attended Yale Divinity School, where we each began a master's program: Scott in philosophical theology/ philosophy of religion and Lindsay in ethics. We chose Yale because there we would each be able to take classes in both theology and our other primary field of interest, in which we were considering pursuing a Ph.D.: philosophy for Scott and political theory for Lindsay. Neither of us were sure of which field to make our primary focus, and Yale gave us an opportunity to explore both. After our first year at Yale, we were joyfully married.

Yale Divinity School was a different Christian environment from those we had previously encountered. While it had not eschewed its Christian roots and become a mere center for the study of religion, the dominant Christian culture, in our experience, tended toward the "progressive" end of the theological spectrum. By this, we mean that the culture was characterized by revisionism regarding sexual morality and an emphasis on doing theology primarily in the service of (or through the lens of) current social and political issues. There were some who accepted "demythologizing" or postmodern readings of Scripture and the early Christian creeds. Nonetheless, it was a genuinely diverse place; there were also faculty and students interested in historical and systematic theological issues and who held more traditional views of Scripture, the creeds, and sexual issues.

It was especially unsettling to me, Lindsay, to encounter deep disagreement regarding the content of Christianity and the opposition expressed toward those who held traditional Christian views regarding sexual morality. While my view of Scripture had been challenged at the TFA, the challenge was positive in the sense that it took the form of a compelling invitation to consider additional themes and facets of the Gospel message within Scripture that I had formerly failed to see. Some of what I encountered at Yale was positive in that sense too. But the goal of some professors, and the majority culture, at Yale was more strongly negative in the sense that the aim seemed to be to undermine traditional understandings of the Christian faith and convert students to the so-called progressive view.

Whereas at the TFA there was a shared assumption that the Bible is God's revelation to humanity and that it is trustworthy, at Yale there was not this shared assumption. While I retained that assumption, the historical-critical method introduced me to additional complexities relevant to biblical interpretation. I had already encountered disagreements regarding biblical interpretation between seemingly faith-filled Christians. But as I encountered disagreements between biblical scholars, especially disagreements that couldn't be settled using the original languages, it became apparent to me that I could no longer assume that by simply seeking to be led by the Holy Spirit in my reading of Scripture, I would arrive at a true understanding of doctrine. This left me in a state of deep uncertainty and restlessness. With respect to ethical issues that were clearer in Scripture, my encounter with Christians who opposed the relevant scriptural views awakened in me a desire to understand why certain behaviors are deemed immoral in Scripture; I no longer found "because the Bible says so" to be a satisfying rationale.

Neither of us found the dominant "progressive" understanding of Christianity at Yale compelling, and this was so for several reasons. First, we were aware of good criticisms of demythologizing approaches to Scripture. For example, such interpretations of texts hold contentious, and in our minds implausible, philosophical assumptions such as that miracles are impossible and that the only valid explanations of events are natural ones. Second, we found unpersuasive the argument that Christian love requires revision of traditional biblical sexual morality. For we found much more plausible and biblical a notion of love that includes willing what is good for the other where what is good in sexual practice is objective and aligns with the traditional Christian view. Third, we found and still find it puzzling why one would remain committed to a Christianity emptied of the traditional content, especially emptied of belief in the Resurrection and an afterlife with the possibility of eternal union with God. As the Apostle Paul said, "If Christ has not been raised, your faith is futile."[5]

So, despite the environment of "progressive" Christianity at Yale, by God's grace, we remained committed to the core tenets of orthodox Christianity summarized in a literal interpretation of the Nicene Creed (although we were not yet thinking carefully about its description of the Church as "one, holy, catholic, and apostolic") as well as to the trustworthiness of Scripture, even as we had significant questions regarding how best to understand such trustworthiness and how to interpret Scripture. We realized that there were many relevant theological questions and issues that we simply hadn't yet considered in much detail or hadn't recognized as open to reasonable disagreement between faithful Christians (e.g., infant vs. adult baptism, the nature of the Eucharist, the significance of apostolicity, etc.). We sought to learn more on these issues, but since neither of us was pursuing a ministerial position and neither of us was already committed to a particular Christian denomination, we had no practical motivation to solidify views on many of the theological issues that divide Christian denominations.

While at Yale, we attended an Episcopal church, to which we were initially attracted primarily because, coincidentally, a number of other Evangelical faculty, students, and affiliates of Yale University (including the Divinity school) were part of the congregation. Our friendships with these faculty and students were dear to us and an important means of support as we worked through the challenges of our studies. The Anglican liturgy of the Episcopal church was foreign to us, but we quickly came to appreciate how full it is of Scripture, beauty, and theological depth. We came to recognize that,

[5] I Cor 15:17.

contrary to our assumptions, we actually heard far more Scripture in the context of an Episcopal service than we ever did in the Evangelical worship services we had attended. We also valued that the content of the pastor's homily was to be directed by the lectionary readings and that its role was to help prepare the congregation for the highpoint of the service, which was the eucharist. We appreciated that the focus of the service was the community gathering to worship God together, to profess our shared faith using the words of the Nicene Creed, and to fulfill Jesus' command to receive his body and blood in remembrance of him. Formerly, we had both (mistakenly) judged that those features were a distraction from what, we thought, should be the exclusive focus of a Christian worship service—namely, the individual's relationship with God.

Through our exposure to the Anglican liturgy, we began to see the typical Evangelical worship service as too narrow, too subject to distortion, and too likely to result in a cult of personality around the pastor. For the typical Evangelical worship service consists almost wholly of praise songs focused on the individual's relationship with God and a lengthy sermon whose content is completely determined by the pastor. Further, despite the intention to allow for greater freedom in worship, the absence of a formal liturgy in Evangelical worship fosters a certain idiosyncratic form of active participation that overemphasizes one's subjective, internal states. While extemporaneous prayer is crucial to growing in relationship to God, we began to see that worship services, such as Evangelical ones, with only extemporaneous prayer also miss an opportunity to help form people's prayer life and beliefs about God through good, formal prayers and the recitation of the Nicene Creed. Some of the advantages of such formal prayers include not only that they can help people form an accurate conception of God and their relation to him and avoid distorted ones, but that they can also be a means of encouragement for those experiencing hardships, doubts, or grief.

The encouragement that can come from a formal liturgy and formal prayers became clear to us as we grieved the death of Scott's father soon after we were married. We took a semester off in order to live with and help his mother. While we remain grateful for the support we received from the pastor and many close friends from his family's Evangelical church, we found the Anglican liturgy and the resources in the Anglican Book of Common Prayer for grieving and praying for the dead to be the most helpful and appropriate for us in our time of grief (with hope) in comparison with the Evangelical worship services and resources we encountered. In addition, due to the difficulty of having the content and even the practice of our faith on the examination table while in divinity school, we found it practically helpful to be able to participate in Anglican worship services that weren't so dependent upon our own subjective states. As I, Lindsay, was especially wrestling with confusion concerning God's intention for the structure and life of the church and the interpretation of Scripture, I found it a great help to my questioning faith to say formal prayers and recite the Nicene Creed, knowing that they had been prayed and professed by other Christians for centuries. In this way, and through reading primary texts of Christians throughout history, I began to have a profound experience of the communion of Christians across time and space, and this greatly encouraged my faith.

After our first year at Yale, Scott decided to pursue a Ph.D. in philosophy rather than theology, and so his academic focus was on developing his philosophical education and preparing to apply to Ph.D. programs. I, Lindsay, came to recognize that my longing for social unity and solidarity that motivated my interest in politics was to be most wholly fulfilled in the church. So, I became much more interested in theology and theological ethics than in political theory. During my first year at Yale, after reading *The Politics of Jesus* by the Mennonite theologian John Howard Yoder, I became an advocate of the sort of Christological peace theology advanced by theologians like John Howard Yoder and Stanley Hauerwas.[6] Given my Evangelical zeal to follow Christ in a radical and distinctive way, my proclivity to be a peacemaker in human relationships, and the influence of some peers and mentors whom I respected, I was easily persuaded by the account of the Christian faith as primarily about taking up one's cross and following Christ in nonviolent resistance to evil forces in the world. An important feature of this peace theology was its opposition to the project of natural theology (i.e., formulating

---

[6] John Howard Yoder, *The Politics of Jesus*, 2nd ed. (Grand Rapids, MI: Eerdmans, 1994). Stanley Hauerwas, *The Peaceable Kingdom: A Primer in Christian Ethics*, 1st ed. (Notre Dame: University of Notre Dame Press, 1991).

arguments for the existence or attributes of God without appeal to
supernatural revelation) and of grounding ethics in the nature of
human beings. But much of the work in the philosophy of religion
and philosophical ethics that Scott was engaging was a form of natural theology or of grounding ethics in the nature of human beings.
As a result, there was a tension between Scott's work in philosophy
and my theological interests, which led to ongoing debates between
us. Throughout the remainder of our time at Yale, my central academic concerns were to consider the systematic implications of such
a Christological focus on peace, to seek out evidence that such was
the view of the early Church (which I assumed would confirm its
accuracy as an interpretation of Scripture), and to consider various
views of natural theology.

While at Yale, I was surprised to discover in my study of the early
Church the reverence that was directed toward the bread and wine
used in Communion; the hierarchical structure of bishops, priests,
and deacons; the significance of apostolic tradition, councils, and
creeds; and the late formation of the canon of Scripture (in the fourth
century A.D.). Those discoveries undermined the misconceptions I
acquired as an Evangelical Protestant that the early Church professed
Scripture to be sufficient alone for our understanding of faith and that
such structures and traditions were merely later human additions to
and distractions from what Jesus revealed. But since these surprising
discoveries cohered with what I found in the Anglican tradition, they
didn't undermine my continuing as a Protestant. I was also surprised
to encounter in early Church writings a deference to the Church of
Rome with respect to matters of faith and Christian practices and to
learn that the Anglican liturgy I had come to value was based on the
Roman rite of the Catholic Church. But I simply passed over those
discoveries. At that time, I still held many of the standard objections
to Catholicism, so those discoveries were not sufficient to lead me to
examine Catholicism directly.

We both were also surprised to find that some of our formerly
Evangelical friends were converting to Catholicism. I, Lindsay,
recall judging (not so humbly) their conversion as a move to replace
their infallible Bible that had come under attack by historical-
critical scholarship with an infallible pope. I didn't understand the
Catholic teaching on papal infallibility, but knowing that the pope

was regarded as infallible in some sense was sufficient for me to dismiss their conversion as reactionary. I also dismissed their sense of confidence in the Catholic Church and her teachings as arrogance and evidence of their failure to accept the messiness of the historical development of Christianity, which, I assumed, resisted what I took to be the kind of tight systematic formulations of Christianity advanced by the Catholic Church or by other denominations, such as Calvinist ones. I, lacking humility, regarded myself as the more intellectually honest.

When it came time to apply for and decide about Ph.D. programs, we decided that Baylor University was the best fit for us because there Scott could continue to pursue his interests in philosophical theology and philosophy of religion in the philosophy department while training in the other philosophical areas, and I could work with theologians in the theology department who were interested in the peace theologies of Yoder and Hauerwas.

Lindsay's Road to Rome

At Baylor University, we realized, as we considered where we would worship on Sundays, that we would be dissatisfied with any Protestant alternative to an Anglican or Episcopal church.[7] After worshipping in an Episcopal church for nearly three years at Yale, we found that our faith in and love for God was most deeply nourished by the beautiful prayers and words of the formal liturgy and, especially, by the central act of each weekly service, which was the reverent celebration of the Anglican eucharist. While at Yale, we didn't pay much attention to the debates that raged within the Anglican Communion, for we didn't regard our attending an Episcopal church while in graduate school as a commitment to the denomination. But once I, Lindsay, was pursuing a Ph.D. in theology, I recognized that I needed to be rooted in some part of the Christian tradition. It was evident to me that a theologian ought to serve the church, and that in order to do so, I needed to commit to some part of it. Since the form of worship in the Episcopal

[7] The Episcopal Church in the United States of America is part of the global Anglican Communion.

church was both personally nourishing and reflected much of what I had discovered about the early Church, I naturally began discerning about committing to the Anglican tradition. But before actively doing so, I found, through my theological studies, my commitment to peace theology lessening and the apparent tension between my theological work and Scott's work in philosophy heightening.

The Baylor theology department was a wonderful context for my theological development. My professors were committed to Christian orthodoxy, valued the whole of Christian history, and were very supportive of me. Thanks to the guidance of one professor, I came to recognize that what was most central to Yoder's (apparently Christological) peace theology was his pacifism rather than the Person of Christ, who seems to be dispensable in Yoder's later work advocating pacifism.[8] I realized that Yoder's commitment to pacifism was the lens through which he interpreted Scripture and that there were plausible alternative interpretations of the relevant biblical texts he used to support his pacifism. I also recognized how narrow and non-traditional Yoder's understanding of Christianity was; the peace for which he advocated was exclusively social and neglected the individual's battle with sin and need for grace to attain peace in relation to God and within the soul.[9] In following Yoder, I went from an overly individualistic understanding of the Gospel message while in college to the opposite extreme of an overly social understanding. Despite having already recognized that Scripture is open to many plausible interpretations, I had been so taken by Yoder's interpretation that I hadn't really critically examined it.

As I came to doubt Yoder's trustworthiness as a guide to understanding Scripture and the Christian life, I began increasingly to rely on another—namely, the New Testament scholar and Anglican bishop N. T. Wright. Wright's work, much of which was confirmed

[8] The professor was Paul Martens, who has since published this critique of Yoder's work in *The Heterodox Yoder* (Eugene, OR: Cascade, 2012).

[9] One of my teachers of Yoder and the Christian peace tradition while at Yale—namely, Joe Jones—had pointed out to me the absence of the concept of grace in Yoder's work, but it wasn't until later in my time at Baylor that I appreciated the significance of that absence in casting doubt on Yoder's trustworthiness as a guide to biblical interpretation. For a traditional understanding of the Christian pursuit of peace in which grace is central, see, for example, Jacques Philippe, *Searching for and Maintaining Peace: A Small Treatise on Peace of Heart*, 1st ed. (New York: Alba House, 2002).

in my study of the early Church's biblical interpretation, had already significantly influenced my understanding of Scripture in many of the ways that Scott described how the New Perspective on Paul influenced his (e.g., the importance of the Jewishness of Jesus and his fulfillment rather than abolishment of the law, of greater continuity between the Old and New Testaments than on a standard Reformation view, and of the New Testament's distinction between "works of the law" and "works of faith"). Wright's biblical scholarship challenged the Reformation understanding of justification by faith alone. Although the view of justification he defended as the biblical view was much closer to the Catholic view, Wright, as a Protestant, saw himself simply following the spirit of the Reformation in pursuing the best interpretation of what is given in Scripture. His work was rigorous as historical scholarship while coming from a perspective of faith that balanced both the individual and social dimensions of the Gospel message. It satisfied my intellectual need for serious engagement with historical-critical biblical scholarship as well as my spiritual need for pastoral guidance regarding the practical implications of biblical theology. It also cohered with the form of worship we had come to value greatly in the Episcopal church.

With Wright as my guide, I began to think seriously about committing to the Anglican Communion. I began to consider directly what it means to be Anglican and to confront the debates that we had previously ignored. The Anglican Communion was in a state of conflict in the wake of the Episcopal Church in the United States' controversial ordination to the role of bishop of a noncelibate self-identifying gay priest in 2003 in defiance of the advisement from representatives of the global communion not to do so. The conflict was not isolated to the single issue of the morality of homosexual activity, but concerned different understandings of Scripture and the core beliefs of Christianity. Bishop Wright held to orthodox views on these issues; that is, he affirmed the immorality of homosexual activity, the trustworthiness of Scripture as divine revelation, and a literal interpretation of the Nicene Creed. He advocated for patience and trust that the Holy Spirit would bring reconciliation to the Anglican Communion, and so, with him, I prayed for patience, trust, and reconciliation for the Anglican Communion. In the fall of 2009, we gathered with our young-adults group from our Episcopal church to discuss a document called the Anglican Covenant, which was intended to help strengthen the relationships between the churches that make up the Anglican Communion by clarifying what they hold in common and specifying ways of assessing the seriousness of conflicts and of resolving conflicts. At that time, we tried to be hopeful about the covenant and its aims. After further consideration, we recognized that the Anglican Communion has no authoritative means to resolve their deep disagreements and so must sacrifice truth for unity—a unity that can only go so deep given that significant disagreements remain unresolved.

In the same semester, I participated in a seminar on twentieth-century Protestant ethics that explored the disavowal of and yet apparent tacit dependence on some form of natural law reasoning in such works.[10] As background to the debates concerning the natural law, we read the treatise on law within St. Thomas Aquinas' *Summa Theologiae*. Upon reading it, I realized that many of the Protestant criticisms of natural law reasoning that I had encountered were not relevant to Aquinas. For contrary to such criticisms, Aquinas did not use the natural law to minimize the distinctiveness or radicality of Jesus' commands nor to dilute the Christian way of life to some lowest common denominator that could be followed by anyone regardless of their beliefs. Rather, the natural law, for Aquinas, concerns the bare minimum that can be expected of humans without the aid of God's revelation in, first, the Mosaic law and, then, the new "law" of the Gospel.

The contrast between Aquinas and the Protestant ethicists whose works we read was stark in my judgment. Aquinas' account of the various levels of law was clearly an attempt to consider carefully and account for the whole of Scripture as well as commonsense observation regarding human action. The distinction (without opposition) between Aquinas' account of the natural law and the revealed laws enabled Aquinas to maintain a distinction (without opposition) between the order of creation on the one hand and the order of redemption on the other. In contrast, by neglecting to analyze the nature of human beings—apart from regarding it as sinful—and by attempting to ground all of ethics in some feature of God's revelation

---

[10] Paul Martens, the professor of my seminar, articulates the view that some Protestant ethicists tacitly depend on natural law reasoning in his "With the Natural Grain of the Universe: Reexamining the Alleged Pacifist Rejection of Natural Law", *Journal of the Society of Christian Ethics* 32, no. 2 (2012): 113–31.

(e.g., the nonviolent resistance or the Resurrection of Jesus), the Protestant ethicists tended to conflate the distinction between the order of creation and the order of redemption and to lack theoretical resources for addressing ethical questions not directly treated in Scripture and for dialoguing with non-Christians about ethics.[11] In contrast, I found in Aquinas a detailed account of created nature, which, far from threatening the significance of grace, is what enabled his robust understanding of grace, sin, and sanctification.

Reading Aquinas at this time was, for me, like taking a breath of fresh air after gasping in a smoggy city. Much of the contemporary theology I had been reading was either overly dense and nearly inaccessible, reactionary in the sense that the views advanced were often at the opposite extreme of the view they opposed, or too sweeping and uncharitable in their claims and criticisms of alternative views.[12] Finding Aquinas to be a helpful interlocutor on theological matters, I began to turn to his writings in consideration of various theological issues.[13]

---

[11] Similarly, in a course engaging the recent work of a theological movement called "Radical Orthodoxy", I found that in an effort to prioritize the grace of God by attacking a certain secular understanding of nature, but without offering a robust alternative theological notion of nature, such theologians lost the distinctiveness and meaningfulness of the theological notion of grace. It turns out that something similar could be said for some twentieth-century Catholic theologians, especially Henri de Lubac, who actually influenced the Radical Orthodoxy theologians whose views I came to question. This is not problematic with respect to the Catholic teaching regarding the infallibility of the Church, for it is not part of that teaching that Catholic theologians are protected from error. It is worth noting that de Lubac also made some very positive contributions to Catholic theology, which also influenced me. Some examples are Henri de Lubac, *Catholicism: Christ and the Common Destiny of Man* (San Francisco: Ignatius Press, 1988); *Medieval Exegesis: The Four Senses of Scripture, Vol. 1* (Grand Rapids, MI: Eerdmans, 1998). For the definitive critique of, and alternative to, de Lubac's understanding of the natural desire for God, see Lawrence Feingold, *The Natural Desire to See God according to St. Thomas and His Interpreters*, 2nd ed. (Ave Maria, FL: Sapientia Press Ave Maria University, 2010).

[12] I realize that many would regard Aquinas' writings as dense and nearly inaccessible (and they can be, especially without guidance regarding their structure and technical terminology). But what set Aquinas apart from the others I was reading was that he was trying to account carefully for and synthesize all of the relevant data, including the whole of Scripture, the Christian tradition of reflection on God's revelation, and commonsense reflection on the world. In his writings, he defines his technical terms and only introduces them when necessary to make relevant distinctions, is careful to distinguish merely apparent from real disagreement, and charitably seeks to identify the truth wherever it can be found.

[13] While in a course on the Pauline epistles, I read Aquinas' *Galatians* commentary and found much of what I had learned from N. T. Wright regarding the Apostle Paul's treatment of the law reinforced in Aquinas' work.

In the midst of all this, I found the apparent tension between my theological study and Scott's work in philosophy heightening. I encountered theological criticisms of contemporary philosophy of religion that suggested that the standard mode of argumentation concerning God used by such philosophers was idolatrous because it somehow put God on the same level with creatures. As I discussed this and other theological criticisms of philosophy with Scott, I often couldn't answer Scott's questions regarding the content and target of the criticisms nor his counterobjections. And I didn't find good responses to them. We found that some criticisms seemed to be based on mistaken assumptions and others were less sweeping than recognized. For example, some theologians were critical of contemporary philosophers for the latter's encroachment into topics traditionally reserved for theology. They were correct that some (but not all) philosophers (and particularly some Protestant ones) were doing theology poorly because of their ignorance of historical theology. As Scott and I discussed these issues, I developed an appreciation for some philosophical tools that I found sorely lacking in much of the theology I encountered, such as the precise definition of terms, use of explicit argumentation, and evaluation of arguments according to basic rules of logic. As I was myself developing interest in philosophical topics, especially insofar as I recognized the partial dependence of theology on them, and a desire to gain the requisite philosophical background for the study of Aquinas' works, the real tension between my theological work and Scott's philosophical work began easing.

In the same semester, I participated in a course on a certain movement within twentieth-century Catholic theology focused on ressourcement—that is, a return to the sources of the Catholic faith, especially Scripture and the early Church Fathers.[14] Although the theology department at Baylor was Baptist, many of the theologians there recognized that there is a great wealth of theological and spiritual resources in the Catholic tradition and that students of

---

[14] These theologians were responding to what they judged to be overly rationalistic formulations of Catholic theology, especially in neo-Scholastic manuals that simply summarized the views and arguments of Thomas Aquinas and his commentators. While these theologians were right to advocate a return to the reading of primary texts as well as the recognition of the limits of reason and the significance of mystery in theology and worship, they seemed to me at times too fierce in their opposition. What we find in the sources of the Catholic faith is a balance between reason and mystery; either one without the other is problematic.

theology ought to engage them. In that course, I read *The Meaning of Tradition* by Yves Congar. In it, Congar distinguishes various meanings of the term "tradition", explains in detail the Catholic notions of "Tradition", and argues that reliance on some tradition of biblical interpretation is inescapable.[15]

Reflection on my own experience contributed to my acceptance of Congar's conclusion regarding the inescapability of reliance on a tradition of biblical interpretation. Throughout my theological study, I had repeatedly replaced one interpretative tradition with another as I found the former fail to withstand scrutiny; first, it was the interpretive tradition of my college campus ministry which viewed discipleship primarily in terms of evangelism, then some of the interpreters I encountered at the TFA, then Yoder who viewed discipleship primarily in terms of nonviolent resistance to social evil, and then Wright (as well as others with lesser influence mixed in). Over and again I recognized that what I thought was merely the plain sense of Scripture was an interpretation that could be reasonably contested using other portions of Scripture and historical or theological resources. I realized that the same was true of other Protestant individuals and denominations who took one or another Christian theologian (or philosopher) as their guide, or else became skeptical that we can arrive at a trustworthy interpretation given the endlessness of historical criticism.

As I read Congar, I recognized how implausible it is to think that one or a few Patristic, medieval, Reformation, or contemporary theologians or individuals had the key to interpreting Scripture correctly, or that further and better historical study of Scripture would lead to the best interpretation. Further, Congar's description of the impoverishment of faith that results if Scripture is regarded as the sole authority rang true to me.[16] In addition, Congar's description of

---

[15] See Yves Congar, *The Meaning of Tradition* (San Francisco: Ignatius Press, 2004).

[16] "How poor our faith would be, and how uncertain, if we were really left with nothing before us but the Biblical text! And who would have given it to us, where would we have gotten it, how would we have found it? How poor and uncertain would be our communion with God, in Jesus Christ, if we were forced to establish it by ourselves, starting from ourselves and God alone, without the Church's maternal initiation, without the Christian community, without the communion of saints! What would become of our faith in the Holy Trinity without Athanasius and Nicaea? How should we pray without the Jewish psalms, without the liturgy, without the example and enthusiasm of the saints? We have received everything unconsciously, in the same way that we benefit from our culture, simply by being born and educated in a society whose culture was built up, treasured and handed down right to us." Ibid., 25–26.

the historical reality of the Church's founding and life preceding the writing of the New Testament struck me in a deeper way than it had when I first realized that the New Testament canon wasn't established for several centuries after Christ's Ascension into heaven.[17]

Having already had most of my objections to Catholicism overcome through my theological study, I was open to the Catholic alternative that Congar presented. Congar explains the Catholic understanding of "Tradition" in its primary sense to be what the Church Fathers and councils have often called the "Catholic spirit" or the "mind of the Church" together with the living manner in which that spirit/mind is transmitted. The Catholic spirit/mind is, in Congar's words,

> the unanimous belief common to the whole Church, considered not only from the aspect of present-day Catholicity, but from that of its continuity and identity even, throughout the ages; it is the practice of the faith common to the faithful today, to the preceding generations from whom they inherited it, and, through them, to the apostles and first Christians themselves. It is the heritage of the Catholic communion, a heritage that is truly "catholic" and total, which greatly surpasses the part that is recorded, and even more the part that we have understood and are capable of explaining. For ... owing to its transmission, what we hold is not merely a theoretic statement, or even a profession of faith, but the reality that is Christianity itself. We received it with our baptism, the beginning of our initiation, and subsequently throughout our life in the Church, in the highest degree in the celebration of the Eucharist, by which Christ delivers himself to us; this reality is entrusted to our fidelity, with the injunction to keep

---

[17] "The scriptural evidence is of a nature to provide endless discussion, and in fact there has been so much argument over its exact meaning that a critical reader of the Bible can always produce reasons for doubting a given piece of evidence, for dating it differently, for attributing it to another writer who was stupid or biased, and so on. What are the 'presbyters' and the 'episcopos'; what is the origin of their institution? The Church could not wait until the critics were agreed among themselves: she had to live. She lived her own life, which had been handed down to her as such, before the texts and together with them, in the texts and yet not limited to them, independently of them. She did not receive her life from them. She *was* the Church from the time of the apostles and not the product of their writings; she used these writings, not following them word for word, as a pupil copies an exercise imposed from outside, but treating them as a mirror and yardstick to recognize and restore her image, in each new generation." Ibid., 21.

and transmit it faithfully, without adding to it anything alien, taking anything away or changing its meaning.[18]

As I reflected on this notion of Tradition, I realized that I had seen evidence of it throughout my theological education—in the writings of the early Church, of medieval and contemporary Catholic theologians (especially Aquinas), and in a number of papal encyclicals—as well as its remnants in the Anglican liturgy and celebration of the liturgical calendar. The Protestant theologians I studied seemed often to emphasize certain themes to the exclusion or even opposition of others (e.g., the individual vs. the social dimensions of the Gospel, the primacy of the soul vs. the body and of faith/mystery vs. reason, the good of family life vs. priestly or religious celibacy). In contrast, I saw in the Catholic Tradition a spirit of balance and peace as well as the coherence of its views and their consistency across time. I found in the Catholic Tradition the most compelling view of Jesus' radical call to discipleship as the call to become a saint, i.e., to be conformed to the image of Christ by cooperating with God's grace to cultivate the virtues and gifts planted in the soul by God, resulting in a union with God characterized by perfect peace and happiness.[19]

Soon after, at a conference hosted by the Institute for Faith and Learning at Baylor University, I introduced myself to a woman who turned out to be a Catholic and a professor of history. As we discussed our academic interests, I expressed to her that I was beginning to think Catholicism might be true, but that perhaps I should "remain" Anglican (though I wasn't officially Anglican) and pursue the corporate reunion of the Anglican Communion with the Catholic Church. I acknowledged, though, that that position might be untenable if I truly came to think Catholicism true. She shared with me about her pious Catholic grandmother's influence on her family's faith as well as her experience in Rome for Pope John Paul II's funeral as the crowds expressed their recognition of his sanctity by chanting "Santo

---

[18] Ibid., 32–33.

[19] Depending on the individual's personal mission, the process of being transformed into a saint may or may not involve evangelism or nonviolent resistance to social evil or any other specific form of concrete service to God. In short, all people are called to be saints, which will include some forms of concrete service, but not all are called to each and every form of concrete service.

subito!" (i.e., ["Declare him a] saint immediately!"). As she shared, I was reminded of what I read in Congar about the living tradition of Catholicism. When we bid one another farewell, she gave me a rosary and a Catholic prayer book. The next day I prayed the Rosary and found that its focus on the mysteries of the life of Christ enabled me to meditate in a profound way, with Mary and through her eyes, on Christ's life and saving work. It was the first time I ever addressed Mary as someone with whom I could commune and whose prayers I could seek. Soon I began to ask other saints, especially the women Doctors of the Church, for their prayers. My feelings of loneliness as a woman in a male-dominated field were transformed into a deep sense of communion with those women saints.

Ten days later (November 4, 2009), Pope Benedict issued the apostolic constitution *Anglicanorum Coetibus*, which allowed for Anglican groups to enter the Catholic Church as a collective and retain some of their Anglican liturgical practices. I was stunned: the corporate reunion of some Anglicans with the Catholic Church was happening. Then, out of the blue, another philosophy graduate student invited us and others to Mass in the extraordinary form (i.e., the traditional Latin Mass as celebrated before the liturgical revisions of 1962). I was eager to go. I had been to Mass only a few times in my life for weddings. When I knelt to pray before the Mass began, I was moved to tears as I had a profound sense of the presence of Christ in the tabernacle,[20] and that it was to his presence in the Catholic Church that God had been leading me through all my restless study and search for the truth about God's revelation. I was moved to an even deeper sense of awe of God through my experience of the beauty and reverence of the Mass.

Afterward, I told Scott that I thought I would become Catholic. We both recognized immediately that this complicated our future plans. I wasn't going to be trained as a Catholic theologian in a Baptist theology department. So, we considered applying to doctoral programs at a Catholic university. We were advised to talk with a local priest. When we went to him to talk about graduate programs

---

[20] The tabernacle is the place where reserved consecrated Hosts—i.e., Jesus present in the Eucharist—are kept, which typically occupies a position of prominence in Catholic churches and is a focal point behind the altar.

in Catholic theology, his first concern, rightly, was my interest in becoming Catholic. He asked me some questions to gauge how I was thinking about Catholicism and whether I was treating it merely as a theory. The response that came to me to best articulate my attitude was, "I trust the Church." With that, it was clear to the three of us that it was only a matter of time before I would enter the Church.

Given that application deadlines for graduate programs were impending, we decided it was best not to apply in such a rush. I was already enrolled in three philosophy courses for the spring semester, including two reading courses on Aquinas. As I spent more and more time with the philosophers and received encouragement in my work, I developed a desire for the training offered in the philosophy department. I was able to apply to the doctoral program in philosophy, was accepted, and made the transfer soon after. I didn't officially become Catholic until over two years after I became committed to the Church in heart and mind, because I discerned in prayer and with confirmation from the priest whom we were consulting that God was leading me to wait on Scott as he evaluated Catholicism.

In the time of waiting and developing as a philosopher, I solidified and gained additional reasons to trust the Church.[21] For example, I found Alexander Pruss' development and defense of Boccaccio's argument for the Catholic faith to both express and strengthen my own reasoning regarding the coherence of the Church's teachings over time and their consistency with Scripture. In short, Pruss argues that the persistence of the coherence and consistency with Scripture of the Church's teachings, and indeed the very survival of the Church, in the face of the corruption of some of its highest ranking officials at various times (who, importantly, themselves never formally taught anything contrary to the Church's teachings), is evidence that the Holy Spirit is the source and protector of the Church and its teaching.[22] In addition, as I awaited my first Holy Communion, I received deep spiritual encouragement and consolation from

---

[21] A particularly helpful resource to me was Alexander Pruss and his blog, which includes a number of posts about the Catholic faith.

[22] Alex Pruss, "Boccaccio's Argument for the Catholic Faith", May 26, 2010, http://alexanderpruss.blogspot.com/2010/05/boccaccio-argument-for-catholic-faith.html.

God, especially at Mass, and experienced the growth of my desire to receive Christ in the Eucharist.

Further, and of great personal significance, I discovered in the Catholic Church the deepest understanding and affirmation of my femininity and my service of the Church as a female intellectual of any I had encountered. Since this may be surprising (it was to me!), I'll briefly explain. The Church's understanding of femininity includes, but is not limited to, her teaching on human sexuality, which I (and eventually Scott) came to regard as true, good, beautiful, and uniquely consistent with what Christians have held throughout history (in contrast with the official views of non-Catholic Christians, especially regarding contraception). The Catholic view of femininity includes, but goes beyond, the biological distinctiveness of women. It regards the distinctively feminine spirit, which is characterized by the receptivity of life and fostering of its flourishing, whether within a woman's body or in her work in the home, the Church, a religious community, or the broader society.

Contrary to what I encountered as an Evangelical, the Catholic notion of the integral complementarity (and equal dignity) of the sexes isn't reducible to a narrow set of gender roles, but rather concerns the integrity of the whole person—mind, body, and spirit—in his endeavors and relations with others. On a practical level, I found this to mean that the Catholic Church affirms the significant value of women's contributions outside the home, in the Church, and in the world. At the same time, because the Church regards the work of raising children (who have immortal souls destined for eternity with God) as of inestimable value, the distinctive roles of women and men in raising children are affirmed with the highest regard. Such a view has, for both Scott and me, ennobled our work of child-rearing and helpfully relativized the significance of our academic work, so that we see the latter as valuable, but subordinated in its value to that of the former.

It is also worth noting that it was crucial for me to recognize the sharp contrast between the Catholic and many Protestant rationales for a male-only priesthood/pastorate. Whereas, in my experience, Protestants tend to explain the exclusion of women from the pastorate in terms of a difference in the intellectual capacities of men and women, the official Catholic view does not focus on the teaching role of the priest, but rather on his sacramental role, which requires him to represent Christ in a particular way that is impossible for women. While some past Catholic theologians (along with the broader culture of their time) may have expressed views suggesting the intellectual or otherwise inferiority of women, the Catholic Church has taken the lead in the modern world in affirming the equal dignity of women and men and the significant value of the distinctiveness of women.[23] For me, it was and is in the Catholic Church alone that I have found the resources and encouragement to embrace and integrate, within a comprehensive understanding of the meaning and destiny of human life, my desires to bear and raise children and to contribute to the pursuit of wisdom, through research, teaching, and other educational endeavors.

While my conversion to Catholicism bears some similarities to my "conversion" to philosophy, it was much more like the growth of my relationship to Scott. My first impressions of Scott and of the Catholic Church were negative—in Scott's case, only somewhat so! Yet over time and after many positive encounters with Scott, on the one hand, and with the Catholic Tradition, on the other hand, I realized that my negative impressions were based largely on misconceptions and I found myself surprised by a strong attraction that I had no idea was developing, but that was based on a growing respect and admiration in light of more accurate evidence. In both cases, the attraction became such that I could no longer imagine my life without its object. Since committing to Scott in marriage and to the Catholic Church as God's representative on earth, my love for each has only grown and has done so with help from the other.

Scott's Road to Rome

When Lindsay told me she thought Catholicism was true, I, Scott, realized that this would be a watershed moment in our lives, however

---

[23] See, for example, Pope John Paul II, apostolic letter *Mulieris Dignitatum* (August 15, 1988); Edith Stein, *Essays on Woman*, 2nd rev. ed., ed. L. Gelber and Romaeus Leuven, trans. Freda Mary Oben (Washington, DC: ICS Publications, 1996); Prudence Allen, *The Concept of Woman, Volume 1: The Aristotelian Revolution, 750 B.C.–A.D. 1250*, 1st ed. (Grand Rapids, MI: Eerdmans, 1997); *The Concept of Woman, Volume II: The Early Humanist Reformation, 1250–1500* (Grand Rapids, MI: Eerdmans, 2002); *The Concept of Woman, Volume III: The Search for Communion of Persons, 1500–2015*, repr. ed. (Grand Rapids, MI: Eerdmans, 2017).

it turned out. Would this constitute a division between us or a new source of unity? As both of us were (and are) committed to following the truth whatever the cost, the possibility of division was real.

I respected Lindsay and knew she had serious reasons for accepting Catholicism. We had often discussed what she was reading and thinking, but not to the extent that I had a similar view of all the relevant details that influenced her. So, I needed to think through my own attitude to the Catholic Church and her teachings and learn more about them. When I first began, I realized that some of my former objections had already been overcome. I found the idea of purgatory fitting already (in part from my reading of George Macdonald). We must be made fit for eternal life in the household of God, and if that process is not completed prior to death, then it must be completed thereafter. My commitment to Scripture as the sole authority in matters of faith was significantly undermined by what Lindsay mentions above—namely, the need for an authority to settle disputes about scriptural interpretation and the role of ecumenical councils in resolving the early Christological debates (among others). The Catholic view of justification by faith and (grace-enabled) works was not a significant obstacle for me, due to my biblical studies through which I learned of different senses of "righteousness" and "faith" in Scripture, which were compatible with the Catholic view of justification. I did not consider the abuse scandals, horrific as they are, and priestly celibacy to be impediments. For I knew the Catholic Church recognizes the moral fallibility of her priests (since they retain free will) and that celibacy is a discipline (a practice based on a prudential judgment that is not binding for all time) rather than a dogma. I soon realized that I didn't know enough about Catholicism to make an informed decision either way. I had to make time to study the teachings of the Catholic Church.

The Catholic Church claims that she is the Church founded by Jesus Christ to safeguard and teach with infallibility what God has revealed in Christ regarding what we must know and do in order to become fit for everlasting union with God and his angels and saints. How was I to assess the credibility of the Church's claim to such divine authority? Jesus, like the past prophets, provided signs for his speaking for God such as prophesying and fulfilling prophecy, performing miracles, and teaching with supernatural wisdom. Each of these acts involves supernatural agency and so points toward God's authorization. Assessing the Catholic Church's claims is more complex than assessing an individual prophet. For in the former case, the testifier is not an individual but the Church, which is a community and an institution. Further, the Church does not claim to receive new revelation but to safeguard and clarify the revelation from Christ.

I already believed in the trustworthiness of Scripture as God's revelation and gave primacy to the early Christians' faith and practice. So, the way I proceeded in my investigation was to test Church teaching against my understanding of Scripture and investigate the faith and practice of the early Christians to test the historical precedent of the Church's teachings. I also looked for the overall coherence of the Church's teachings as a necessary condition for its truth. I was not just looking for a single knockdown argument for the Church's teaching authority, but sought to accumulate enough evidence from an array of areas to judge whether the Church is worthy of trust with respect to her teachings.

The process I followed was akin to how I sought to learn many things about Lindsay's beliefs, actions, and character in order to know whether or not to trust her with the lifelong commitment of marriage. In the case of the Catholic Church, I came to recognize that the beliefs, actions, and character that were relevant to my assessment were not simply those of just any set of individual Catholic laypersons or clergy, but rather the Church's official teachings and the actions and character of the people the Church identifies as exemplars of the faith—namely, the canonized saints.

Lindsay and I quickly learned that for the health of our marriage Lindsay should not bear the burden of being my primary teacher of Catholic beliefs or defender against my objections. The main sources for my learning about Catholicism were Church documents, especially texts of ecumenical councils, Church Fathers and Doctors (especially St. Thomas Aquinas), the *Catechism of the Catholic Church*, personal conversations,[24] and Lawrence Feingold's extensive online

---

[24] These conversations were mostly with friends among the students and faculty at Baylor, including some of the contributors to this book: Logan Gage, Trent Dougherty, and Frank Beckwith. In addition, Michael and Alexandra Foley, Alexander Pruss, and Father Timothy Vaverek were especially helpful.

audio lectures for the Hebrew Catholic Association.[25] My investigation gave rise to many questions, initial objections, and important
discoveries. I'll discuss first a general obstacle to my accurately understanding Catholic teaching and then turn to some specific obstacles
and their resolutions.

The first general obstacle was that I encountered particular arguments for Catholic doctrine that weren't strong enough to show the
truth of the given doctrine, but I assumed they were thought by Catholics to be sufficiently strong. Once I recognized some important distinctions between two different kinds of arguments, their respective
authoritative status, and the strength of belief they warrant, I was able to
overcome this mistake. The two different kinds of arguments are arguments from authority and fittingness arguments. In this context, an
argument from authority appeals to the teaching of Christ and the
apostles, as interpreted by the Church, as the support for the relevant
conclusion. Such an argument from authority warrants certain belief
in the conclusion given that the person believes (with warrant) that
what the Church proclaims to be the true teaching of Christ and the
apostles is in fact revealed by God, who is perfectly trustworthy.

A fittingness argument is an argument for why a given claim fits
with God's character and past revelation. This kind of argument is at
least in part meant to provide an answer to the question, why did God
do this? Fittingness arguments can lend credibility to the argument's
conclusion, but they do not warrant certain belief in the conclusion in
the way that an argument from authority does.[26] For example, while
Catholics are bound to believe on the basis of the Church's authoritative teaching that Mary was assumed into heaven with both her body
and soul, Catholics are not bound to believe in Mary's Assumption
on the basis of arguments that theologians may make in support of

---

[25] I believe I was pointed to these by the website Called to Communion (overseen by Neal
Judisch and Bryan Cross, fellow contributors to this volume), which I found helpful as well.
Feingold's lectures provided a good overview of Catholic teaching that was systematic and
precise enough for me to trust that Feingold both knew the tradition and could present it
with plausibility. Where the lectures didn't go into sufficient detail or address objections raised
in my mind, I sought answers elsewhere but with more informed questions and objections.

[26] Lawrence Feingold and others helped me to appreciate fittingness arguments. For a discussion, see his *Faith Comes from What Is Heard: An Introduction to Fundamental Theology* (Steubenville, OH: Emmaus Academic, 2016).

its fittingness (e.g., the argument that Mary was assumed into heaven because it is fitting that Jesus would honor his mother by preventing her body from corrupting). It was helpful for me to recognize that the basis for believing Church teaching did not depend on fittingness arguments. For fittingness arguments are—and often seemed to me— too weak to establish that a claim must be believed.[27]

Fittingness arguments and arguments from authority warrant different strengths of belief. This was relevant to my understanding the Church's teaching that belief by faith requires certainty. Arguments from an infallible authority warrant beliefs that ought to be held with the certainty of faith. Fittingness arguments can at most warrant what are sometimes called "theological opinions", which ought not to be held with certainty. Informed theological opinions may be warranted by forms of reasoning, such as fittingness arguments, that do not ground whatever claim is the object of opinion directly in divine revelation but in philosophical, theological, or empirical considerations that go beyond revelation and which at most give probable but not certain support for a given claim. An example of a mere theological opinion is when a person believes that God is a Trinity of Persons, and his belief is based not on God's revelation but on his reflection on the nature of perfect love. Belief by faith, in contrast, is based on divine revelation. Since God is the perfect testifier (i.e., he is perfectly honest, sincere, and truthful and is maximally competent to know), believing God's testimony with certainty is both reasonable and normative.

Aquinas illustrates the distinction between mere theological opinion and belief by faith in his discussion of the phenomenon of doubt with respect to an article of faith. Aquinas says that the one who doubts one article reveals that he holds to each article of faith not by faith that God revealed it but according to his own opinion of its plausibility.[28] For by doubting one article, one shows that one believes the articles based on reasoning that at best provides probable but uncertain support for the articles. The way for a believer to be reasonable in holding to the articles of faith with certainty is to hold them by faith in God—that is, on the basis of trust in God, the perfect testifier, having revealed them to the Church. The distinction

---

[27] See, for instance, Aquinas' *Summa Contra Gentiles* 1.9.2.
[28] For example, see *Summa Theologiae* II–II, q. 5, a. 3.

between informed theological opinion and belief by faith proved helpful in my thinking about the certainty of faith, which I discuss more below. It also helped to clarify for me that my investigation was not merely a matter of my coming to have theological opinions in accordance with Church teaching but required my submitting to the Church's God-given teaching authority.

Now I'll turn to some of my specific obstacles and objections, beginning briefly with some that were less significant and then discussing in detail more significant ones. We had been attending both Catholic Mass and our Episcopal church on Sundays after Lindsay judged Catholicism to be true. I formed an initial, uncharitable impression that many of the Catholics I observed were neither devout nor duly reverent toward what they putatively believed was happening on the altar. While some may not have been duly reverent, I say my impression was uncharitable because I wasn't sensitive enough to internal forms of devotion that may lack affective expression. I was biased due to my Evangelical background, with its particular overt expressions of devotion. As we continued to go to Mass, I came to recognize different expressions of devotion, which helped to overcome this cultural clash.

I was also initially put off by some Marian devotion because I thought some of the language used to address Mary and her accomplishments attributed to her what I took to be the sole work of Christ. I was also puzzled by the Church's dogmatic Marian teachings because they didn't appear to have clear scriptural warrant. But I came to see that there is scriptural warrant, the attestation of Tradition, and good fittingness arguments for the Marian dogmas and that Mary's place in the story of salvation as the Mother of God Incarnate and the New Eve warrants such high praise. Further, rather than her elevation diminishing the work of Christ, I came to recognize that it reveals the beauty of both the way humanity can cooperate with Christ's work and the destiny of those God redeems.

Now for the more significant issues. Like many Evangelicals, I had assumed that it was Evangelicals who held to and practiced the teachings of the early Christians. Through my investigation of the early Church, I came to see that this view did not withstand scrutiny for at least two reasons: distinctively Catholic beliefs and practices were clearly present in the early Church, and they show credible continuity with what God had done in forming the people of Israel. This stands out in two areas: the priesthood and the Eucharist.

I learned that the Church affirms the priesthood of all believers in a certain sense (i.e., the common priesthood). She also holds that there is a ministerial priesthood that is not common. The difference is that, while all priests minister and serve the Lord through prayer, good deeds, thanksgiving, and offering their own spiritual sacrifices, the ministerial priests have a special role involving ministering to the Lord through offering a special sacrifice—the Eucharistic sacrifice, which makes present the one sacrifice of Christ. This distinction between common and ministerial priesthood was also present in the people of Israel, "a kingdom of priests and a holy nation".[29] All of the Israelites were priests, but some were also ministerial priests and their assistants who are of the house of Levi. Ministerial priests of Israel offered drink, grain, and animal sacrifices to the Lord. Catholic priests offer the Eucharist and administer sacraments. It was illuminating to find that the structure of the priesthood in Catholicism is isomorphic with the structure of the priesthood in Israel.[30] I found that belief in this distinction between common and ministerial priesthood was present very early in Christianity and was accepted as the teaching of Jesus Christ and the apostles.[31]

With respect to the hierarchical structure, I recognized that the Church claims that priests are appointed servants who occupy an office that has certain powers exclusive to that office. Jesus founded a

---

[29] Ex 19:6.

[30] There is a parallelism between the high priests and ministerial priests (of the line of Aaron) in the people of Israel and the bishops and priests in the Catholic Church, between the assistants to the ministerial priests (those of Levi but not Aaron) in Israel and deacons in the Catholic Church, and between the non-Levitical nation of Israel (common priesthood) and the laity in the Catholic Church.

[31] For example, St. Clement I (the fourth bishop of Rome) writes on this in about A.D. 96 in his *Epistle to the Corinthians* (chaps. 40–44). St. Clement says that offerings are to be made by the early Christians in the proper place, at the proper time, and by the appointed people just as in Israel. He claims this order of duties (holy orders) is from God in both cases. He explicitly draws the parallel to Israel and says daily sacrifices are not to be offered by everyone but only by those appointed to do so (the apostles or the successors they designate) and in the proper way. He makes an argument from analogy that just as there was contention about who would be priests at the time of Moses, so there will be contention about who will be priests in the early Church. The first apostles settle this dispute by directly appointing bishops and deacons to serve in a ministerial priestly role.

visible organization that included a structure of offices that bestowed certain powers, were ordered hierarchically, and had a means of succession for the occupants of those offices. This is not a strange idea but a nearly universal organizational practice, and both was held by the early Church to be the teaching of Christ and was continuous with God's will for Israel.

The Church teaches that Christ gave to the apostles an office that had powers that include the power to make Christ truly present in the Eucharist. I was attracted to the idea of the Real Presence of Christ in the Eucharist and that his Presence should be respected and adored. I thought it beautiful and awe-inspiring to be able to genuflect (i.e., to go down on one knee) to Christ, if he was really there. I desired to be like Catholics in this way, although I wasn't yet sure it was true. For the Eucharist provides a location, in a sense, for directing one's worship and provides the privilege of practicing with our bodies the highest form of respect and union. So, it seemed like a good idea and a fitting way for Christ to remain with us always.

The Anglican Communion also claims to affirm the Real Presence of Christ in the Eucharist and that his presence there is a mystery.[32] But I found that there is an important difference between the Catholic and the Anglican view, which has significant practical implications. The Anglican Communion affirms Christ's Real Presence without specifying the nature of that presence in terms of whether Christ is present with his Body, Blood, Soul, and Divinity and whether the bread is really absent. The Catholic priest who was mentoring us posed an objection to the Anglican intentionally ambiguous view of the presence of Christ in their eucharist. He pointed out that because the Anglican Communion has no authoritative teaching on the nature of Christ's presence in the eucharist, they also have no standard practice for how the eucharist is to be treated. This allows for a serious practical contradiction between Anglicans during the very act that is supposed to be a sign and means of their unity: those Anglicans who regard Christ's presence in the eucharist as worthy of worship genuflect and adore

---

[32] Pope Leo XIII's 1896 papal bull *Apostolicae Curae* states the position of the Catholic Church that Anglican holy orders are invalid. The Church's position was confirmed by Pope John Paul II in his 1998 *Ad Tuendam Fidem*. Given the invalidity of the Anglican priesthood, Anglican priests do not have the power to make Christ truly present.

him there, while those who do not, do not. And those who reflect on the different intentions behind the treatment of the eucharist—whether Christ's presence there is to be worshipped or not—may well regard those whose practice is opposite from their own as either idolatrous or irreverent. This practical contradiction was a living reality in the Episcopal church we attended in Waco. I did not see a way for Anglicans to overcome this disunity. This isn't to say that the Anglican Communion should be more authoritative about the matter if it thinks it has no grounds for such authority. But considerations such as this raised the question, did God leave an authority to provide a clear teaching on issues like these that are central to Christian belief and practice and that are often the source of divisions between Christians?

An experience made me feel the keenness of this problem. Our Episcopal church in Waco used leavened bread for communion. One day, the bread was particularly dry, and so it was crumbling as people were receiving communion with crumbs falling on the ground. People ignored the crumbs that were accumulating on the ground; some crumbs may have even been walked on by people. The crumbs remained there until the end of the service. After the service, Lindsay, a friend of ours, and I went up and picked up the crumbs. We weren't sure whether Christ was really present in the full sense at that point, but we thought that if he was, then just leaving him on the ground to be walked on was irreverent. From this experience, I could see that the Anglican and Episcopal lack of clarity on the nature of the eucharist had important, practical ramifications. I was, for that reason, attracted to the Catholic Church's claim that God has provided a clear teaching on the presence of Christ in the Eucharist and a corresponding clear standard for how the Eucharist should be treated.

As I read SS. Ignatius, Justin Martyr, and Irenaeus, I discovered that belief in the Real Presence of Christ in the Eucharist and the transformation of the bread and wine was present very early.[33] It

---

[33] For example, Irenaeus in *Against Heresies* 5.2 gives an argument against a form of Gnosticism that denies the possibility of the salvation and regeneration of our bodies. His argument depends on a view of the Eucharist according to which ordinary bread and wine is transformed into Christ's actual material Body and Blood, the consuming of which contributes to the redemption of the human body. For the Eucharist actually bodily unites us to Christ and our bodies are regenerated by this union. If this was not his view, then it is not clear why he would use the Eucharist in his argument against Gnosticism.

became clear that at least some among the leaders of the early Church held to the view of the Catholic Church that the bread is transformed and Christ is made really present in the Eucharist (even if they didn't use the term "transubstantiation"). Further, I recognized that the sixth chapter of the Gospel of John was easier to understand in this light, and I came to see, as Lindsay had, that the Catholic view wasn't a late innovation.

After a year and a half of study, I reached a point where I believed that the Church's teachings (including her claim to divine authority) were plausible and probably true. But our priest mentor told me that a judgment that the Catholic faith is probably true was distinct from the kind of faith needed to become Catholic, which is faith that everything that the Church teaches is revealed by God. So, I began to pray to receive such faith, which I took to be a gift from God, and I did so for about six months. During that time, Lindsay and I had the privilege of traveling throughout Italy. Our experience of the ancient presence of the Catholic faith; the genuine catholicity or universality of the Catholic Church (witnessed by us especially at the Pentecost Mass at St. Peter's Basilica in Rome); the beauty of Catholic art, architecture, sacred music, and worship; and the fittingness of certain forms of Catholic devotion (e.g., the Liturgy of the Hours, the honoring of relics, penitential practices) increased my belief that the Catholic Church is probably what she claims to be and my desire for the gift of faith that I was awaiting from God.

Eventually, I realized that I was confused about what was essential to such faith. I believed that it required a psychological (or felt) certainty characterized by complete peace and lack of doubt with the decision to become Catholic. I had assumed that I should ask for the gift of faith, that God would, in his time, give it to me, and that the sign of its presence would be such certainty. Then, I could responsibly choose to enter the Catholic Church. Since I lacked such certainty, I waited. What I misunderstood was the relation between the choice to enter the Church and the certainty that is characteristic of faith. I assumed that the requisite voluntary act of placing my faith in the Church as God's representative could responsibly come only after God gave me a felt sense of certainty and peace.

My misunderstanding became clear to me one Sunday at Mass. The Gospel reading that day was the story of Jesus and the centurion who asked for the healing of his servant.[34] Jesus offers to go home with him, but the centurion begs him to simply say the word and trusts that his servant would be healed. Jesus praises him for his faith, for the centurion did not need to see Jesus heal his servant directly. The centurion trusted that Jesus had the supernatural authority to heal at a distance in contrast to others who needed to see and touch Jesus to be healed. While I did not take this Gospel story to be about an act of faith despite uncertainty, it was the occasion for to me to see that my waiting and praying for a sense of certainty before entering the Church was similar to the behavior of those with weaker faith who needed to see and touch Jesus to be healed. But the centurion, with his greater faith, needed no such thing.

I saw that my waiting for certainty was akin to holding out for the kind of certainty that St. Thomas the Apostle seemed to desire after the Resurrection.[35] He refused to trust the other apostles' testimony to the Resurrection of the Lord. For me to be certain in the way of St. Thomas would require that I "see for myself" in some way that would likely require an extraordinary act of grace from God—a special revelation from God just for me showing me that the Church was the mediator of his revelation. While God may grant such things, Jesus says, "Blessed are those who have not seen and yet believe."[36] In this, I understood God to be saying to me, "Blessed are you if you choose to trust my revelation through the Catholic Church when you have sufficient evidence to do so and without waiting to be granted a special privilege." I did have sufficient evidence for it to be reasonable for me to trust the Church. To do so would not be a blind leap. For I regarded the Church as credible and was certain enough that the act of trusting the Church to be God's mediator of revelation was a reasonable action. I did not need a greater sense of certainty in order for my choice to trust the Church to be reasonable and pleasing to God.

Having recognized this, I had sufficient peace to choose to trust the Church. So, I did. That afternoon I told Lindsay I was ready, and we were received into the Church two weeks later on the Sunday before Lent began in 2012. After I was confirmed and received my

[34] Mt 8:5–13.
[35] Jn 20:24–29.
[36] Jn 20:29.

First Communion, by God's grace, I felt the complete peace and certainty I had been waiting for, and since then I have never doubted my decision. I recognized that the certainty I had initially waited for was not a necessary condition for responsibly choosing to become Catholic but rather a fruit of the choice to trust the Church—a choice that is only possible with the help of God's grace. I found to be true the *Catechism*'s statement that "believing is possible only by grace and the interior helps of the Holy Spirit. But it is no less true that believing is an authentically human act ... contrary neither to human freedom nor to human reason."[37]

Conclusion

Upon reflection on our journey to the Catholic Church, we have been struck by how God's providence was at work throughout our spiritual and intellectual development. Many potential obstacles to the Catholic faith were removed before we were even thinking about the possibility of becoming Catholic. The answers to many of the questions that drove our desire for further education prepared us for the Church and found their most complete answer only in the Catholic faith. Further, the process knit us together in mind and heart in unforeseen, unplanned, and significant ways. We were surprised to find in the Catholic Church an integrated and comprehensive understanding of reality, Scripture, history, and the meaning of life, and an inspiring wealth of spiritual resources for growth in our relationship with God. As philosophers, Catholicism was and is good news indeed. Many of our prior theological opinions were transformed into truths of faith once we accepted the Church's authority as our basis for belief. We also acquired by faith important truths that we did not seek but that have become dear to us. Rather than stifling thought, we have found these additional truths to provide helpful guidance in our philosophical and theological inquiry and to enable in our pursuit of wisdom a freedom characterized by peace. Similarly, the wealth of spiritual resources in the Catholic tradition have guided us deeper and deeper in our closeness to Christ. These resources have

[37] *Catechism of the Catholic Church*, no. 154.

also guided us in the formation of our children through our development of a family culture built around living according to the liturgical calendar in concrete ways and integrating our faith in all areas of life. We have found the Church to be like a great mansion with mansions within mansions as its rooms. Not only is it filled with spiritual and intellectual resources to guide our family's faith, hope, and love, but it is occupied by great heroes and heroines of the faith, who inspire us by their example, encourage us by their prayers, and point us to closer union with God.

9

Traditions as Paradigms: A MacIntyrean Approach to the Catholic Question

Bryan R. Cross

Leaning on the Everlasting Arms:
My Time in the Pentecostal Tradition

I was raised from infancy in the Pentecostal tradition. On both my mother's and father's sides my grandparents were involved in the early stages of Pentecostalism in North America in the first part of the twentieth century. In our family, it was considered essential to know Scripture. My siblings and I were consistently taught Scripture since as early as I can remember, even memorizing complete chapters of the Psalms and Gospels. We attended church twice Sunday, again on Wednesday evenings, and also attended Sunday school weekly. We went to all the revivals and all the Vacation Bible Schools. So my family and the Pentecostal tradition gave me a thorough familiarity with the Bible, a healthy fear of God, and a disposition to be sensitive to the prompting of the Holy Spirit.

During church one Sunday morning early in the final semester of my senior year in high school, I experienced a unique sense of God's presence and calling. But what this meant was unclear to me at the time. Later, I went to our youth pastor and told her about this experience. She recommended that we meet regularly for prayer and Bible study, which we began to do and continued to do until I left for college in the fall of that year. Through these weekly meetings I began to own my faith in God for myself, as a choice I made for myself, not merely as something I believed and practiced because it was what I had been taught. At the age of eighteen, I was seeking to grow closer to God, in part to determine what God wanted me to do, so that I could live my life in his service.

During my undergraduate education at the University of Michigan in Ann Arbor, where I met my future wife, I was exposed to Christians of all different traditions in various Christian campus ministries and fellowships. These included charismatics, Presbyterians, Baptists, Catholics, and charismatic Catholics. We often worshipped, prayed, and studied the Bible together, trying to focus on what we had in common, rather than trying to debate the points on which we disagreed. This experience raised a number of questions for me, but at the same time, it helped me see more clearly how sincere Christian faith extended beyond my own particular tradition.

At this time, I also began to rethink the relation of ethics and religion. I had grown up thinking that right and wrong were based entirely on divine commands and could be known only by knowing divine commands. At that time, I did not understand that divine commands concerning ethics were related to the natures of things, and that we can know the natural law by the natural power of reason.

During Thanksgiving break of my junior year, I stayed up until almost three o'clock in the morning talking with my younger brother, who was home from his first year as an undergraduate philosophy major at Wheaton. We sat in the family room debating divine command theory: I was defending it; he was opposing it.

Drawing from Plato's *Euthyphro*, my brother asked: "Are ethical truths true because God commands them, or does God command them because they are true?"

I replied, "They are true because God commands them."

To which he replied, "Why does God command these and not others? If rape is wrong only because God commanded us not to do it, then if God commanded us to do it, rape would be right and good. (And we may replace the word 'rape' with any other term referring to some heinous atrocity—for example, genocide, cannibalism, incest, pedophilia, necrophilia, abortion, blasphemy, and so forth).

"And in that case," continued my brother, "how would God be morally distinguishable from the devil?"

"But," I protested, "God wouldn't do that."

"Why not?" he replied.

"Because," I said, "that's not his character."

"Well," he replied, "then at least we now agree that the wrongness of rape is not because God commanded us not to do it, but rather because it is contrary to God's character. But what is it about the act of rape that makes it contrary to God's character?"

"Well," I replied, "God is loving and good, and rape is an act of selfishness and violation, completely disregarding the good of the other."

"So," he said, "rape is wrong because it is not good and loving, and whatever is not good and loving is contrary to God's character?"

"Yes, I think so." I said.

He replied, "Well, now you are agreeing that rape is wrong because of something about the nature of rape; and that God commands us not to do that act because of the nature of that act in relation to his character."

At that time, I believed that humans, through our natural power of reason, could come to knowledge of, say, botany or mathematics or cell biology or quantum physics. But I believed that unlike the truths in those sciences, ethical truths were fundamentally and entirely divine commands, and that therefore we could not have a true ethical system without basing it on the ethical prescriptions and prohibitions laid out in Scripture. Even our conscience, according to my theology of the time, was simply a God-implanted blueprint of those divine commands, like pre-loaded software—that software had been corrupted by original sin, but the original code was a kind of database of divine commands.

My brother did not persuade me that evening, but his criticisms were strong enough that I was less confident that I was right. I had an inkling that I was bringing philosophical assumptions to my interpretation of Scripture, but what those assumptions were, and how I was to evaluate them, was an inscrutably dark mystery to me, extending into an area that could be symbolized as one large question mark. Even the word "philosophy" elicited defensive and highly skeptical affections within me, because the term "philosophy" was for me associated with deception and human wisdom.[1] I subsequently read Plato's *Euthyphro* and saw how Socrates presented Euthyphro with

---

[1] Cf. 1 Cor 1:18–25; Col 2:8.

that fundamental dilemma: Is something good because God loves it, or does God love it because it is good? I could give a glib answer: It is good because it conforms to God's nature, but I did not know what that meant; it was a bit of semantic jargon to patch over a gaping intellectual hole. It left me with more questions, and I did not know how to answer them, or even how to begin to answer them.

Over the next few years, I started reading books on the ethics of euthanasia and assisted suicide. I went to hear Dr. Jack Kevorkian ("Dr. Death") give a talk near campus. He was in the prime of his publicity around that time, and the issues of euthanasia and assisted suicide were hot topics for that reason. To the best of my knowledge, nobody seemed to have good arguments against his positions. Most of the books I was reading that opposed euthanasia were written by Evangelical Christians. And these books generally approached ethical questions from the point of view of *sola scriptura*, which was the only Christian point of view I knew at the time. I noticed that the Christian authors whose arguments were more cogent and persuasive were incorporating philosophical claims into their writing; they were not being fully consistent with *sola scriptura*, at least in the "sufficiency" sense of *sola scriptura*—namely, the notion that Scripture is sufficient in matters of faith and conduct.

I could see that the merely *sola scriptura* approach was not sufficient to deal with moral questions about beginning and end-of-life issues, especially those involving medical technology—that is, those falling under the category of medical ethics. I also noticed that another problem with the *sola scriptura* approach is that in a democratic society in which the majority of citizens do not believe in the authority of Scripture, a *sola scriptura* Christian's only solution to the problem of the legalization of assisted suicide and abortion is evangelism—that is, conversion. It seemed to me at the time that in order to persuade in the public square regarding such moral questions, the only recourse available to a *sola scriptura* Christian was to open the Bible and start pointing to verses. And if other people did not accept the Bible, the only recourse for a *sola scriptura* Christian was to convert them to Christianity so that they accepted the Bible as authoritative. But these problems did not cause me to doubt the doctrine of *sola scriptura*. At the time, they were merely difficulties, and I had no alternative paradigm.

By my senior year, I was attending a nondenominational charismatic church, where my wife-to-be worshipped. The pastor of this church had recently moved toward Reformed theology, and by the end of my senior year, I was reading various books on Reformed theology, and eventually became convinced that Reformed covenantal theology was more biblical than the dispensational theology in which I had been raised.

In the three years following the completion of my undergraduate education, my wife and I led an international student fellowship composed of mostly Indonesian students at Eastern Michigan University and the University of Michigan. During this period, I continued to read as many books as I could find on Reformed theology. By the end of those three years, I came to see that if I was going to be a pastor or missionary, I needed formal theological training. So we moved to St. Louis, Missouri, so that I could begin studying at Covenant Theological Seminary, a Presbyterian seminary deeply committed to the Reformed theological tradition, and belonging to the Presbyterian Church in America.

In Christ Alone: My Time in the Reformed Tradition

When we moved to St. Louis, we began attending a vibrant nondenominational charismatic church. At this time our first child, Joshua, was ill with a terminal illness. When he died the following year, at the age of two and a half, the people of the church enveloped us with support and comfort. But the loss was traumatic for my wife and me. Even returning to the church building where he had been with us was a painful reminder of his absence, especially for my wife. For me this event also continued to elicit and press theological questions that only began to grow during my time in seminary.[2]

On one particular Sunday morning not long after our son had died, a woman performed a voice solo at the church. She went up to the front of the church, was handed a microphone, and began to sing the traditional hymn "Holy, Holy, Holy, Lord God Almighty".

---

[2] Bryan R. Cross, "God in the Dock: Tragedy and Trilemma", *Strange Notions* (blog), November 12, 2013, https://strangenotions.com/god-in-the-dock-tragedy-and-trilemma/.

But from my point of view, she sang it as if she were in a night club, with a forced gravelly voice, and sensual, bodily motions. The poignant contradiction of form and content was too much for me. I had been growing more and more disturbed by the irreverence of the form of the worship, without being able to identify consciously what it was that was troubling me. Finally, during this song the contradiction was for me directly palpable and undeniable. As we left the service that day, I decided that I could not continue to worship there.

After leaving the charismatic church, we started attending a Presbyterian church belonging to the Presbyterian Church in America (PCA), and joined it shortly thereafter. I knew that there, at least, my family and I would not be getting the night-club version of "Holy, Holy, Holy". Here we settled in and made this church our home. I was now firmly Reformed, a five-point Calvinist endorsing the Westminster Confession of Faith. I began teaching Sunday school and eventually completed a pastoral internship there.

In my third year of seminary, I took a graduate philosophy class at Saint Louis University on the problem of evil, motivated in part by questions that lingered from the death of my son. At this point, I began to think more carefully and intentionally about the role and relationship between theology and philosophy. Prior to that, I was for theological reasons distrustful and suspicious of philosophy and of reason in general in any theological matters. This was in continuity from my Pentecostal tradition. From my point of view now as a Calvinist committed to total depravity, I had even more reason to believe that reason was fallen and untrustworthy. At the same time, I knew that I could not persuasively respond to philosophical objections to the Christian faith merely by quoting Scripture or the Westminster Confession of Faith. In order to answer philosophical objections, I first had to understand those philosophical objections. So my initial motivation for studying philosophy was merely instrumental, to understand and refute philosophical arguments against the faith.

In my last year of seminary, I took a graduate philosophy class at Saint Louis University on the metaphysics of St. Thomas Aquinas. Studying St. Thomas raised many questions regarding the Reformed tradition, particularly in those ways in which the Reformed tradition differed from the Catholic tradition. Although I could not answer those questions at the time, it was clear to me that there was at least a deep tension between the philosophical and theological positions and methods of the Reformers, and those of St. Thomas.

My belief as an early seminarian was that other Christian traditions did not agree with us (Presbyterians) primarily because they did not know exegesis (i.e., the interpretation of the text of the Bible) as well as we did. At the seminary, we believed that exegesis was on our side—that it was exegesis that validated our position over and against that of all the other Christian traditions. I had believed that a rigorous study of the biblical languages and Scripture would provide the means to resolve interpretive disagreements dividing the various Christian traditions. So I had poured myself into exegesis with that hope, so much so that at graduation the seminary faculty honored me with the exegesis award awarded to one graduate each year.

But especially in my last year of seminary, I began to see the implicit but determinative role that philosophy was playing in our interpretation of Scripture. We were calling what we were doing exegesis, as if it were an entirely objective activity, but we were tacitly importing many philosophical and theological assumptions into the process by which we arrived at our interpretations. I had not realized this until I began to study philosophy, which allowed me to become more aware of the implicit philosophy present in our hermeneutical practice.

This became clearer to me when I took a class at the seminary on the Westminster Confession of Faith (WCF). One of the assignments at the end of the semester was laying out, explaining, and justifying any "exceptions" we had to the WCF. Students variously had different exceptions and different numbers of exceptions. My list of exceptions was somewhat larger than average, and when I showed it to another student, he asked me why I came to this seminary in the first place, rather than going to another seminary that more closely matched my theological views. It was at this point that I first began to be aware of the problem of ecclesial consumerism, though at the time I could not have identified it as such or explained precisely what is wrong with it.[3] But I had thought that the solution to interpretive

---

[3] See Bryan R. Cross, "Ecclesial Consumerism", Called to Communion, July 5, 2010, http://www.calledtocommunion.com/2010/07/ecclesial-consumerism/.

disagreements was turning to the text of Scripture and allowing exegesis to illuminate the solution.

Now I began to realize that the belief that exegesis was sufficient to resolve interpretive disagreements was protected and insulated by a prior sorting of persons into distinct groups that shared sufficiently similar interpretations. When the exegesis did not resolve the disagreement, one was supposed to have chosen another group that more closely matched one's theology, and one was supposed to leave the nonmatching group so as not to attempt to compel even subtly that present group to accept one's personal interpretation of Scripture. In this way, the belief in the sufficiency of exegesis and the perspicuity of Scripture was insulated from falsification by a continual partitioning and sorting of persons on the basis of their theological beliefs.

When I began to see the degree to which philosophy was playing an implicit role in our interpretation of Scripture, my belief that exegesis was a neutral objective science, and that it was sufficient to adjudicate interpretive disputes, began to weaken. So I decided to pursue a formal program of graduate philosophical study in order to acquire a better understanding of the relation of philosophy to theology throughout the history of the Church. If I could not avoid bringing philosophy into exegesis, at least I was going to do my best to bring in true philosophy.

This conclusion was complemented by another experience, shortly thereafter. A few weeks after I graduated from seminary, some young Mormon missionaries came to our door. My wife invited them in, and we started talking. But we were just getting into the important questions when we ran out of time. So we agreed to meet with them the following week. They ended up coming weekly for the rest of the summer. Since I had just completed four years of training in biblical theology, Greek and Hebrew, I was quite confident that I could persuade these teenage missionaries by exegetical arguments from Scripture that Mormonism is false and that the Gospel, as I understood it then, is true.

Over the course of our discussions with these Mormon missionaries, when I argued that their teachings were contrary to Scripture, they would counter by appealing to the Book of Mormon, and I would respond by saying that the Book of Mormon is contrary to

Scripture. But they viewed Scripture *through* the Book of Mormon—that is, in light of the Book of Mormon. They claimed that very shortly after the death of the apostles (or maybe even *before* the death of the last apostle) the Church fell into utter apostasy, and that the true Gospel had been preserved in North America where Jesus had come to preach to certain peoples living here at that time. For that reason, according to the Mormons, the Bible had to be interpreted and understood in light of this additional revelation that Joseph Smith had recovered, and not according to the teachings and practices of the early Church Fathers. That was because in their view the early Church Fathers had corrupted Christ's teaching by incorporating into it both Greek philosophy and pagan rites in syncretistic fashion. So our conversation at some point reached fundamental questions such as, "Why should we believe the Book of Mormon over the early Church Fathers?" and "How do you know that the Church Fathers corrupted Christ's teaching?"

I realized at the time that I too, as a Protestant, could not appeal to the early Church Fathers or the councils in a *principled* way to support my position against that of the Mormons. Of course, at that time I agreed with Nicene Trinitarianism and Chalcedonian Christology, but like the Mormons I too believed that shortly after the death of the apostles the Church had begun to fall into various errors, minor at first but progressively more serious. So in my mind, everything any Church Father said had to be tested against my own interpretation of Scripture.

Where did I think the early Church had gone wrong? I agreed with the Mormons that the early Church had been influenced by Greek philosophy. The Church had made use of Greek philosophy with terms such as *homoousious, hypostasis,* and *physis* to explain and defend the doctrines of the Trinity and the Incarnation. Of course, I believed those doctrines to be true, but the use of such Greek notions worried me because it suggested an implicit syncretism. Protestants I respected had told me that they questioned or rejected parts of the Nicene Creed (e.g., saying that Christ was "eternally begotten") as being both extrabiblical and based on Greek philosophy. I knew that Greek philosophy had been quite influential in Alexandria, and I believed that this is where the allegorical method of interpretation was introduced. This was a method, in my mind, that was at least partly responsible for the Church's departure from the Gospel, and the subsequent need for the Reformation. From my *sola scriptura* point of view, there was no difference between bishop and elder, no basis for the papacy or even Roman primacy, not even a real distinction between clergy and laymen. So the whole hierarchical organization of the early Catholic Church seemed to me to be a corruption, a departure from what was taught in the New Testament.

Similarly, I believed that the Catholic liturgy, holy days, almost everything in the liturgical calendar, vestments for clergy, veneration of saints and their relics and icons, prayers for the dead, and prayers to departed saints were all accretions from pagan holidays and practices. Even the idea that some Christians are saints in some greater way (with a capital "S") than that in which all Christians are saints was, in my opinion, a corruption, because I thought that egalitarianism followed from our being saved by grace. This was epitomized, in my view, by the Catholic Church's veneration of Mary, treating her as "Mother of God", and claiming that she remained a virgin after the birth of Jesus, as though marriage and sexual intercourse were in some way evil or tainted with evil.

From my point of view at that time, the early Church had somehow been led astray from the finished work of Christ and come to believe in what I thought was a magical conception of the sacraments, presumably also imported from paganism. This magical way of conceiving of the sacraments explained why the bishops who wrote the creeds treated baptism as forgiving sins, why at some point they came to believe that the bread and wine really became the Body and Blood of Christ, and why they transformed the *agape* love feast into the "Eucharistic sacrifice".[4] That, along with their failure to adhere to *sola scriptura*, explained why they treated things like confirmation, marriage, penance, and ordination as sacraments. From the *sola scriptura* point of view, all these "additions", like purgatory, the exaltation of celibacy, mysticism, monasticism, and asceticism, had to have come from paganism and were therefore a corruption of the purity of the Church and the Gospel, just as Israel of the Old Testament had

---

[4] Cf. *Didache* 14; 1 Clement 44; St. Justin Martyr, *Dialogue with Trypho* 41; St. Irenaeus, *Against Heresies* 4.17; St. Cyprian, *On the Lapsed* 26; St. Cyril of Jerusalem, *Catechetical Lectures* 5.18.

played the harlot with the gods of the other nations. As I saw it, the Church had started to deviate from orthodoxy by the second century, and the pace of that deviation only accelerated when, according to this narrative, Constantine legalized Christianity through the Edict of Milan in A.D. 313 and Theodosis made Christianity the official state religion in A.D. 380. Christ had said that his kingdom was not of this world, but in my mind, the Catholic Church had tried to turn it into an earthly kingdom with bishops and popes assuming monarchical prerogatives.

So when the Mormons claimed that a great apostasy had overcome the Church by the time of the death of the last apostle, I had no ground to stand on by which to refute that claim. The Mormons believed that the true Gospel was recovered in the early nineteenth century by Joseph Smith. I believed, as a Reformed Protestant, that the true Gospel was recovered in the early sixteenth century by Martin Luther. But to my frustration, we both agreed that the early Church Fathers and the councils were suspect and not authoritative in their own right. Over the course of our meetings with the Mormon missionaries that summer, I realized that with respect to our treatment of the early Church Fathers and ecumenical councils, there was no *principled* difference between myself and the two young Mormon missionaries sitting in my living room.

What troubled me was something I had learned in my philosophy graduate seminar on St. Thomas Aquinas. In his arguments, St. Thomas continually appeals to the tradition of the Church and to the Church Fathers. I found myself frustrated by his theological method. I wanted him to be doing exegesis from Scripture when making theological arguments, not appealing to the Church Fathers. The professor teaching the seminar responded to my objections by explaining that St. Thomas believed that divine providence guided the Church Fathers and the development of the Church. This professor pointed out that St. Thomas was not a deist about the Church (that is, God does not abandon the Church to her own devices). That short answer provoked me to do a great deal of reflecting, because I realized then that I did not share St. Thomas' nondeistic way of conceiving of the development of the Church. My position at the time regarding this particular point was again not different *in principle* from that of the Mormons.

Of course, I firmly believed in divine providence, but I distrusted all the Church Fathers to whom St. Thomas appealed. That is why, in my mind at the time, appeals to the Church Fathers did not establish anything at all, because if the Church were being corrupted and falling away from the purity of the Gospel, then appealing to the Fathers was like appealing to heretics. But for St. Thomas, if the Church Fathers taught something, especially if they were Doctors of the Church or if the claim in question was held and taught widely by the Church Fathers, that showed it to be authoritative for us as a kind of patrimony precisely because the Holy Spirit was unfailingly guiding the development of the Church into all truth. On this point, I discovered a very deep difference between myself and St. Thomas. The more I studied his writings, the more the difference was noticeable to me. St. Thomas believed that faith in Christ necessarily involves trusting the Church, because Christ cannot fail to guide and protect the development of his Church.

In January 1999, Pope John Paul II visited St. Louis. One of my philosophy professors had two extra tickets to attend the papal Mass and offered them to a fellow graduate student and myself. We accepted. My purpose in accepting the ticket was not on account of interest in becoming Catholic. I respected Pope John Paul II for his philosophical writings, for his leadership with respect to the culture of life, and for his role in the defeat of communism. I attended the papal Mass more as an observer, interested in hearing what he had to say, and wanting to participate in a civic event in which a prominent world and religious leader visits my city. I found myself uncomfortable when, in my impression, many of the Catholics present seemed to treat him like a rock star. That was unintelligible to me theologically. At the end of the Mass, I left seemingly unchanged, viewing it as an interesting and valuable life experience, but in no way as attracting me to Catholicism.

I completed the internship required for ordination and continued to teach Sunday school at the Presbyterian church we were attending. But at that point, I decided not to pursue ordination, because for me there were too many unanswered theological questions. I was no longer confident that the Westminster Confession of Faith was the correct interpretation of Scripture, let alone authoritative.

The year after finishing seminary, my youngest daughter went through a very serious illness in which she required chemotherapy and many months of hospitalization. And during the following year, I went through what I would call an intellectual crisis concerning theology and the ecclesial practice of Christianity. It was not a personal faith crisis; my belief in Christ and love for him was never in question.

At the time, I could not have explained exactly what the problem was. Anglicanism and Catholicism were not even on my conceptual horizon. But as a graduate student studying major figures in the history of philosophy, especially figures such as St. Augustine, Boethius, St. Anselm, and St. Thomas, I found that they far overshadowed the musings of any man who took the microphone on Sunday mornings. And so I was becoming more and more aware that the Presbyterian service was simply not feeding my soul. Yet I could not identity what was missing. One thing I did know, the whole service seemed to be man-centered in its form and activity. So much of what took place involved handing a microphone to a human being, and letting that person give his thoughts about something. These could be welcoming comments particularly to visitors, an explanation of who we were as a church, and what our mission was in the community, and various reports by lay persons on activities and outreaches. There was a children's sermon, a regular sermon, and exhortations about stewardship and being generous to God by an elder, before the offering plate was passed.

I was weary of all this man-talk. I cared about the needs of the people present, but that was not fundamentally why I was coming to church. I wanted no more words of men, no more handing around of the microphone. Even beyond the announcements, church seemed to me at the time to be fundamentally intellectual and theological, because for me at the center of church was the sermon. But even there what was being served intellectually and theologically fell far short of what I could be getting reading the medieval Christian philosophers and theologians. I knew that I did not want to go to church to hear any more "man-talk"—that is, opinions of human beings. If church were primarily about "man-talk", I could go to the library and find much more erudite thinkers and writers. From what I was learning from the writings of ancient philosophers and medieval theologians, I found myself mentally challenging and even refuting Sunday sermons point-by-point as they were being delivered during every service, and I could sense that that kind of disengaged cynical disposition was soul-destroying.

Of course, I knew we are not supposed to forsake the assembling of ourselves together, and yet existentially I could not see any good reason to "go to church". Fellowship I could obtain from my fellow graduate students who were Christian. And my theological knowledge I could obtain from the books of far greater theologians. So what was the point of going to an institutional church? I had been coming to church for something else, not to hear people give their opinions or talk about what they were doing. I did not want to be in merely a religious club; I wanted something other than that. I became so increasingly critical and disengaged during church services that I stopped going to church entirely for about a year in frustration and fear of what a persistently cynical attitude would do to me, and because I was so frustrated with the whole scene, a scene that to me seemed spiritually vacuous and human-centered in its continual "man-talk".

Lo! He Comes with Clouds Descending: My Time as an Anglican

That year a fellow graduate student suggested that I visit an Anglican church, so I did. I went by myself. The moment I walked in, I noticed a complete difference. It was quiet and reverent before the liturgy began. People were not talking before the service started. People were kneeling and praying silently, on kneelers. The liturgy itself was beautiful, rich, and meaningful. All the words of the service were already written down, as the liturgy, in this case the Book of Common Prayer, which is beautiful and reverent and drawn largely from Scripture. The liturgy is God's speech spoken back to him by his people or by one representing them. The only occasion in which a person spoke his own opinion was the homily, and the homily was only about five minutes long, compared to the thirty- to forty-minute sermons with which I was familiar. Here for the first time I found freedom from "man-talk". There was no human personality at the front of the church with a microphone saying whatever came into his mind at that moment. There was no speculative exegesis or theological argumentation that I could critically dismantle.

The climax of the Anglican liturgy was what was referred to as "Holy Eucharist".[5] We walked forward between the choir, and received the bread and wine at the front of the church, while kneeling. The very form of worship communicated something altogether different from the way of taking communion I had previously known. I found God to be present there in the beauty, reverence, and silence of the liturgy. Here was something that went beyond men's opinions. I could not be cynical about the liturgy or critique it. This was not "man-talk". It was nonpropositional; it was sacramental—that is, the Gospel embodied. It did not lend itself to rational evaluation or refutation. In that respect, this sacrament almost bypassed my intellect and went directly to my heart. In this sacrament, God was speaking to me not through words and propositions, but through a physical action, giving himself to me in a very intimate way. This was not something toward which I could take a critical, disengaged stance. I could only receive it and be grateful.

I realized that this is what my soul had been craving—to be fed on God. In the sacredness of the liturgy centered around the "Holy Eucharist", my heart, which had been starved under a diet of mere propositions, was drawn anew toward God. The form of this aesthetic and liturgy clearly fit the serving of the bread of heaven. In the liturgy, my soul was drawn up to God by its majesty and beauty. When the priest said, "Lift up your hearts," we replied, "We lift them up unto the Lord." The form of the liturgy and the music helped us lift our hearts up to heaven.

I invited my wife to attend, but we learned that this Anglican church seemed to have no position on certain important moral issues involving marriage and the sanctity of life, matters on which we could not compromise. I was in survival mode, and I was willing to put up with (unspoken) laxity regarding formal doctrine in order to have my soul fed on the beauty and richness of the liturgy. Eventually

---

[5] At that time, I was not aware of *Apostolicae Curae*, in which Pope Leo XIII explains that Anglican orders are "null and void" because the Edwardine Ordinal of 1552 introduced by Thomas Cranmer during the reign of King Edward VI was deficient in the form necessary for the validity of ordination, and thus that the Anglican "Holy Eucharist" was not truly the Body and Blood of Christ.

we found an independent Anglican parish that was in agreement with the natural law on these moral issues, and we were confirmed there in 2003. To be clear, for me, in this case it was not fundamentally or primarily *doctrine* that moved me from the Presbyterian to the Anglican tradition; it was liturgy. Here again, as aesthetics had played a role in my move from charismatic to Presbyterian, so aesthetics again played an important role in my becoming Anglican. And yet philosophy played a role too, because it helped me see the implicit role philosophy played in the Calvinistic theology I had once held. And that removed, for me, that theology's apparent authority, allowing me to look openly, carefully, and sincerely outside the Calvinist model.

At the same time, I was still thinking and praying about the question of unity and what divides Christians, and had started reading the early Church Fathers. Becoming Anglican required that I examine more closely the question of ecclesiology and apostolic succession, because the Anglican tradition, but not the Presbyterian tradition, distinguished between bishops and priests. And it became clear to me that the Anglican liturgy was connected with this distinction in holy orders. Both the liturgy and holy orders were traditions that claimed to extend back to the early Church. Embracing them required reconsidering the ecclesial deism I had presupposed as a seminarian. And this drew me back to the Church Fathers, whom I had studied only in a cursory and filtered way while in seminary. I dug into them seeking to understand how they conceived of apostolic succession and of the unity of the Church.

Already by the following year I found myself with serious questions about Anglicanism, as I sought to understand the underlying reason for the obvious disunity among Christians. A friend of mine asked me the following question: "Why aren't you Catholic?" I gave him a reply that involved my disbelief in the papacy and the Marian dogmas. But I was not entirely satisfied with my answer, because the very question carried the hint of a different paradigm, according to which I needed a good reason not to be Catholic, a reason that did not presuppose the falsity of the Catholic tradition. That was followed by a year of reading voraciously everything I could get my hands on about the differences between Catholics and Protestants.

My Anglican bishop seemed to have almost no interest in dialogue with the local Catholic bishop with a view to eventual full communion with the bishop of Rome. That troubled me. I had learned from reading the Church Fathers that the bishop of Rome had a unique authority and role as the Church's principle of unity, because of his succession from the Apostle Peter. When I asked myself why I was following this Anglican bishop, rather than the successor of St. Peter, I did not have a good answer. When I asked my Anglican bishop which ecumenical councils we (Anglicans) accept, his answer also troubled me. He said something like "we believe the first four, but are selective about what we believe from the others." His answer seemed entirely arbitrary to me. Nor could I find a good answer in all the Anglican theology books I studied. How could we pick and choose from an ecumenical council, or from among ecumenical councils? Either we should treat them all as merely good advice, or we should accept them all as authoritative. Picking and choosing from them on the basis of our agreement or disagreement with them, and then saying that the ones we have chosen are authoritative, was to my mind self-deceiving, like shooting an arrow and then drawing a target around the embedded arrow.[6]

By the middle of 2004 I was trying to determine what exactly was the referent of the line in the Creed: "We believe in one, holy, catholic, and apostolic Church." I was wondering whether what we were meaning by that phrase was what the early Church Fathers meant by that phrase. Finally, every Sunday while reciting the Creed, when we would get to the line "one, holy, catholic, and apostolic Church", I discovered that I could not say this line. I had to remain silent when we said it, because I was concerned that I was being dishonest if I were to say the line. My conscience was telling me that we (as Anglicans) were not saying the word "one" with the same meaning that those bishops who wrote the Creed intended it. We were treating what was a collection of groups of particular churches not in full communion with one another, as though it were a true unity. But I had come to believe from studying the Church Fathers that this was not how the early Church conceived of the unity of

---

[6] This is one form of the Texas sharpshooter fallacy. See Bryan R. Cross, "Clark, Frame, and the Analogy of Painting a Magisterial Target around One's Interpretive Arrow", Called to Communion, January 14, 2014, http://www.calledtocommunion.com/2014/01/clark-frame -and-the-analogy-of-painting-a-magisterial-target-around-ones-interpretive-arrow/.

the universal Church. True unity included full communion of the
bishops of the particular churches.[7] And this raised the question of
how, in the event of a schism among the bishops, to determine which
group of bishops was the continuation of the one, holy, catholic, and
apostolic Church, and how Christ intended believers to know the
answer to that question.

Of course, this question led to the consideration of the Catholic
claim regarding the unique authority and role given to St. Peter and
to the bishops of Rome in succession from St. Peter. Through study
of the early Church Fathers, it became clear to me that they recognized the bishop of Rome to have a unique authority, not because
Rome was the capital of the empire, but because they recognized that
this unique authority entrusted to St. Peter, and the unique charism
he had been given by Christ, had been preserved in his successors in
the Apostolic See.[8] This became evident especially in studying the
various schisms, such as the Novatian and Donatist schisms, and
the writings of Church Fathers who addressed these schisms. In the
event of a schism, the bishop of Rome served as the *principium unitatis*
(principle of unity) by which to distinguish the continuation of the
Church from schisms from the Church.

Adoro Te Devote: Becoming Catholic

The most important aspect of this Protestant-to-Catholic transition for me involved recognizing that the Protestant and Catholic
traditions were rightly intelligible as "paradigms"—that is, as complete theological-conceptual frameworks that must be considered all
together as a whole in order to be understood rightly. Once that is
clear, then an important conclusion follows. If we try to compare
two paradigms by presupposing the truth of one of them, we are
not authentically comparing them on their own terms. Criticisms
of one paradigm on the basis of assumptions of the other paradigm

---

[7] See Bryan R. Cross, "Christ Founded a Visible Church", Called to Communion, June 7,
2009, http://www.calledtocommunion.com/2009/06/christ-founded-a-visible-church/.

[8] See, for example, Dom John Chapman, *Studies on the Early Papacy* (New York: Benziger
Brothers, 1928).

are question-begging; that is, they are an exercise of circular reasoning, presupposing the very point in question—that is, which is the true paradigm. One cannot rightly adjudicate rationally between two paradigms merely by presupposing the truth of one of them. Doing so is a kind of self-deception, because one makes it seem as though one is *arguing* for a position, say, the Protestant position on a particular doctrinal question, when, in the paradigmatic assumptions underlying one's argument one is merely *assuming* the truth of the Protestant paradigm within which a Protestant answer to that doctrinal question unsurprisingly is either entailed or at least can find support. And we typically engage in these question-begging criticisms of positions in another paradigm because we are not yet *seeing* the other paradigm, because we are viewing only pieces of it, from the point of view of our own paradigm. And that in turn is typically because we are not seeing our own paradigm; we are seeing only its material constituents.

This understanding of the relation of paradigms or traditions can be seen in a 1977 work of the philosopher Alasdair MacIntyre.[9] Here MacIntyre drew from Thomas Kuhn and Imre Lakatos to propose that Kuhn's solution to the problem of competing scientific paradigms be applied to competing ethical traditions in moral philosophy. According to MacIntyre, the resolution of an epistemological crisis involves determining which available narrative is more intelligible or more adequate. The more intelligible narrative is that which better explains the competing traditions and better explains how persons can be misled to believe the other tradition. The more intelligible tradition has superior explanatory resources for resolving the problems and inadequacies internal to the other tradition. MacIntyre writes, "It is more rational to accept one theory or paradigm and to reject its predecessor when the later theory or paradigm provides a standpoint from which the acceptance, the life-story, and the rejection of the previous theory or paradigm can be recounted in more intelligible historical narrative than previously."[10]

---

[9] Alasdair MacIntyre, "Epistemological Crises, Dramatic Narrative and the Philosophy of Science", *Monist* 60, no. 4 (October 1, 1977): 453–72, https://doi.org/10.5840/monist 197760427.

[10] Ibid., 467.

When one encounters other paradigms, one can come to see the same data from the point of view of those other paradigms. Seeing the data from different paradigms allows one to see weakness, failures, or problems internal to one's own paradigm, and to see explanations for those weaknesses and failures, from the point of view of another paradigm, according to criteria mutually accessible to the paradigms in question. This allows one to compare paradigms in a noncircular way.

Through my Protestant paradigm I had interpreted all the data from Scripture and from Church history in such a way that supported uniquely Protestant doctrines regarding justification, the law, the work of Christ, the exclusive sufficiency of Christ's work and intercession, the nature of the sacraments, the role and authority of tradition, Church authority, ecclesiology, the Reformation, the marks of the Church, etc. In that paradigm, all these hung together as interconnected doctrines, mutually supporting. And therefore, from within that paradigm the Catholic Church had seemed so wrong on so many things. But when I began to see the Protestant paradigm as a paradigm, rather than as simply the plain truth straight off the pages of Scripture, then it became intellectually possible for me to consider all of the same data of Scripture, in light of the Catholic paradigm, and compare the two paradigms in a non-question-begging way.

The Catholic paradigm includes the authoritative role of Sacred Tradition and the Church Fathers in the interpretation and understanding of Scripture. In this paradigm these are not derived from one's interpretation of Scripture, but established by Christ. Even the theological methodology between the paradigms is distinct. The Protestant paradigm seeks to resolve theological disagreements primarily by scholarly analysis of the text of Scripture. The Catholic paradigm turns to the Tradition and the magisterium.[11] Moreover, the Catholic paradigm is incompatible with ecclesial deism and ecclesial consumerism. In the Catholic paradigm, what belongs to the articles of faith comes to us through the Church. That is how we know what to affirm by faith, through what the Church delivers to us,

---

[11] See, for example, Bryan R. Cross, "The Tradition and the Lexicon", Called to Communion, February 10, 2010, http://www.calledtocommunion.com/2010/02/the-tradition-and-the-lexicon/.

just as the early Christians would have done by believing what the apostles taught them were the truths delivered to them from Christ and the Holy Spirit. Among the articles of faith are the four marks of the Church specified in the Creed, in contrast to the Reformed marks of Gospel, sacraments, and Church discipline. From the Catholic point of view, the Protestant move of making discipline a mark of the Church was an unauthorized addition to the four marks given in the Creed. So then from the Catholic point of view, the Protestant appeal to discipline as a mark of the Church, for example, used against the Catholic Church, presupposes the very point in question between the two paradigms—namely, the possession of the authority to establish the marks of the Church and determine how they are to be understood. This was especially made clear to me by St. Francis de Sales' *The Catholic Controversy*, which allowed me to see the ideas and actions of the Protestant Reformers from the perspective of the Catholic paradigm.

By the spring of 2005, I was coming to see, first, that every single one of my Protestant objections to the Catholic Church presupposed the Protestant paradigm, and thus was evidentially and argumentatively question-begging. These objections implicitly and paradigmatically presupposed the very point in question. I was also coming to see that the Catholic paradigm was able to incorporate the patristic data in a far more coherent way, without having to adopt an ecclesial deism, and without thereby implicitly calling into question the divinity of Christ. The Catholic paradigm, unlike the Protestant paradigm, made schism intelligible and thus made intelligible what the Church Fathers said about schism.[12] The Catholic paradigm made Christ's atonement compatible with God's justice.[13] The Catholic paradigm made intelligible what the Church Fathers said about baptismal regeneration,[14]

---

[12] See, for example, Bryan R. Cross, "Michael Horton on Schism as Heresy", Called to Communion, October 6, 2011, http://www.calledtocommunion.com/2011/10/michael-horton-on-schism-as-heresy/.

[13] See Bryan R. Cross, "Catholic and Reformed Conceptions of the Atonement", Called to Communion, April 1, 2010, http://www.calledtocommunion.com/2010/04/catholic-and-reformed-conceptions-of-the-atonement/.

[14] See Bryan R. Cross, "The Church Fathers on Baptismal Regeneration", Called to Communion, June 15, 2010, http://www.calledtocommunion.com/2010/06/the-church-fathers-on-baptismal-regeneration/.

about merit,[15] about the distinction between mortal and venial sin,[16] and about many other things. It was clearer to me that being in communion with the bishop of Rome was the default position, and that I needed some good (at least non-question-begging) reasons not to be in communion with the bishop of Rome.[17]

On April 22, 2005, having reflected on these questions in light of the proceedings surrounding the death of Pope John Paul II and the subsequent election of Pope Benedict XVI, I reached the conclusion that the Catholic Church is the Church Christ founded, and I found that I had no good reasons not to be Catholic. I decided that day to seek full communion with the Catholic Church. But my wife was not yet ready, and it took her about a year to do her own reading and be ready to enter the Church. The following year she and our two daughters and I were received into full communion with the Church on October 8, 2006, at the Cathedral Basilica of Saint Louis.

[15] See Bryan R. Cross, "The Doctrine of Merit: Feingold, Calvin, and the Church Fathers", Called to Communion, November 14, 2011, http://www.calledtocommunion .com/2011/11/the-doctrine-of-merit-feingold-calvin-and-the-church-fathers/.

[16] See Bryan R. Cross, "Why John Calvin Did Not Recognize the Distinction Between Mortal and Venial Sin", Called to Communion, November 10, 2011, http://www .calledtocommunion.com/2011/11/why-john-calvin-did-not-recognize-the-distinction -between-mortal-and-venial-sin/.

[17] Here, I am not alone. Thus, Westminster Theological Seminary's Carl Trueman explains, "Every year I tell my Reformation history class that Roman Catholicism is, at least in the West, the default position. Rome has a better claim to historical continuity and institutional unity than any Protestant denomination, let alone the strange hybrid that is Evangelicalism; in the light of these facts, therefore, we need good, solid reasons for not being Catholic; not being a Catholic should, in others words, be a positive act of will and commitment, something we need to get out of bed determined to do each and every day." Carl Trueman, "Is The Reformation Over?", *Reformation 21*, November 2005, http://www.reformation21.org /shelf-life/is-the-reformation-over.php.

IO

A Spiritual Autobiography

Candace Vogler

I am grateful to Hank Vogler and Father Stephen Brock for comments on this piece in draft, and for their friendship and support.

Origins

It is hard to know where to start a story about faith. We all come from God. If things go well, by God's grace, we are all headed back to God. But the road is almost never very clear, and it is the ruts and hurdles that make up the stuff of a story. Mine started in Seattle more than half a century ago in a family quarrel.

Elizabeth, who would one day be my mother, had just introduced the man she meant to marry, Donald, to her mother, Blanche. There must have been some sort of meal. There must have been some sort of conversation. Elizabeth had grown up the unwanted second and last child of a relatively wealthy couple. Her best friend from school came from a big loving family that provided a refuge for Elizabeth growing up, and she wanted that life for herself. She had been engaged once before to a well-placed young man who shared her dream, but he had died of leukemia. Now she had found Donald. Unfortunately, Donald had told her that they could not marry unless she gave up on having children. And now her mother was telling her that something about Donald was "not right". In a spirit of defiant optimism, Elizabeth married Donald over Blanche's objections. I was born ten months later.

Elizabeth had thought that no one could really object to a baby. She had imagined that, once I arrived, her mother might reconcile with Donald, and he would realize that children are the greatest blessing a couple can have and would want still more of them. Elizabeth was wrong. Although Blanche welcomed her only grandchild, she told my mother that my birth meant that my mother would be bound to my father for life, and would likely end up regretting the match. My father did his best to steer clear of me. And my mother went into a profound depression. She put me in a crib in a back room. I gather that she did not feed me—she remembers my father trying to make her feed me, and remembers this as spousal abuse. My father took over care-taking duties. My maternal grandmother, realizing that my mother could not cope, decided to take part in seeing to it that I was fed, and clean, and clothed. She found bloody diapers. The sense in which something was wrong with my father began to come clear, as did the reason he did not want any children.

Both of my parents were Christians—my father had even been a Presbyterian minister briefly before becoming a schoolteacher. He taught me to read and write, paint and draw, when I was very young. He insisted that we go to church every Sunday, but was in flight from the social changes happening around us in the 1960s and early '70s, and so kept us moving from church to church, denomination to denomination, in search of an appropriately conservative and staid congregation. My mother kept having children, and he tried to manage by distancing himself more and more from each new arrival. I was his. And I had the benefit of having to develop a complicated relationship with a primary caretaker who had a serious moral and spiritual struggle at the center of his life.

I read the Bible a lot. I thought that God had written a book, and that someone called "King James" had translated it into English. I especially loved the stories about Jesus, and I thought about them a lot, trying to put them together with my experiences. I had learned a lot by the time I was eight. I had learned most of it from my father. It seemed perfectly clear, watching him with my mother and grandmother, that men did not like women. From his relationship with me and my sisters, it seemed clear that the way that men liked children, when they happened to like a child, was not always good. Watching the Vietnam War on television every night made it clear that men did not even like each other. But when God decided to become human and walk with us and teach us as a fellow human being, God came as a man.

Jesus held me. He loved me. He loved my father. He loved my increasingly distracted and chaotic mother. He loved my grandmother who tried her best to teach me about the world in her faintly ruthless way. He loved my sisters and brother, whose care fell to me much of the time. He knew as well as I did that men were dangerous. And I thought a lot about the depth of the sense in which he came to teach and to heal. He taught us that the ones who are most in need of teaching and healing are the ones who are suffering the most and the most in need of help. And I realized that in Jesus we have an actual model of a human masculinity that is not toxic to itself and to everyone else. We have a model of a man who humbles himself so that he can come to us from love, a man who sacrifices himself from love. For everyone.

Struggles

I grew up. My grandmother died when I was ten. And although I was often too ill or injured to attend school, I studied hard, I read voraciously, and I kept up with my schoolwork. The fact that both of my parents were schoolteachers and that I performed well on homework and tests made it the case that no one questioned my frequent absences. We had a veritable parade of pet dogs—two of them prevented my father from getting near me one very dark day when I hid in a thorny berry patch after he stabbed me. They disappeared a few weeks later. It seems very likely that my father had them put to sleep. He took two others away, females, as soon as they reached maturity.

My father did not want me to get pregnant, and so altered his conduct toward me when pregnancy became possible. I think that I had some sort of breakdown around that time. I was in the basement, feeding the current crop of dogs who had a dog door in the laundry room. I had filled their food bowls with kibble, and replenished the water in their drinking bowls, and they had started in eating when

they suddenly rushed outside, leaving me alone. I turned around to
see what had scared them, saw what looked like me, suspended in
midair, older than I was, with my head cut off. The head was floating just above the neck. The apparition was trying to scream, but
couldn't because the vocal cords were severed. I stared at the thing
that somehow was me, saw my father coming in right behind it, and
started screaming. Apparently, I fainted. When I regained consciousness, I was upstairs in our living room and the whole family was
gathered around staring at me. And I was afraid.

What I was most of the time for the following few years was afraid.
I was afraid to look in any reflecting surfaces. I was afraid to walk to
the end of the driveway to take out the trash. I was afraid to be alone.
I was afraid of the other children in school. I was afraid of the other
children in the neighborhood. I feared that an evil thing had attached
itself to me, and could injure anyone who got close to me. And still I
prayed and prayed. I got over the paralyzing fear by forcing myself to
do the things that had come to seem impossibly dangerous, reciting
psalms in my head and whispering the Lord's Prayer all the while.
Bit-by-bit, over the course of a few years, I overcame the terror. And
although I had very little contact with people outside the immediate
family, I realized that all of this was abnormal and strongly suspected
that I was not a sane person. Jesus still loved me. I was very scared
of myself and for my brother and sisters because they had to rely on
me for a lot, and children should not have to rely on a crazy person
to feed them and get them safely to and from school; but Jesus was
not afraid of me, and I was not afraid of him, and I felt sure that he,
at least, could help shield my brother and sisters from my mental
instability.

Thanks to my younger sister Debz, who started attending my high
school in my sophomore year, I started to know people my own
age. Debz had loads of friends and was willing to let me be part of
her social world. By then, none of my siblings wanted anything to
do with Christianity. I was still Christian, but had lost any optimism
I once had for churches. I had deep respect and admiration for a
lot of people who belonged to one or another congregation. But
I understood myself to be an ugly and undesirable creature tainted
by my history in ways that made me unfit for the clean and well-
lighted worlds of local churches. Jesus was the sort of person who

embraced lepers. It was a bit much to expect that sort of thing from the local churches.

Looking for a Church

I had drifted away from church services by the time I graduated from high school. I applied for undergraduate admission to Mills College in Oakland, California, and to places like Princeton and Yale. My parents insisted that I stay on the West Coast, so I went to Mills. I wanted to be a painter. My high school art teacher, who had let me use a corner of his studio space, told me not to major in art. He suggested that I take courses in a lot of subjects, and major in the one that was the most difficult for me. I followed his advice. Philosophy was the most difficult subject. It dealt with crucial questions in human life, work, and thought—questions that had been with us a long time and become acute for me over the course of my childhood and adolescence. Best of all, philosophy was an area in which you might be remembered for a thousand years if you managed to make an interesting mistake rather than a stupid one. The only sane aspiration in the field was to hope to one day make a useful mistake. This suited me.

Mills was a strange place—a small women's liberal arts institution on a beautiful campus in East Oakland. Apart from my sense for what was at stake in my philosophy classes, coursework was not especially challenging. I got in the habit of working through everything on the syllabus in the first two weeks of term, and then going to office hours to discuss the assigned work with my professors, and get advice on how to build on what I had done. I took a couple of art classes and managed to talk the faculty into letting me use a studio with a wall of windows overlooking a beautiful meadow next to the stream that ran through the campus. I had a place to paint.

Mills had a van service that shuttled students back and forth from the University of California at Berkeley campus several times a day. It was 1978, and the Second Wave Women's Movement was gaining strength in Northern California. I joined the Mills Feminist Alliance. I helped to staff crisis phone lines in Berkeley. I took part in the first Take Back the Night March in San Francisco. I volunteered at a women's health center in Oakland. I went on retreat to a women's commune in Albion on the coast. We were working against violence. And in the meanwhile, I reveled in the things that had never been possible for me before. I went to concerts and museums. I spent hours in cafés and used bookstores. I heard lectures, attended poetry readings, and hid myself away in magnificent libraries.

I had, by then, learned a lot about the situation of women in various corners of the world, and about ways in which various religious institutions had contributed to circumstances in which women of every race and ethnicity and creed, alongside colonized men, were denied rights to property, had no effective security in their persons, and were very fortunate if they managed to attain the status of second-class citizens in modern nations that were nominally democratic. It was inconceivable to me that this could have been the will of the God who had held me together my whole life and taught me about love. These were, instead, human institutions with all the homely qualities familiar from human beings—the very qualities that made it important for God to come among us as one of us. Still, I respected the aspirations of religious institutions. I was glad they were around. It wasn't my place to say how God had worked in and through them, much less to insist that God could not be working in and through some of them.

Particularly painful experiences of being rejected and received with suspicion and fear in some of the churches I had attended as a child and adolescent had made it natural for me to separate my faith in God from the doctrinal and other contours of the institution in which I happened to be engaged in shared worship. The churches I knew were Protestant. I believed in transubstantiation even though my pastors did not, because that was what the Book said and because, after all, pastors are just human beings and transubstantiation is from God. God could work it even if the man in charge of handling grape juice and bits of pie crust did not mean for it to happen. But I also believed that respect for churches required that I not take communion unless I had gone through the relevant confirmation process. In the childhood and adolescent migration from church to church, I had been confirmed in four different denominations. Mills had a chapel, and different pastors held services in the chapel each week. I tried most of them. The Catholic services were the best because of the Eucharist. Once I found that service, I attended weekly. The fact that I was the only person who came every week, and that there were never more than two other people there, made it very disappointing for the priest that I could not share in the sacrament.

I took a junior year abroad at the University of Edinburgh and found a home with the Quakers. The meditative stillness of silent service, the absence of wall hangings and choirs and carvings, the opportunity to be quiet and get far enough out of the way to be available to God suited me, as did the effort to be of use to people outside of worship service.

Life as a floating nondenominational Christian had its drawbacks, but the Incarnation was unimaginably big. I did not see how God's work with us and among us could be subverted by the wrong interpretation of a line of Scripture—which, I had come to understand, was not a book written by God and translated into a language I could read by a person I had never met. I did not see how his ongoing life with us could hang in the balance if we had the wrong understanding of the rituals at the center of shared worship. After all, the work of grace in sacraments does not offer itself up to ordinary human understanding very readily. I knew that God loved my family. I knew God loved me. I knew that Jesus was willing to die to give each and every one of us a chance for a life with him. This seemed to me to be a very small, intimate, and deeply personal instance of the really important point—trying to take that point in, trying to learn how to live from that point, was hard.

I tried to belong to some community while I was at Mills. Shared worship with the disappointed priest wasn't it. The British Quakers were British, and a junior year abroad, however transformative, is a form of tourism. The women's community at Mills and in the Bay Area more generally wasn't it either. I learned through painful experience that they did not like me—a thing that I managed to hide from myself for more than two years. My father was distant. My mother was so rattled and disorganized at that point that the fact that she had long ago ceased to seem capable of telling the truth except by accident had become a serious barrier to pursuing any meaningful relationship with her. My sisters had, understandably, come to associate me with my father and were accordingly scared of me. My brother was trying to find some way of living without the taint of fear and shame that were part of the lives of all the women in the family and was, accordingly, aspiring to a kind of middle-class normalcy that had never been possible for the rest of us.

Friends

The people who welcomed my company were gay men, starting with a man I had met in my senior year in high school. We loved each other. We had tried to date. Call him "B". B came from a happy family in Edmonds, and his mother and father opened their doors to me. B and I corresponded regularly while I was at Mills and all through my junior year abroad. We both got jobs doing maintenance work for the local public school system in the summers. When I was raped by an acquaintance, got very sick, was ordered to stay in bed (thereby requiring that I stay behind when the rest of my family went away for vacation), B came. He brought me food and kept me company after work each day. I sat beside him when he told his parents that he wanted men, not women. His mother was unhappy. His father pointed out that I was the one who was most directly affected by the situation, and that it had not seemed to interfere with my love, so it ought not interfere with theirs. B's family gave me most of the personal experience I have had with a well-ordered family. Up until very recently, B's family was the only such family in my experience.

Through B's good offices, gay men adopted me. I learned that most of the young men I had known in high school were now self-identified gay men, and I reconnected with another of them who was attending Catholic services through an organization called Dignity.[1] I started going to Dignity Masses. B, who had given up on religion entirely, would not come along.

The summer that Dignity brought me into Masses with more than three people in attendance, I began wondering what I would do after graduating from Mills. I was about to enter my senior year, and I realized that I did not know why I was there. I decided that I would leave Mills and try to make my way in the world for a while. And

---

[1] At the time, I did not know that Dignity is not an organization approved by the Catholic Church and no longer are allowed to meet in Catholic facilities.

somewhere in all of this, I was introduced to the most charismatic person in the Dignity congregation: Vincent.

We took an instant dislike to each other. Vincent was a writer who worked behind the desk at the largest homeless shelter downtown. He was loud and showy and smart. He loved crowds and he loved Mass. He was going to do a radio play for a local station, and he needed a female voice. I may not have been the *only* woman he had met in town, but I was the only one who counted as a friend of a friend *and* a person from church, so he asked me to be the female voice. I agreed. Around the edges of rehearsing and recording his play, we fell into conversation and ended up friends.

I returned to Mills in September, left halfway through my senior year, and moved back to Washington State. B had taken a job and an apartment in Seattle. I moved in with him and started looking for work. I found a job at the Winchell's donut house a few blocks away from his place on Capitol Hill and got used to going to work with a pocketful of change so that I could buy coffee and donuts for the homeless people who came in. I liked the job. I liked my co-workers.

Vincent and I had been planning to find a place together once I was more settled. We wound up renting a small house in Fremont from my high school art teacher. B didn't like Vincent. My family didn't like Vincent. But Vincent wrote like an angel and loved and feared God. We had a household. We had a community at church. I knew a lot of people and got on well with them. We went out to bars and restaurants and movies together. It was the closest I had ever come to having a social life that I was not borrowing from my younger sister.

Feeding donuts and coffee to the downtrodden on Capitol Hill put me in contact with some of the difficult aspects of their lives. One of my customers was a tiny younger woman—Chris—a born-again Christian lesbian from Appalachia with a strong singing voice that sounded a lot like Anne Murray's. Chris slept on the floor of the back room of the toughest bar on the street—the "206". She was in love with the lady bartender. I was walking toward the bus stop late one night after work and there was a commotion near an alley. A group of men had cornered Chris and were holding her down and preparing to rape her. Something in me snapped. There was a wine bottle on the ground next to the brick wall. I grabbed it, broke it, and headed in. The men fled. Chris was badly beaten but too afraid to let me contact the police. We went back to the Winchell's, and I looked after her as best I could.

She showed up at the door of the Winchell's very late again a few weeks later. This time, men had tried to cut out her right eye. She would not go to a hospital. She would not let me phone the police. Winchell's had a first-aid kit on the wall. I prayed like mad as I got out alcohol, a tube of antiseptic cream, the sealed plastic bag with a length of suture threaded through a curved, sterile needle, and the surgical gloves from the first-aid kit. There was a lot of blood. I cleaned the wound as best I could. I think it took four stitches to close the cut, but I don't really remember. I was inwardly terrified of making anything worse. Happily, one of the excellent things I had gained from childhood was an ability to be focused, methodical, and steady when faced with a physical emergency. I used the last of our gauze and some white tape from the kit to bandage her up afterward. Then I bought her some orange juice and a plain donut and sat with her a long time while she ate and drank and began to calm down, singing a hymn to herself softly.

Life in my new home was getting more complicated. Vincent had invited a man to move in with us. Vincent wanted romance. Our new housemate, Peter, did not. The household had never been calm, but it had been optimistic. It was a place for art. We wrote. We read. We used colored chalk on our blackboard in the hall to make elaborate pictures for each other. We left each other jokes on the dining room table. We criticized each other's work. We went to Mass together. Peter had just graduated from Northwestern—he grew up somewhere in Illinois. I never did find out why he moved to Seattle or how he met Vincent, but the household began falling apart.

Around that time, I was heading to the bus stop late one night after work, walking past the 206, and heard a commotion inside. They had a round window in the front door, so I looked in. Some men had hoisted Chris onto the bar where she was standing, looking miserable, while they poked at her and demanded that she sing for them. In I went. I headed for the bar and started joking with the men. They relented and I helped Chris climb down. She ran away to the back room, crying. And then the men arranged themselves in a circle around me. I realized that I was about to be beaten. I stood very still, avoided making eye contact, and prayed silently. Before anyone could throw a punch, the largest man I had ever seen rose at the back of the bar and said, "She's with me."

The men around me mumbled some apologies to the big man and returned to their seats. I went over to join the big man's table. He was celebrating his release from prison. I learned that the 206's clientele was made up primarily of active duty and retired policemen. The big man, Larry, explained that none of them would give him trouble because he had been in a maximum-security prison. I didn't understand this and suspected that his size was likely more of a deterrent than his criminal history, but I didn't argue. We talked for a while, then I headed home.

Larry showed up outside the Winchell's as I was getting off work the next afternoon. I was glad to see him, and we went for a walk. This began a stretch of some weeks in which Larry sought me out wanting romance and I tried to figure out how to cope. He said that he wanted marriage and children. I couldn't imagine such a thing. He showed me photographs of two women. One was recovering after someone burned her face. The other was recovering after someone cut up her face. He told me that these were the other women who had refused him. And I decided that it was time to leave town.

Debz was attending The Evergreen State College and was willing to let me come and stay with her while I resettled in Olympia. She still moved with a big crowd of friends. She still was willing to share her social world with me. She wanted to be an actress and was working with a well-known filmmaker who was an artist-in-residence at Evergreen. Her friends were exciting—musicians who were in the process of developing the music that came to be called "Grunge"; painters and critics; collage artists; photographers; and writers. They let me tag along. I had a sort of brief romance with the filmmaker, got involved making props for the movie he was making, and learned a lot about cameras and lenses, light, and wooden boats. I got a job at the Dairy Queen up the street and took a small apartment in the complex where my sister lived—a place called the Angelus. The Angelus sat above a row of commercial buildings, above the pizza parlor and a café and the tiny storefront that a group of women artists rented called Girl City, across the street from the Oddfellows lodge and a few other small businesses. In those days,

from my point of view, Olympia was paradise. It was small. It was
exciting. We did things. A photographer, Suzanne, and I became
good friends. She was involved with Victor, a man who was out of
town visiting his relatives in Oklahoma. Victor lived in a barn on the
rural outskirts of town, a space he shared with a man called "Hank".
Victor was due back from Oklahoma, and Suzanne hatched a bold
plan to fix me up with Hank, so that when she went out to see Victor, I could go along and see Hank. She thought that she and I could
garden out there.

If you ask Hank, he will tell you that he decided to marry me
two weeks before we met. Suzanne arranged for the four of us to
have dinner in the barn. Victor, who was opposed to matchmaking
schemes, invited a lot of other people. Hank and I managed to have
a conversation at one edge of the most boisterous dinner I had ever
attended. I talked about Plato and complimented him on his boots.
He told me he wrote poetry. We played chess. I learned that he had
his morning coffee at a café on his side of town, up a long hill from
the Angelus, and I went there the next morning. We sat across a table
from each other, writing in our notebooks, and occasionally getting
coffee for each other that morning, and the next, and the next. On
the fourth morning, he walked me down the hill to the Angelus. I
invited him up and heated up a can of soup for us on my hot plate.
After we finished our soup, he asked if I wanted to marry him. I
told him that I thought you should know each other for at least two
weeks before getting engaged. He asked again two weeks later, and
I accepted. We were engaged for nine months. My cousin John,
a Presbyterian minister, performed the ceremony, and my friend B
gave us a honeymoon for a wedding present.

Marriage

Things were hard. Hank went into a profound depression shortly
after we got back from the honeymoon. The two of us began discovering the physical wreckage left behind by my history of abuse
during my first nonviable pregnancy—there were three nonviable
pregnancies eventually. The emotional residue obtruded in night ter-
rors and the beginnings of what would be my thirty-year struggle

with chronic insomnia. My spiritual life became wide-ranging. I still prayed, but as often as not, the first prayer was just "Help."

People our age in Olympia and other places we lived thought that I was a witch. I wasn't a witch, but I did engage in a wide variety of spiritual practices in a haphazard and superstitious way. My life as a sexual being had never been very far from my life as a spiritual being, and I was still haunted by the sense of being surrounded by dark forces and looking for a light in my dealings with other people—a light that was there with my husband, but elusive with everyone else. Hank and I moved back to California so that I could finish my degree at Mills. I won a fellowship for doctoral study in philosophy, and we took that to the University of Pittsburgh.

A lot of things happened. Back in my parents' home, things were deteriorating at an alarming rate. My brother found refuge with the family of his sweetheart. My youngest sister, Lisa, was at the mercy of the middle child, Cynthia, who was by then a serious heroin addict. Cynthia sent Lisa on heroin buys because if Lisa was caught, she would be tried as a juvenile (whereas Cynthia would be tried as an adult). My father sold Lisa's mattress and dog to get money for prostitutes. Both parents gave Lisa the job of answering the phone to deal with creditors. Lisa was fourteen.

Hank and I conspired with Debz, and begged money from our friend David, to bring Lisa to Pittsburgh. She arrived with a broken wrist and almost no clothing (my father had destroyed most of her clothing). She was terrified and terrorized. We kept her out of school for a year to help her get her balance. A member of the counseling staff at the local family services organization, the Whale's Tale, took one look at her and set her up with free counseling services. When she was ready to reenter the world, we moved to the neighborhood with the good high school for her.

No one in the family in Washington had so much as remembered when her birthday was since I left home when she was seven. We celebrated her birthday. We celebrated Christmas with her. We taught her to live with people who cared what happened to her enough that we needed to hear from her if she was going shopping or going out. She had a successful social and academic life at her high school, and we did what we could to make her home life orderly. Neither of us understood how to make a well-ordered home from scratch. But the bar was set low enough for anyone coming from my family that even our chaos counted as a real home in Lisa's eyes. By then it was clear that she was as close as we were going to get to having a child.

I did not talk to her about faith. She shared my siblings' deep mistrust of Christianity, and I was afraid to broach the topic with her. What she saw in me was instead a drive to understand things through study. I prayed *for* her but not with her. I think that I thought that nothing about me could count as a good example, and the thing that seems obvious to me now—that God can work through a deeply flawed person whose manifest struggles are unattractive—did not enter my understanding then. Such order as there was in my spiritual life in graduate school came through work in various 12-step programs aimed at one or another aspect of codependency. What Lisa *did* hear was frank discussion of the need for a Higher Power.

I was a graduate student for a long time. I wound up doing two doctoral tracks—one in philosophy with an emphasis in ethics, and one in English literature, with an emphasis in cultural studies, along with taking a year out on a fellowship studying formal economics. Hank completed his undergraduate degree at Pittsburgh.

Things continued in a downward spiral for my mother, father, and Cynthia. My parents lost the house in bankruptcy. Everything that could be sold had been taken and sold by Cynthia for heroin or my father for prostitutes. My father, mother, and Cynthia moved into a shabby apartment. And my father started stalking and attacking other people's children. He came up behind them when they were alone in parks and playgrounds and assaulted them. The local police were, by then, tracking him, but his victims could not identify him. At that time, in Washington State, an apparently dangerous person could be involuntarily committed to a psychiatric facility three times and held for seventy-two hours each time. The state had three chances to get you and keep you institutionalized on a more permanent basis. My father, believing that he was probably HIV positive because of his life with prostitutes, took to biting the police officers who apprehended him for involuntary commitment. On the third commitment, a clever psychiatrist told my father that, since it seemed that my father did not know what he was doing or had done, the psychiatrist was going to have to declare my father mentally incompetent. This so offended my father's pride that he asked for an attorney and someone to record their conversation. Then he began a recitation of what he had done to children.

I gather that it took hours for him to recite a list of what he had done to me. I do not know how long it took him to say what he had done to Lisa. And then the police and social service agencies in Washington State started phoning Pittsburgh. The State of Washington offered me counseling and other services, and wanted to make these available to Lisa as well. He had not raped Lisa, but he was the source of scar tissue around her neck that still gives her trouble, and he had terrorized her. Her abuse fell within the statute of limitations. Hank and I talked about it, and talked with Lisa, who was terrified at the prospect of having to go back to Washington to testify against our father. We did not take Lisa back to Washington State. But my father stood trial and was committed to the psychiatric ward of the state penitentiary under the then-new, and now-defunct, sexual predator law in Washington State.

It was a relief to everyone. When justice is meted out to someone with the kinds of trouble my father endured and perpetrated, that justice is *itself* a mercy to the perpetrator. Hiding and shielding a perpetrator, as we had done for years, is not a kindness.

By the time that my father was in prison, I had decided that the whole of my philosophy doctoral dissertation was a defense against admitting how much I had been damaged by my childhood. I destroyed my dissertation and started reading John Stuart Mill, because I needed a philosopher who had broken under the weight of a heavy father and used philosophy to pull himself back into life again. It was the summer before I was scheduled to hit the job market, and I started writing a new dissertation (I had completed my work for English Literature the previous year; the Program for the Study of Culture was not yet independently degree-granting, but I had my doctoral certification from them). I wound up going to UCLA to teach Warren Quinn's classes—he had committed suicide and left my friend Michael Thompson stranded there. Hank and I separated while I was away in Los Angeles. Michael and I looked after each other. And I got a lot of good job offers and accepted the one from the University of Chicago. Hank and I reunited over the summer and moved to Chicago together, sending Lisa off to college in Vermont.

Our struggles were not over in Chicago. Hank worked harder than one would have thought possible starting a woodworking business while I started teaching. After two years, Lisa left college and came home to us. My father died suddenly, having been moved from the prison to a secure psychiatric institution in the San Juan Islands. Lisa did the office work for Hank's business for a few years before entering DePaul to pursue her degree, specializing in urban elementary education. I started spending a lot of time with Psalms and the Gospel of John.

Hank moved away from the business, and it was clear that we needed to separate again. He went back to Santa Cruz to stay with his father and work through the remains of his own traumatic childhood while Lisa was finishing up her degree at DePaul. I had started leaning heavily on the Serenity Prayer when I was a graduate student. It continued to help me a lot.

Separations

After my father died, my mother fell in with Cynthia. Cynthia had stopped using heroin and had stopped using the varieties of speed that she took up while getting off heroin. She did some extra schooling and got a job as a surgical tech person. My mother found work as a receptionist at a local hospital. Cynthia talked my mother into cashing in some of her retirement. They used the money to buy an SUV and move to Denver, where Cynthia hoped to study to be an exotic animal veterinarian with a firm she had seen advertised on Animal Planet. The plan failed. The school was too expensive. The climate was too harsh. They lost all their remaining belongings when their U-Haul trailer was stolen the night before they were scheduled to make their move to Portland, Oregon. They moved anyway.

Lisa and I were sharing an apartment in Chicago while she completed her degree. We discovered that Cynthia and our mother had taken out credit cards in Lisa's name and run up as much debt as they could. Lisa and I managed to get the debt cleared. I sent Cynthia and my mother housewares for their new place. And Lisa and I began a long process of trying to figure out what to do about our mother. In that space of time, Lisa was betrayed by her boyfriend, but decided that she wanted to have a child. She explained that it is very rare to have unconditional love from someone who knows you inside out. There is nothing you can do with that except find someone else to love unconditionally and know as well as one person can know another. She had that love from me. "What you do with a love like that," she told me, "is have a baby and pass it to your child. Consequently, I have to have a baby and it's your fault."

We were priced out of the rental market in the neighborhood near my university. I bought a large condominium farther south— big enough that we could raise her child there, if need be. I brought Hank back for visits a couple of times a year, and went to see him in Santa Cruz when I could.

Returns

While Hank was in Santa Cruz, he became deeply involved in an Afro-Brazilian spiritual practice called "Umbanda", and his life in Umbanda became my way of finding my way back to an ordered community-based spiritual practice—a religion. I followed Hank into Umbanda from a distance. Perhaps because of my own difficulties, I have always respected syncretic religious practices. They are a place to feel how people who have suffered horrors I cannot even imagine negotiate a spiritual life with God in the face of ongoing hideous trouble that I have never known.

I had started reading work by philosopher G. E. M. Anscombe in graduate school. I loved *Intention*. It seemed likely that there was a ghost writer at work in that slender volume, and it seemed clear that it wasn't Aristotle. I knew that Anscombe was a devout Catholic, a convert, so I suspected that the ghost author could be Aquinas. I had started reading Aquinas our first summer in Chicago, and it was the best philosophical work I had ever read, so I just kept reading him. By the time that I had been working with Aquinas and Anscombe for more than a decade, and understood the depth of the strand of Catholicism in the syncretic spiritual practice that was the sort of Umbanda I knew, I started to be able to imagine the Catholic Church as a possible place to be.

By then, I understood that the stories of Jesus that had been my one hope as a child would not have been there for me without the Catholic Church. The Church had preserved the texts. The Church made the decisions about which texts belonged to the Scriptures that nourished me, and which texts did not. They had a bigger Bible than the one I had known as a child, but I recognized their Bible as Bible.

Hank came back to Chicago, officially because my sister Lisa found her true love, married, and was expecting her first child, Nora. Hank wanted to be part of Nora's life. He brought his spiritual practice with him, and I took part. We lived apart for a few years, then he moved into the spare room, and we started making a new life together.

We had divorced when he was in California. He said, "I keep looking over my shoulder toward Chicago, and I need to divorce so that I can do what I need to do here."

It was horrible. He later told me that what he really wanted was to free me to marry someone else. This turned out to be unimaginable. Hank and I decided to remarry, but to do it very quietly. The only person we told about it was my friend Father Kevin Flannery. Father Kevin had said a small Mass asking for us to reunite when he was meeting with Pope Benedict at the Vatican several years before. We wanted to let him know that his prayers had been answered. I wrote to him first thing in the morning—around 4 A.M.—the day we were headed for the courthouse. He wrote back so quickly that I assumed he was in Rome, but Father Kevin was in Chicago. He had never met Hank, but knew that I had never stopped looking to Hank as my husband. We met Father Kevin for a drink at the Drake Hotel the night we remarried and learned that he and his fellow Jesuits had celebrated a Mass for us at about the time that we were saying our vows in the courthouse downtown.

By the time Hank came home, things were very bad in Portland. Cynthia had gotten pregnant and had a baby, Sadie. She phoned to tell me she was pregnant, and I became involved in trying to help. My mother, Cynthia, and Sadie were living with Sadie's alcoholic father in a house owned by Sadie's paternal grandfather. My mother had a stroke and had barely recovered when she found herself responsible for most of Sadie's care. Children are differently at risk with my mother than they were with my father. It is hardest for the children that my mother likes best—I have always had an easier time than Debz or Cynthia, because our mother doted on them. I understand how my father hurt children. My mother's ways are sometimes clear, but often mysterious to me. I asked her about my early childhood with my father once, and she said, "I knew what he was doing to you, and it would have killed me, but you were such a strange, silent, staring child that I didn't think it was affecting you the way that it would affect a little girl."

Cynthia kept taking as much of my mother's limited income as she could get hold of to try to keep the household afloat. Sadie's father grew increasingly unhappy with both Cynthia and my mother. And Lisa and I made the decision to try to bring my mother to Chicago. It seemed to us that everyone in our family had suffered enough, and that our mother might be able to experience a few years of security, and possibly even some sort of happiness, before she died if we got her out of Portland. The time we had needed her to be other than she is was when we were children. We were grown. We had lives. And I started the long project of getting my mother to Chicago, as much for Sadie's sake as for my mother's. It took two tries. In between the two, she took a bad fall in Portland and had a brain bleed in exactly the area where the stroke had struck. She was a wreck.

All through this time, I kept reading Aquinas. If you work long enough and hard enough asking for discernment with Aquinas, you find yourself in powerful Catholic intellectual circles where many of your fellow thinkers and students have exactly the kind of intellectual life that you dreamt about in graduate school. They are honest. They are humble. Their intellectual lives are animated by deep devotion to God. They are erudite in ways that you can only dream about. They have reasonable moral compasses. And they welcome questions and argument. Father Kevin was the first of my scholarly priest friends.

My mother lived with Hank and me for several years. She had spent some time living with Lisa, her husband, and little Nora when they were renting a large apartment on the Northside, but was persistently psychologically abusive to Nora—Sadie was the good grandchild; Nora was the unjustly privileged one; Nora needed to be discouraged and kept down verbally. We needed to put some distance between Nora and her grandmother.

Sharing a household with my mother was hard. She is, understandably, very needy. She is desperate for approval. She is very talkative. And she has had to work so hard for so long to keep a lifetime of disappointment and loss from stopping her efforts to lay hold of whatever seems like it might make something bearable that it is hard

for her to function without having something or someone to envy
or despise. She lavishes hollow praise on people and later speaks ill
of them behind their backs. It is still unwise to take her accounts of
things at face value. And Jesus loves her enough to have died for her.

Nora had recovered some and regained some balance by the time
that Lisa and her husband bought the apartment above ours. Nora
enjoyed being able to go up and down the building stairs and see her
aunt and uncle and grandmother whenever she liked. She learned to
take some benefit from seeing her grandmother without being hurt.
Lisa developed a relationship with our mother that seems to be about
as good as such a relationship can be. We both developed a more
accurate sense for what is and what is not possible with our mother.

My work with Aquinas, my association with Dominicans, and
being adopted into the family surrounding the Witherspoon Institute
in Princeton were bringing me closer to the Church. My mother had
a horror of Catholics, but came to feel secure enough to have suppers
with priests when my friends were in town.

I was blessed with a growing number of Catholic friends and colleagues. One of them, Father Thomas Joseph White, made a lot of
space for me in the Dominican circles where he lives and works and
inspires those around him. We both wound up invited to the Sym-
posium Thomisticum in Paris.

I have always hated Paris, even though my own work is deeply
indebted to French thought. My two trips through Paris during my
junior year abroad were both pockmarked by encounters with men
who were hurting or about to hurt young women, so for me it had
become a place marked by monstrous academic politics at the surface
and a dark underbelly of violence in train stations and alleyways.
Father Thomas Joseph loves Paris, so I asked if he would come early
to the conference and show me a Paris one could love. He agreed,
and we prayed our way across the Left Bank.

I do not share Father Thomas Joseph's love for the architecture of
the churches of Paris, although I share his enthusiasm for walking in
the footsteps of saints. The unadorned silent Quaker circles, and the
praying in song and dance in Umbanda, will probably always be more
to my taste than genuinely marvelous big stone buildings. But Father
Thomas Joseph and I had an opportunity to engage in Eucharistic
Adoration at a lovely, empty church—our second stop—and in the

meditative peace of the Real Presence, I asked Christ if he could hold me in the Catholic Church. He let me know that he could. Then we went to the Chapel of Our Lady of the Miraculous Medal, which was filled with African congregants who were, in turn, so filled with the Spirit that the air was fairly humming. And then we made our way to the Chapel of Saint Vincent-de-Paul, a church filled with the stillness of the Father. It was a Triune day of prayer.

On our way back to the hotel, Father Thomas Joseph mentioned that I could just come into the Church, that I even could enter at the Dominican House of Studies in Washington, D.C., where several of my friends were. I sent him an email that evening, asking if this was true. He said that it was. And he undertook the work with his superiors and a canon lawyer to make it possible. I was under instruction with him all summer. I stopped practicing Umbanda, and Hank agreed to come to Mass with me if he got to pick the church. He chose Saint Sabina, and the two of us started attending Mass there. It's an African American church with a profound social justice mission that meshed well with community work we have been doing since we first arrived in Chicago.

I was received into the Church the day after Trump was elected president, and my friends at the Dominican House of Studies in Washington made a proper fondue supper for everyone. Friends and colleagues came from Catholic University of America across the street. Luis Tellez came from the Witherspoon Institute. Father Kevin came. My colleague and friend Jennifer Frey came up from South Carolina. Our friend Father Raphael Mary was my sponsor. It was a joyous day.

Father Thomas Joseph once told me that he thought that I had been given special graces by Jesus all my life. I have. But it is an extraordinary blessing to get to enjoy the ordinary graces of sacramental practice after years of just reading, praying, worshipping God in this place or that, and following along in the Rosary with Mother Angelica and her sisters on television. I have come here from hard places. I am not clear of the difficulties and may never be.

My mother is now settled into a retirement home that she likes, and Hank has shouldered almost all the burden of overseeing her finances and her care. Jesus is holding us. Hank does most of the hard work with my mother. I am with her once or twice a week. She has more security than she has known since leaving her home and striking off with my father, and my nieces are growing up at a safe distance.

As for me, I enjoy a kind of peace now that I could not have imagined before. I am the luckiest person I know.

CONTRIBUTORS

Francis J. Beckwith is professor of philosophy and church-state studies, and associate director of the graduate program in philosophy, at Baylor University. A graduate of Fordham University (Ph.D.) and the Washington University School of Law in St. Louis, he is the author of over a dozen books, including *Defending Life: A Moral and Legal Case against Abortion Choice* (Cambridge University Press, 2007), *Taking Rites Seriously: Law, Politics, and the Reasonableness of Faith* (Cambridge University Press, 2015), and *Never Doubt Thomas: The Catholic Aquinas as Evangelical and Protestant* (Baylor University Press, 2019).

J. Budziszewski is a professor of government and philosophy at the University of Texas, Austin, where he also teaches courses in the law school and the religious studies department. He specializes in natural law, with a special interest in moral self-deception, and more generally the ethical foundations of political and social life. His most recent books are *Commentary on Thomas Aquinas's Treatise on Law* (Cambridge University Press, 2014); *Commentary on Thomas Aquinas's Virtue Ethics* (Cambridge University Press, 2017); and *Commentary on Thomas Aquinas's Treatise on Happiness and Ultimate Purpose* (Cambridge University Press, forthcoming).

Lindsay K. Cleveland resides in Bismarck, North Dakota, with her husband, Scott, and their two children. She received an M.Div. from Yale Divinity School and her Ph.D. in philosophy from Baylor University (2018). She works from home on research projects in the areas of metaphysics, philosophy of religion, and analytic theology. She enjoys participating in the community at the University of Mary (Bismarck, North Dakota), where she has been invited to adjunct teach there in philosophy and looks forward to doing so in the future.

W. Scott Cleveland is director of Catholic studies and assistant professor of philosophy at the University of Mary (Bismarck, North Dakota). He and his wife, Lindsay, are the grateful parents of a daughter and son. Scott received his M.A. in religion, specializing in philosophical theology and philosophy of religion, from Yale Divinity School and received his Ph.D. in philosophy (2014) from Baylor University. His research interests are in philosophy of religion, ethics, and moral psychology, especially the study of the virtues and emotions, the relation between the two, and the role of each in the moral and intellectual life.

Bryan R. Cross is an associate professor of philosophy at Mount Mercy University. His research centers around the role of tradition in philosophical practice and its implications for the role of philosophy in higher education. He and his wife and two daughters were received into full communion with the Catholic Church on October 8, 2006.

Brian Cutter is an assistant professor of philosophy at the University of Notre Dame. His research is primarily in the philosophy of mind and metaphysics, with a focus on the nature of consciousness, intentionality, and perception. He lives in South Bend, Indiana, with his wife and three children.

Edward Feser is associate professor of philosophy at Pasadena City College in Pasadena, California. He is the author of many academic articles and books, including *The Last Superstition: A Refutation of the New Atheism* (St. Augustine's Press, 2008); *Aquinas* (Oneworld Publications, 2009); *Scholastic Metaphysics: A Contemporary Introduction* (Editiones Scholasticae/Transaction Publishers, 2014); *By Man Shall His Blood Be Shed: A Catholic Defense of Capital Punishment*, co-authored with Joseph Bessette (Ignatius Press, 2017); and *Five Proofs of the Existence of God* (Ignatius Press, 2017).

Logan Paul Gage is assistant professor of philosophy at Franciscan University of Steubenville. He holds a B.A (philosophy, history, and American studies) from Whitworth College and an M.A. and Ph.D. (philosophy) from Baylor University. His academic work is primarily in epistemology and philosophy of religion.

Neal Judisch is associate professor of philosophy and academic director of multidisciplinary studies at the University of Oklahoma, where he specializes in metaphysics, action theory, and philosophical theology. A lifelong Christian, he was received into the Catholic Church in 2008 with his wife and six children.

Robert Koons is a professor of philosophy at the University of Texas at Austin, where he has taught for over thirty years. He has degrees from Michigan State, Oxford, and UCLA, and he is the author, co-author, or co-editor of six books, including most recently *The Atlas of Reality: A Comprehensive Guide to Metaphysics*, co-authored with Timothy Pickavance (Wiley-Blackwell, 2017), and *Neo-Aristotelian Perspectives on Contemporary Science*, co-edited with William Simpson and Nicholas Teh (Routledge, 2017). He specializes in metaphysics, epistemology, and philosophical theology.

Peter Kreeft has been professor of philosophy at Boston College since 1965, has published seventy-plus books on philosophy and religion, loves his six grandchildren, four children, one wife, one cat, and one God, and hates only mimes, computers, and Yankees. He finds this planet a nice place to visit but would not like to live here.

Candace Vogler is the David B. and Clara E. Stern professor of philosophy and professor in the college at the University of Chicago, and principal investigator on "Virtue, Happiness, and the Meaning of Life", a project funded by the John Templeton Foundation. She has authored two books, *John Stuart Mill's Deliberative Landscape: An Essay in Moral Psychology* (Routledge, 2001) and *Reasonably Vicious* (Harvard University Press, 2002), as well as essays in ethics, social and political philosophy, philosophy and literature, cinema, psychoanalysis, gender studies, sexuality studies, and other areas.